The First Yankees Dynasty

ALSO BY GARY A. SARNOFF

*The Wrecking Crew of '33:
The Washington Senators' Last Pennant* (2009)

The First Yankees Dynasty

*Babe Ruth, Miller Huggins
and the Bronx Bombers
of the 1920s*

GARY A. SARNOFF

McFarland & Company, Inc., Publishers
Jefferson, North Carolina

LIBRARY OF CONGRESS CATALOGUING-IN-PUBLICATION DATA

Sarnoff, Gary A.
　　The first Yankees dynasty : Babe Ruth, Miller Huggins and the Bronx Bombers of the 1920s / Gary A. Sarnoff.
　　　　p.　　　cm.
　　Includes bibliographical references and index.

　　ISBN 978-0-7864-4966-8 (softcover : acid free paper) ∞
　　ISBN 978-1-4766-1718-3 (ebook)

　　1. New York Yankees (Baseball team)—History—20th century.　2. Ruth, Babe, 1895–1948.　3. Huggins, Miller, 1879 [sic; 1878]–1929.　I. Title.
GV875.N4S27　2014
796.357'64097471—dc23				2014035349

BRITISH LIBRARY CATALOGUING DATA ARE AVAILABLE

© 2014 Gary A. Sarnoff. All rights reserved

No part of this book may be reproduced or transmitted in any form or by any means, electronic or mechanical, including photocopying or recording, or by any information storage and retrieval system, without permission in writing from the publisher.

On the cover: New York Yankees baseball team October 19, 1926 (George Grantham Bain Collection, Library of Congress)

Printed in the United States of America

McFarland & Company, Inc., Publishers
　Box 611, Jefferson, North Carolina 28640
　　www.mcfarlandpub.com

In memory of Michael Fellman:
A great teacher, writer, and baseball fan
who touched so many lives.

Table of Contents

Acknowledgments — ix
Introduction — 1

1. Babe Ruth to the Yankees—1920 — 5
2. Ruppert and Huston — 13
3. Fifty-Nine Home Runs and Five Suspensions—1921 and 1922 — 21
4. Miller Huggins — 34
5. World Champions—1923 — 45
6. The Bellyache Heard Around the World—1925 — 53
7. Crash!—1925 — 64
8. Suspension—1925 — 77
9. Comeback Season—1926 — 85
10. Yankee Pride—1926 — 100
11. The 1926 World Series — 107
12. Babe Ruth, the Legend—1927 — 121
13. Lindy! Lindy! Lindy!—1927 — 133
14. Baseball's Greatest Team—1927 — 143
15. Break Up the Yankees—1928 — 155
16. Collapse—1928 — 169
17. Completing the Dynasty—1928 — 180
18. Tragedy—1929 — 194

19. Remarried—1929	202
20. The End of the Road—1929	213
21. Legacy	220
Chapter Notes	227
Bibliography	247
Index	249

Acknowledgments

All authors need support when writing a book, and I was fortunate to have a good group of people who worked hard to help make my story into a book. I want to thank the staff at the Library of Congress, St. Petersburg Museum of History, St. Petersburg Public Library, the Boston Public Library, Watertown (Massachusetts) Public Library, New York City Public Library, the Sudbury (Massachusetts) Historical Society, and the A. Bartlett Giamatti Library at the Baseball Hall of Fame in Cooperstown, New York.

Introduction

"'He's an old man. He isn't the Babe that he used to be,' the fans say."
—Ford Frick, *New York Evening Journal*

"The Yankees are a collection of individuals who are convinced their manager is a sap."—Westbrook Pegler, syndicate sportswriter

Babe Ruth was old, washed up, and would never be the player he once was.

Miller Huggins was a bad manager who had failed to earn the respect of his players and won three consecutive American League pennants (1921–1923) by benefiting from the bankrolls of the Yankees co-owners.

This was the consensus among the majority of the fans and sportswriters. The greater number also believed that the glory days of the New York Yankees were finished, and hard times were ahead for the proud franchise that capped their first American League dynasty by winning the 1923 World Series championship.

In 1925, the New York Yankees hit rock-bottom, and so did Babe Ruth, whose career, personal life, marriage, and health had suffered through a turbulent year that included an operation to delay the start of his season, a separation request from his wife, a hefty fine with a suspension by his manager, and his worst season since coming to the Yankees. To add to his headaches, the New York Yankees, the team predicted to return to the top of the American League in 1925, plunged to a seventh-place finish.

Was there hope for Babe Ruth's career? A minority believed there was, including Babe Ruth, who was hungry to regain his superstar status and show up his critics.

Was there hope for the Yankees? Miller Huggins was confident that his team, and Babe Ruth, would bounce back, and like Ruth, he wanted to show the detractors, who had ridiculed him through the Yankees' glory years without ever crediting him for his team's success, that their prognostication for the future of the Yankees was incorrect.

The rise of the Yankees began when two millionaires named Jacob Ruppert and Tillinghast Huston purchased the ball club in 1915: a club that lacked discipline, leadership and direction, were accustomed to finishing in the lower tier of the American League standings, and served as an afterthought in New York to the powerful Giants. However, due to the owners' burning desire to succeed, their investments in the team's future through wise transactions, and Rupert's decision to hire Miller Huggins to manage the Yankees, the team's fortunes began to change. When Babe Ruth came on board, the Yanks were on their way.

Before becoming a Yankee, Ruth had reached stardom by hurling ninety-two victories for the Boston Red Sox in an era when "sharp quick [batting] strokes proved effective," "hitting home runs were frowned upon by the fraternity," and teams played scientific baseball through a base hit or walk, a stolen base or sacrifice, and another hit to score a run. But Ruth proved the fans craved to see the long ball, and his uncanny ability to hit the ball far beyond the distant outfield fences packed the ballparks with patrons with hopes of witnessing a Ruthian homer with their own eyes.

The course of baseball history changed forever on January 9, 1920, when Jacob Ruppert announced the details of the greatest blockbuster transaction in sports history before a packed room of sportswriters. In 1920, the impact of Ruth spiked home attendance to over one million to make the Yankees the first franchise to eclipse that number. They also surpassed their landlords—the Giants—in popularity to become the toast of New York City and make them unwelcome tenants at the Giants' home field, the Polo Grounds. No longer welcomed to do business with the Giants, the Yankees' co-owners quickly moved to build baseball's greatest cathedral, Yankee Stadium.

But while the team was winning, played at Yankee Stadium, won a world championship, continued to keep the turnstiles clicking with winning baseball and the greatest drawing card in Babe Ruth, life was far from perfect. There was dissent among the team's co-owners, especially over one owner's managerial choice. Miller Huggins, a former ballplayer who had worked hard to prove he could play in the major leagues in spite of his handicap of standing 5'4" and weighing only 140 pounds, was caught in the owners' conflict. With one owner's disapproval, and viewed unfavorably by the press, he was forced to fight an endless battle for respect of his ballplayers, and he had the difficult task of managing the unmanageable Babe Ruth. However, as long as the Yankees were winning, and as long as Ruth was producing league leading batting totals, the manager believed it was unnecessary to enforce the discipline.

That was until 1925, when the Yankees were losing and Babe Ruth was having his worst season. The manager finally took action against Ruth with a decision that made the great slugger extremely unhappy.

As the 1926 season approached, the pressure was on Ruth, Huggins, and the Yankees to return to contention. And in addition to a battle to save his career, Ruth had his life to rectify.

Would Babe Ruth be able to become the great player he once was? Would he be able to tolerate his manager? Could he save his marriage, and be a good father to Dorothy, his one and only child? What about the other lady in his life? Did he love her?

Could Miller Huggins guide the Yankees back to the top? Would he be able to keep his job if the Yankees fell short for another season? Would his relationship change with his best player? What was he going to do in order to obtain the respect he desired from his team?

This is a story about the career and life challenges of Babe Ruth and Miller Huggins, and the relationship of the great ballplayer and the Yankees manager. It is the story of a successful franchise during the "roaring twenties," their path to victory and recovery, and their becoming one of the greatest dynasties in baseball history during one of the most exciting decades in American history.

1

Babe Ruth to the Yankees—1920

"Gentlemen, we have just bought Babe Ruth from Harry Frazee of the Boston Red Sox. I can't give the exact figures, but it was a pretty check—six figures. No players are involved. It is strictly a cash deal."
—Jacob Ruppert speaking to the New York sportswriters on January 9, 1920

"You can't do this to me, Harry," complained Red Sox manager Ed Barrow. "Why, Ruth is the biggest attraction in baseball."

"I'm sorry, Ed; I've got to do it," said Red Sox owner Harry Frazee in an apologetic voice.

Harry Frazee was a theater man without a box office hit during the few years prior to the sale of Babe Ruth. He had taken a financial risk when he had purchased the Boston Red Sox in 1916 at a high cost of $675,000. In addition, two of his backers had made half their payment in notes, putting the owner in a bind from the beginning. "The Ruth deal was the only way I could retain the Red Sox," he would later say. Other transitions would follow between the two teams that led to the Yankees' obtaining Waite Hoyt, Herb Pennock, Everett Scott, Wally Schang, Joe Dugan, and George Pipgras. The Boston Red Sox, the toast of the American League before 1920, collapsed to the bottom of the American League while the Yankees won three consecutive pennants (1921–1923) with a team built on a foundation of former Red Sox, thus making Frazee extremely unpopular in Boston. "Those are the only friends that so-and-so has," said a disgruntled Red Sox fan upon viewing a poster in the Fenway Park concourse promoting Frazee's play, *My Fair Lady*.

Confirming rumors that the Boston owner needed money, Yankees manager Miller Huggins advised the Yankees' owners about Ruth's availability. The deal for Ruth, strictly cash, was for $100,000 plus a $350,000 loan.

The Yankees got the greatest player in baseball as well as an attitude problem. Miller Huggins, aware of Ruth's history of poor behavior, was concerned. The first meeting between the manager and the player took place on the Griffith Golf Course in Los Angeles. Ruth was on the West Coast to appear in movie shorts, and he played golf in between shootings. Huggins had traveled to Los Angeles to introduce himself and talk about a contract. Shaking his head over a sub-par game, Ruth was heading to the first hole to play another eighteen holes when he was interrupted.

> HUGGINS: "I'm Miller Huggins of the New York Yankees. I'd like to talk to you."
> RUTH: "I don't have any time. I've got somewhere to go."
> HUGGINS: "Babe, how would you like to play for the Yankees?"
> RUTH: "Have I been traded?"
> HUGGINS: "[hesitates] ... The deal has yet to be finalized."
> RUTH: "I like Boston and playing for the Red Sox, but I will give you my best if traded, just like I did in Boston."
> HUGGINS: "Babe, you have been a pretty wild boy in Boston. In New York you will have to behave."
> RUTH: "I already told you I will play the best I can. Let's get down to business. How much are you going to pay me?"
> HUGGINS: "You have two years left on your contract for $10,000 per season."
> RUTH: "I want more dough than that."
> HUGGINS: "All right, if you promise to behave yourself, Colonel Ruppert will give you a new contract."

Their next meeting was in a conference at the Yankees' office with owners Jacob Ruppert and Tillinghast Huston. "Huggins' word is the law," one of the owners told the ballplayer. Ruth took a puff from a cigarette before responding: "Look at ya! Too fat and too old have fun!" he told Huston. "And that goes for him too," he told Ruppert. "As for this shrimp," he said of Huggins, "he's half dead right now."

Huggins knew what he was in for. He had a great ballplayer with a lot of baggage, something that the Red Sox were happy to be away from. "He is one of the most selfish and inconsiderate ballplayers to ever put on a uniform," Frazee said after the deal. Most experts agreed. "He thought of only himself," wrote a sportswriter from the *Chicago Tribune,* who also added that Ruth "is not a good influence for good team play."

Discipline was a problem for George Herman Ruth from the beginning while growing up in Baltimore, most likely because his parents, George Herman, Sr. and Katherine, were too occupied to give parental guidance. George Sr. was running his saloon; Katherine, who was often ill, was busy with taking care of her health or dealing with her pregnancies. "I learned to fear and hate the coppers and to throw apples and eggs at the truck drivers," said Ruth. He also stole, chewed tobacco, played hooky, and once took a dollar from the till of his father's saloon to buy ice cream for his friends. His dad responded by taking his son down to the cellar to give him a thrashing. The lesson went unlearned, as Babe continued to take from the till.

On June 13, 1902, a Friday the 13th, the course of seven-year-old Babe's life changed when his parents sent him across town to live at St. Mary's Industrial School for Boys, a Roman Catholic training school for orphans, delinquents, runaways, incorrigibles, and boys from broken homes. The home housed over eight hundred boys and was run by about thirty Xaverians. Ruth, listed as incorrigible, and the other boys, were expected to abide by the rules. If they failed to obey, they were punished. "These we used on Babe Ruth," a friend of Ruth's was told when guided to a room with straps hanging on the walls during a tour of the home in later years. "I used to get my discipline the old-fashioned way," said Ruth. "I knew when I had it coming." His offenses were usually for smoking or chewing tobacco.

Once in awhile, Ruth was permitted to return home, but only for a short period. "He just wouldn't go to school," said Mamie, Ruth's only sibling to live beyond childhood. History says he never got a visit from family, although Mamie claimed she and her mother visited on a monthly basis. The visits stopped following Katherine's death in August of 1910. The story is his dad never did stop by. "I guess I am too big and ugly for anyone to come see me," he once told another resident.

At St. Mary's the boys attended classes and workshops every day, and they religiously played the great game of baseball. Each boy was assigned to one of the forty-four intra-school teams, and each had a goal to be good enough to play on the school team, which played against other schools. "I was a catcher," Ruth said of his first position at St. Mary's. He was a left-handed catcher. "Sure it was awkward. I used a regular [right-handed] catcher's mitt on my left hand and when I wanted to throw to the bases I just shook off the mitt and threw left-handed. I could toss the ball back to the pitcher well enough with my right hand."

One day, Ruth was amused over his team's pitchers taking a shellacking. As he rolled over with laughter, a Xaverian known as Brother Matthias called time out to talk to his catcher. In his gentle manner of speaking to the boys, Brother Matthias asked Ruth what was so funny.

"That guy out there—getting his brains knocked out," Ruth answered as he laughed.
"All right, you pitch," responded Brother Matthias.
The laugher came to an abrupt end.
"I never pitched in my life," Ruth said with fear. "I can't pitch."
"Oh, you must know a lot about it," answered Brother Matthias. "You know

Babe Ruth (far left in top row) with the St. Mary's interschool league champions, coincidentally named the Red Sox. Although he is wearing the catcher's mitt on his left hand, Ruth claimed to be a left-handed throwing catcher (National Baseball Hall of Fame, Cooperstown, New York).

enough to know your friend isn't any good. So go ahead out there and show us how it's done."

Ruth traded his catcher's gear for a fingered mitt, and much to his surprise, he felt very comfortable, including having enough confidence to throw a few curves. He did so well that he was converted to a fulltime pitcher. "I pitched to everyone I could get to catch me. If I was going to be a pitcher, I was going to be a good one."

Ruth was bound to be a great ballplayer from the beginning. Soon he was playing with teammates three to four years older and was eventually placed on the school team. In his final season playing for St. Mary's, he went undefeated and hit a home run in almost every game. Jack Dunn, the owner and manager of the Baltimore Orioles (of the International League), was told by a friend about Ruth. During Ruth's undefeated season of 1913, Dunn saw him strike out twenty-two batters while hurling a shutout. He spoke to Ruth after the game, and paid a visit to St. Mary's the following February to officially sign him. Although his dad was still alive, the Xaverians had full responsibility of his affairs, and since Ruth was just nineteen, Dunn became his legal guardian. "He can do anything," Brother Matthias assured Dunn. Ruth began that way with the Orioles and established himself as a hot prospect for the major leagues.

At last! Ruth said goodbye to St. Mary's for good. He was now out in the real world, and he found reality to be greater than he could have ever imagined. Ruth was awed over actually being paid to play baseball. The power of trains amazed him to the point where he would spend hours watching them depart and arrive at the nearest train stations. He loved riding up and down elevators. Best of all, Ruth could sign the checks in the hotel dining room at the team's expense. "You mean I can eat anything I want, and it won't cost me anything?" he asked. "Sure, anything," a teammate clarified. That was all he needed to hear. Ruth went to town and didn't come up for air until he was devouring his third serving of wheat cakes and ham when he noticed his teammates were watching in awe. "I wouldn't have believed it if I hadn't seen it," a teammate would later say of the rookie's appetite. An amused Jack Dunn walked over with a smile and put his arm on Ruth's shoulder. "We've got twenty-seven other fellows on this club, George. Leave them a little food, will you?"

Ruth was like a big kid with poor manners, which made him unpopular with his teammates. He would belch and fart and think nothing of it. He was loud, raucous, vulgar, and obscene. "Excuse me, I have to piss," he announced at a table full of teammates and their wives. One teammate took him aside when he returned to explain that his comments were inappropriate and he ought to apologize, especially to the ladies. When he returned to the table, he said he was sorry "for using the word piss."

"I can't live with this man Ruth," said a teammate who had the misfortune of rooming with him. When asked why, he said, "I told him he was using my toothbrush, and he said 'That's all right, I'm not particular.'" There was more: "A man wants privacy in the bathroom."

The Orioles were in first place. A pennant was in their grasp, but Dunn was uninterested. His team was taking a beating at the ticket window since 1914 marked the year that major league baseball returned to Baltimore in the form of the Federal League. The city of Baltimore had craved for another major league team ever since their Orioles of the American League were relocated to New York City in 1903 and become the Highlanders (and later the Yankees). The new Federal League offered the city another chance, and the Baltimore newspapers and fans focused on the major league franchise, making the Orioles an afterthought. With a dramatic decline in attendance, Dunn looked to sell his prospects. He offered Ruth to his good friend Connie Mack, the manager and part-owner of the Philadelphia Athletics, who was guiding his team to a fourth pennant in five seasons, but was having problems of his own. His attendance was down and his players had drained his savings by demanding new contracts in mid-season, using the threat of jumping to the Federal League as leverage. "Jack, you have a great young pitcher in Ruth," Mack told Dunn, "but I can't give you what he is worth. My players have me broke. Why don't you go to Joe Lannin? He's got lots of money."

Joe Lannin, the owner of the Red Sox before Frazee, never hesitated. On July 8, 1914, Ruth was purchased by the Boston Red Sox. He was heading to the major leagues at the age of nineteen.

Three days later, Ruth and a teammate arrived in Boston. They exited the Back Bay train station and walked across the street for breakfast at Lander's Coffee Shop, where they were served by a sixteen-year-old waitress.

Her name was Helen Woodford. She was from a close-knit Catholic family in South Boston. She was pretty, with a piquant face, pretty blue eyes, and a slender figure. She was polite; a nice girl. Ruth immediately fell in love and she fell in love with him. One morning, Ruth asked her to dine with him. Miss Woodford accepted, and soon the two were dating. However, their romance took a detour when Lannin announced that he was sending Ruth to his Providence team to help them win the International League pennant. Ruth was reluctant but had no choice. He wanted to remain in Boston, to be in the majors and to be with Helen. To him she was the loveliest girl, his sweetheart, a startling beauty, quiet, reserved, and an inspiration. To her he was happy-go-lucky, modest, and kind.

While pitching for the Providence Grays, Ruth would travel to Boston to be with Helen. Before the end of the 1914 season, Ruth was recalled by the Red Sox. When the season concluded, Ruth was with Helen before heading back home to Baltimore. He hated the idea of being away from her until the following season. While with her at Lander's for the last time, he asked, "Hon, how about you and me getting married?" She accepted. It was probably a decision of which her family disapproved. Likewise, Ruth may have faced disapproval from the Xaverians at St. Mary's, since the couple elected to marry in Ellicott City, Maryland.

On October 17, 1914, Ruth and Helen officially became husband and wife. They were teenagers, naïve, and unaware of the difficulties to come. But for now they were happy to have one another.

Ruth was in the majors to stay in 1915. He won eighteen games that season for the pennant-winning Red Sox, although he was disappointed when he did not get to pitch in the World Series. He won twenty-three games the next season, hurled nine shutouts, and posted a league-leading 1.75 ERA. This time he pitched in the World Series and was outstanding. After giving way to a first inning inside-the-park home run, he shut out the Dodgers for the next 13⅓ innings in a 2–1 Boston win. Two years later, when Boston returned to the World Series, Ruth shut out the Cubs in Game One. In his next start, he held the Cubs scoreless for seven innings before finally giving up a run to snap his scoreless string at 29⅔ innings, a record that would stand for the next forty-four seasons.

A proud Mrs. Ruth cheers for her husband. Helen was always well-dressed and neatly groomed when she appeared at the ballpark (National Baseball Hall of Fame, Cooperstown, New York).

Just twenty-four years old after the 1918 season, Ruth owned eighty victories with a lifetime ERA of 2.09. He was on his way to becoming one of the game's greatest pitchers when his career took a different path that would change the game forever. Ed Barrow received the credit for brainstorming the idea of moving Ruth from the pitcher's mound to the outfield in order to get his powerful bat into the everyday lineup. "I can't take credit for changing the game," said Barrow. "After all, Ruth hit the home runs."

Ruth claimed the change was his idea. "In the spring of 1919 I had a sore arm. I didn't know when I would pitch again, and I didn't want to sit around doing nothing, so I told Ed Barrow that I would like to play in the outfield. He told me I could."

Ruth's transformation from pitcher to outfielder began in 1918. From

1914 through 1917, he had hit nine home runs in 361 at bats. Harry Hooper, Everett Scott, and a few other Boston players had voiced their opinions to Barrow about putting Ruth's bat in the everyday lineup. Barrow agreed, but was unsure. After all, Ruth was one of the best hurlers in baseball. On May 6, 1918, the manager took a chance, and Ruth went 2 for 4 with a home run.

Barrow continued to place Ruth in the starting lineup. By mid–May he made 20 hits in 42 at bats. He also continued to pitch Ruth until the heavy workload, combined with the player's active night life, put him in the hospital for a few days with a high-pitch fever. He continued his double duty after returning.

Playing against Babe Ruth during his Boston days can best be described by Bucky Harris:

> He pitched the first game against us and won it with a triple. The King of Sluggers held us to one run. I managed to get a hit off of him and considered myself lucky.
>
> He played in the outfield in the second game. Jim Shaw held him in check until the seventh. Then Ruth connected with one of Shaw's fast ones. The ball landed high in the right field bleachers. Perhaps Ruth has hit longer homers, but I never saw him, or anyone else, drive a ball so far.
>
> Straw hats and cushions flooded the playing field. The fans cheered for fully five minutes. The crowd carried Ruth off the field at the end of the game and followed his automobile for blocks after he left Fenway Park.

On the morning of August 25, 1918, Ruth received a phone call. The caller told him his dad had been killed in an accident. The mishap occurred when George Herman, Sr., who had remarried following Katherine's passing, was involved in a confrontation outside of his saloon with a brother-in-law who said Ruth Sr. had charged him, knocked him down, and kicked him. The brother-in-law claimed that he scrambled to his feet, threw two punches, and Ruth, Sr., landed head first onto the pavement, fracturing his skull. The story was mysterious but never investigated. George Herman, Sr.'s death was ruled an accident.

2

Ruppert and Huston

"When Ruppert and Huston agreed to buy the Yankees, then a sorry excuse for a major league ball club and chronic tenant in the second division, it must have been the only time they ever did agree, because they never agreed on anything in my presence."

—Ed Barrow

"At last, I've written my John Hancock on those papers," said Tillinghast Huston, who then placed two-hundred and twenty-five one-thousand-dollar bills on the table. Jacob Ruppert reached into his coat pocket, pulled out a check for $225,000, and handed it to Bill Devery. "Money talks," he said with a smile.

On January 11, 1915, Jacob Ruppert and Tillinghast Huston became co-owners of the New York Yankees. Their path to achieving their dream of owning a major league baseball team was as different from the "usual" as the two millionaires were as persons.

Jacob Ruppert was wealthy from the beginning. His family, one of the Original 400 (a reference to New York's social elite in the nineteenth century), had earned their social status through the success of their brewery business, which became very prosperous under the direction of Ruppert's father. Planning to go to college to study to become an engineer, young Ruppert was accepted to college into the School of Mines at Columbia University, but opted to follow his dad's footsteps into the family business, where he discovered that he would have to learn the business from the ground up. Jacob's first job was as the lowest position of keg washer. One year later, he was running the business, and sales soared under his direction.

In 1886, Ruppert joined the Seventeenth Regiment National Guard, serving as a private until 1889, when New York Governor David Hill, who knew Ruppert from when he had worked on the governor's staff, appointed him as colonel of the regiment. In 1899, he was elected to the U.S. House of Representatives, where he served for eight years, but he never put politics above his business.

Tillinghast Huston had three things in common with Ruppert: financial success, the love of baseball, and having been born in the summer of 1867. Unlike Ruppert, he was born without wealth and prestige; unlike Ruppert, who wore the best suits, kept his mustache neatly trimmed, and looked like a successful businessman, Huston wore the same suit for several days; unlike Ruppert, his title of captain was earned rather than politically granted. Early in life, he went to work with his father on the Louisville and Nashville Railroad until his dad encouraged him to seek better opportunities, which he found as a city engineer in Cincinnati. His break came with the outbreak of the Spanish-American War: he organized a regiment of engineers to help the war effort, and served as captain of his Second U.S. Volunteer of Engineers.

Huston remained in Cuba after the war to seek new opportunities. Going into business for himself with little capital, he sought government jobs to make harbor improvements in Havana and surrounding cities. "The way to make money is to put others to work for you," said Huston. "Never do anything you can hire someone else to do for you. It's the one who tells the other fellow what to do who reaps the profits."

During a visit back home, Huston met John McGraw when attending a Giants game and the two become fast friends. Later, McGraw contacted Huston before a trip to Cuba. During his visit, Huston told his friend of his desire to own a ball club one day. McGraw told him he had another millionaire friend who shared the same interest.

When Huston came home for good, McGraw arranged for his two friends to meet one evening to discuss investing in the New York Yankees. They were unimpressed. As far as Ruppert and Huston were concerned, the Giants were the only team worth owning. "No chance," said McGraw, who kept pushing the Yankees by explaining about the possibilities that existed through proper direction and fresh money.

McGraw wanted to see his two friends, and the Yankees, succeed. With two wealthy owners in charge, there would never be a worry over the Yankees' rent payment at the Giants' stadium, the Polo Grounds. In addition, a contending Yankees team might rub off on better attendance for his Giants, and there was the thought of a Giants-Yankees World Series in the future.

Something that never entered McGraw's mind was the possibility of the Yankees taking the majority of New York City's fan base. The popularity of McGraw's team had made them number one in the hearts of most baseball fans throughout the country, and led to the Giants' setting baseball's all-time home attendance record of 970,000 in 1908. He believed the Yankees would get better, but that would take time, and no matter how good they became, the Giants would continue to be America's team.

Ruppert and Huston decided to speak to Bill Devery and Frank Farrell, the two current owners of the Yankees. The co-owners were open and receptive to selling the team, mostly because they wanted to rid themselves of one another, their working relationship having soured since the time they had purchased the ball club for $18,000 in 1903. They had tasted success in 1904 when the New York American Leaguers had barely missed winning the pennant, and again in 1906, but after that the two owners were said to have become more focused in micromanaging, leading to dissent among players and managers with the owners. Soon the two owners were criticizing each other. With no direction or leadership, the team became a cast of misfits. During the 1914 season, Frank Chance became the latest manager to quit, leaving the managerial duties to twenty-three-year-old Roger Peckinpaugh, one of the few decent players on the roster. "It was an orphan ball club without a home of its own, without players of outstanding ability, without prestige," is how Ruppert described the Yankees at the time of the purchase.

American League President Ban Johnson and the American League owners were delighted to have the Yankees under the direction of wealthy ownership. Wanting to see the new owners succeed, Johnson talked to the other league owners about building a stronger team in New York. Frank Navin, the owner of the Tigers, was the only one to respond by sending two players to the Yanks for $7,500. One of the two was a promising first baseman named Wally Pipp, who would blossom into a star in his new surroundings.

The first order of business was to hire a manager. Unsure where to look, the new owners asked a few sportswriters, and they suggested Bill Donavan, Babe Ruth's manager in Providence in 1914 when the team had won the International League pennant.

Following a losing season in 1915, the Yankees won eighty games in 1916 for just their fourth winning season in team history. They also set a team attendance record by surpassing 469,000, but their success would be short-lived. In 1917, the Yankees suffered another losing season. "I like you, Donavan," said Ruppert, "but we have to make some changes around here." Eager to win as soon as possible, the two owners fired the first manager they had hired.

Before the 1917 season, Huston organized the Eighteenth Engineers and took his new unit to France to help in the Great War effort by building bridges and roads. For his outstanding work and service to his country, he was promoted to lieutenant colonel. While away, he kept in touch with Ruppert, and he was all for hiring a new manager. His choice was his drinking and hunting buddy Wilbert Robinson, the manager of the Brooklyn Dodgers,

Opposite: Colonel Jacob Ruppert and Miller Huggins. Ruppert was impressed with Huggins from the first time they met and remained loyal to the manager to the end (National Baseball Hall of Fame, Cooperstown, New York).

who had impressed Huston when his team won the 1916 National League pennant.

During his playing days, Robinson was a star with the old Baltimore Orioles of the National League. Teaming up with John McGraw and Wee Willie Keeler, the Orioles won three straight pennants during the 1890s, and were pronounced as baseball's greatest team. Now at age fifty, Robinson was as energetic as ever, full of vigor, and could take on any of his players if he had to.

As far as Huston was concerned, it was a done deal. All Robinson had to do was meet Ruppert at his brewery, sign a contract, and he was the next Yankees manager. But Colonel Ruppert was unimpressed. He did ask a few questions and pretended to listen to the answers before saying, "No, you won't do. For one thing, you're too old." Too old! Robinson was insulted. Never did he think of himself as old, even at fifty. He picked up his hat and coat, growled goodbye, and headed to the door.

When Huston heard from Robinson, he fired a cable across the ocean. Ruppert read it, shrugged his shoulders, and contacting Ban Johnson for advice. "Get Miller Huggins," the league president told him.

Johnson did believe that Huggins was a fine manager, but he had another motive: the National League stole a good baseball man from his league, Branch Rickey. Luring Huggins offered a chance to even the score. Johnson had been in contact with Huggins during the 1917 season upon hearing he was unhappy as manager of the St. Louis Cardinals. Huggins happened to be in New York City in December for the baseball winter meetings when he heard that Colonel Ruppert wanted to see him. He knew what it was about; however, being apprehensive about managing in New York City, he declined the invitation. Taylor Spinks, a St. Louis resident and writer for *The Sporting News*, told Huggins he should consider the opportunity. "All right, to please you, I'll go," Huggins said.

Ruppert liked Huggins from the very beginning and wasted little time in offering him the job. And to his own amazement, Huggins accepted the offer. "There is something about that fellow that I like," said Ruppert. "I like his businesslike way he spoke to me. He's young—and businesslike."

Baseball was thriving prior to the 1920s. In 1919, all sixteen major league teams enjoyed a spike in attendance. The excitement of the 1919 season could be attributed to the troops coming home, and to Babe Ruth hitting an unthinkable twenty-nine home runs to set the new home run record. He did it in just 430 at bats, and he pitched eight victories in fifteen starts (the plan in New York was to make him a fulltime outfielder).

Babe Ruth had proved that the fans craved for the long ball instead of scientific baseball, whereby teams would play for a run per inning with a hit, a stolen base, a sacrifice, and another hit to score one run. Owners saw the numbers of fans packing Fenway Park and other parks in the American League in hope of witnessing a Babe Ruth home run. In an effort to capitalize on the power game, trick pitches like the spitball were banned, with a grandfather clause exempting major league pitchers currently using the spitter from the rule. Another change in discussion among the baseball owners was the hiring of a commissioner to govern the game. The idea came about after exposed scandals left the owners feeling embarrassed. Rumors were hot that during the previous fall that the White Sox had sold out to gamblers to fix the 1919 World Series. Although the Reds did indeed upset the favored White Sox, the general feeling was that Chicago was tired after battling the Indians and Yankees in a close pennant race. Former President Howard Taft was considered the leading candidate for the job of baseball commissioner. Another candidate was a hard-working Chicago judge who was said to preside over the courtroom "in which juries never sleep."

Ruth's first spring training with the Yankees in the rowdy town of Jacksonville, Florida, was a party. Without a curfew set by Huggins, his players took advantage of the night life, especially Ruth. "I don't room with him. I room with his suitcase," answered Yankees outfielder Ping Bodie when asked what life was like as Ruth's roommate. In an exhibition game in Miami, a hung over Ruth was kayoed after colliding with a palm tree. That was the final straw for Huggins. He called for a team meeting to lay down the law. Not only did he implement a mandatory curfew rule, he required that every player make a daily appearance in the dining room for breakfast before nine o'clock.

When the 1920 season began, Ruth hardly did anything to back up his transaction and new contract. (He had agreed to honor his Boston base salary of $10,000 per season for the next two years, but he also received a $1,000 signing bonus and another $20,000 to be paid in $2,500 lump sums during the 1920 and 1921 seasons.) In the season opener at Philadelphia, he dropped a fly ball in the eighth inning to allow the winning run to tally. He was presented with a brown derby the next day, a symbol in baseball awarded to the player who makes the misplay of the game. Ruth took it like a good sport, and even wore the hat to go along with the gag. In the game that day he whiffed with the bases loaded. In New York's home opener, Ruth wrenched his side during batting practice, yet he insisted on playing. After striking out in his first at bat, he withdrew from the game.

Following his slow start, Ruth got hot and so did the Yankees. He went 14 for 34 with eight home runs during a New York ten-game winning streak. Ruth went on another hitting tear during another New York winning streak

2. Rupert and Houston

in June that moved New York into first place. Less than halfway into the season, Ruth was batting .385 with twenty-four home runs, leaving little doubt that he was going to shatter his record. The question was, how many would he hit in 1920?

On July 6, the first-place Yankees won at Washington, 17–0. Afterwards, Ruth, who had driven his four-door sedan on the road trip, was driving back to New York with Helen and three other passengers. As the party laughed and sang during their ride, Ruth failed to react in time to a sharp turn in the road. The car spun out of control, turned over, and threw the passengers from the vehicle. Ruth emerged from the wreckage and shouted to the others. All passengers responded accept for Yankees coach Charlie O'Leary. Then Ruth noticed O'Leary flat on his back in the middle of the dirt road. "Oh God, oh my God, please bring Charlie back," cried Ruth as he ran to the coach and fell to his knees. "Speak to me, Charlie. Speak to me." O'Leary opened his eyes, looked around, and asked, "What the hell happened? Where's my hat?"

The party walked a half mile along the road to a farmhouse where the owners welcomed them to spend the night. With their car totaled, they headed to nearby Philadelphia the next day where they saw the headlines of a newspaper: "Ruth Reported Killed in a Car Crash."

At the Polo Grounds on July 15, Ruth tied the home run record in just eighty-three games. Four days later, he set a new record when he hit two more.

Why was Ruth hitting so many home runs? Why were many players hitting home runs? Pitching restrictions helped, but others questioned changes to the actual baseball. A.J. Reach, the company that manufactured baseballs for the major leagues, denied that any changes had been made, but better materials available after the Great War, which could be wound tighter, and mechanical improvements in winding and sewing machines, made for improved quality of baseballs that led to greater spring.

As the Indians, White Sox, and Yankees battled for the American League pennant, rumors of a fix in the 1919 World Series began to heat up. On September 7, a grand jury was hired to look into allegations. At the Polo Grounds on August 16, tragedy occurred on the field when Carl Mays, a controversial Yankees pitcher, threw a fastball that skulled Ray Chapman of the Indians. The injured player died the next morning to become the first and only onfield fatality in baseball history.

Mays, a temperamental hurler who had worn out his welcome with the Red Sox before coming to the Yankees, had a reputation for brushing back hitters. His hot temper and reputation had made him detested by opposing players, and even by his own teammates. His several enemies used the tragedy as an opportunity to attempt to organize a boycott throughout the league with all teams refusing to play against him, but that lost its steam when the incident was clearly ruled an accident. Yankees pitcher Jack Quinn agreed:

> Most fans got the wrong idea of the play. They imagined that Mays tried to dust Ray off the plate, as he had a reputation for that. The truth is poor Chapman was at fault. Mays had two strikes on him, both pitches being outside. Chapman always crowded the plate when he hit and he would lean his head over it. Mays' fatal pitch cut the heart of the plate. Chapman made the mistake of ducking his head in hope the ball would go over his neck, but instead it hit him in the temple.

The game was postponed the next day, but the series resumed the day after with Huggins giving Quinn the starting assignment:

> The accident crushed the two teams' spirit, and the feeling seemed to spread to the spectators. You could hear a pin drop as I pitched the first ball of the game. I was nervous and afraid that I might lose control and hit a player. I had one close one with Steve O'Neil at bat. The ball got away from me and went straight for O'Neil's head and in a second I thought I had pitched another tragedy, but O'Neil ducked. I won the game, but it was a nightmare for me.

Quinn allowed just three hits in seven innings and struck out six, but was not credited with the win. Wally Pipp hit an inside-the-park home run in the bottom of the ninth for a 4–3 Yankees victory.

The grief-stricken Indians went into a tailspin while the Yankees won eight of nine games in September to reclaim first place, with Carl Mays, after taking time away to recover from the accident, hurling two shutouts in his four wins during the winning streak. New York traveled to Chicago for a huge three-game series, but lost their momentum and their league lead after being swept in the series. Cleveland recovered from their brief slump to win 16 of 19 games to clinch the pennant, and then went on to defeat Brooklyn in the World Series.

Ruth set a new home run record with fifty-four, more than any other American League team had combined for. However, the excitement of Ruth's home-run record and pennant race were buried during the final week of the season when members of the White Sox testified before the grand jury that they did conspire to throw the 1919 World Series. Needing to come clean in order to restore the integrity of the game, the owners quickly moved forward on their plan to hire a commissioner, and their choice was that Chicago judge, named Kenesaw Mountain Landis.

3

Fifty-Nine Home Runs and Five Suspensions— 1921 and 1922

"Probably nowhere in all the imaginative field of fiction could one find a career more dramatic and bizarre than that portrayed in real life by George Herman Ruth."

—A New York sportswriter

Some claimed Babe Ruth was bigger than life, but while his popularity reached a new high, his marriage was sinking. Helen was having a rough time coping with her husband's fame. "She was just a kid when they got married, and now her husband was bigger than the president," a teammate said. Ruth's love of spending money and his poor handling of the family finances is where trouble first began. Treating his wife like she was less important than baseball, his endorsements, and his night life added more fuel to the fire. And then there were the other women.

The ladies were plentiful with open invitations. They'd call Ruth in the Yankees' clubhouse. He'd take their calls, and arrange to meet them on the condition they agreed to sex. His teammates would occasionally take the phone calls when Ruth was absent, tell the ladies they could hit the ball and had lots of money, and asked if they could meet in the Astor Hotel lobby at eight o'clock. "We made more dates for Babe than he could have ever dreamed of," said Waite Hoyt. "We often wondered how many of those girls waited all night for Ruth to show up."

To get away from the crowds, or perhaps as an apology to Helen (some have said), Ruth purchased a home in the quiet community of Sudbury, Massachusetts, known as Home Plate Farm. Ruth invited Waite Hoyt and a few other teammates to see his new home. Hoyt recalled seeing antiques in the home that he estimated to be worth more than the property. The next time

Hoyt and the others stopped by they were impressed to see new concrete floors, new wings added to the outer buildings, and the addition of livestock that included turkeys, chickens, cows, and horses, but Hoyt couldn't help but wonder what had happened to those beautiful antiques. "Oh those," answered Ruth, "I paid a guy to move them the hell out. It was just junk."

The hiring of Landis was a relief to owners, fans, and everyone associated with baseball. "Landis was a personality, a man of great mental strength, and one who sincerely loved America's great national sport," said Taylor Spink.

The news was anything but gratifying before the 1920 World Series for baseball. It was announced in late September that eight members of the White Sox were indicted, and their case would head to court. How would this affect the future of the game? "Baseball men were pretty scared. And I mean scared," said Spink, "so was everyone connected with the game. We didn't feel so happy about the situation in our *Sporting News* office. We talked

Judge Landis, baseball's first commissioner, cleaned up the game and showed Babe Ruth who was in charge (National Baseball Hall of Fame, Cooperstown, New York).

3. Fifty-Nine Home Runs and Five Suspensions—1921 and 1922

bravely, but we saw plenty of stormy weather ahead. Thanks to Babe Ruth skyrocketing his home run record from 29 to 54, baseball enjoyed a bountiful 1921 season."

The Yankees were busy during the winter in finding players that could help win the pennant. In a multi-player trade with the Red Sox, New York acquired switch-hitting catcher Wally Schang, and an erratic, hot-tempered, hard-throwing right-hander named Waite Hoyt. Late in the 1919 season, Huggins had watched Hoyt retire nineteen of his Yankees in a row en route to a three-hit shutout. Knowing the youngster possessed great potential, he pounced on the opportunity to bring him to the Yankees.

Born and raised in Brooklyn, Waite Hoyt was so good at Erasmus High School that he was invited to throw batting practice to the Dodgers at Ebbets Field. One day, dressed in a sleeveless shirt, knickerbockers, and black stockings as he threw batting practice, he caught the attention of the Dodgers' owner with his fastball, sharp curve, and accuracy. "Who is he?" asked Charles H. Ebbets.

"Oh, just some pupil at Erasmus; he's fourteen and comes here every day."

"Why don't you sew him up for future delivery?" asked Ebbets.

"He's too young, and I wouldn't like to take him away from school."

A year later, the Giants invited him to pitch at the Polo Grounds. He was signed at the ripe age of fifteen. "The Giants gave me $5 for signing and my dad took it away from me immediately. He felt it was too much money for a kid to have at one time."

He was sent to the minor leagues for "seasoning," and pitched with unspectacular results for three seasons. Before the 1919 season, John McGraw told him he was going to send him back to the minors. "Not me," replied Hoyt.

"What the hell do you mean not me?" screamed McGraw.

"Just what I said," replied Hoyt. "Not me."

His contract was sold to New Orleans of the Southern Association, but Hoyt refused to report. He signed with the Baltimore Dry Docks, an independent baseball team. Red Sox manager Ed Barrow, tipped off about a youngster with blazing speed and pinpoint control, decided he needed to see Hoyt for himself. After watching him pitch batting practice to his Red Sox, he offered a contract. Before signing, Hoyt insisted on never being farmed out, starting a game within a week and one the following.

"Your pretty fresh kid, aren't you?" responded Barrow.

"I guess so, but that's it, Mr. Barrow," said Hoyt.

A few days later, Barrow gave Hoyt his first starting assignment. "It's an easy one, kid. Detroit and Ty Cobb," Barrow told him. Pleased that his new manager kept his word, Hoyt came through by pitching a 2–1 win in twelve innings.

Following the 1920 season, the Yankees had a project to build a new stadium. "They are moving to Goatsville," snickered John McGraw. The ten-acre tract of land in the Bronx purchased by the Yankees was isolated, "and before too long they will be lost sight of. A New York team should be based on Manhattan Island." The site had once been considered by the old Brotherhood League of the nineteenth century, and by Farrell and Devery in 1903. The land around the ten-acre plot remained undeveloped, but potential for businesses and housing existed, since the area now had a subway stop.

With Babe Ruth, the game's best drawing card, the Yankees became the first team in history to draw more than one million fans in a season. Their final 1920 home attendance of 1,289,422 shattered the Giants' 1908 record and made $864,830 in gate receipts. The Giants also surpassed the 1908 attendance record, but drew 359,000 fewer than their tenants, and this did not sit well with McGraw or the Giants' owner, Charles A. Stoneham.

McGraw's hunch was correct. The success of the Yankees' new ownership did help the Giants' home attendance. However, he underestimated how the rise of New York's American League ball club could reduce his Giants to New York City's second favorite team.

The Yankees were now unwelcome to rent the Polo Grounds. They were welcome to play there until their new stadium was completed. At a higher rent amount, of course. "We aim to make our new park the finest baseball plant in the world," said Ruppert. The two owners intended to make their new stadium a palace, the crown jewel among major league baseball stadiums.

Baseball quickly learned that the fans were forgiving, and believed in the new commissioner. Right from the get-go of the 1921 season, the fans packed seven major league parks for a combined opening day attendance of 160,000. Forty thousand fans invaded the Polo Grounds to see the Yankees open the season. Another 15,000 were turned away. Ruth didn't homer, although he went 5-for-5 in a Yankees 11–1 win over the Athletics.

Ruth and the Yankees got off to a good start, winning five of their first six games. Through the first ten games, Ruth was ahead of his 1920 home run pace with five. He hit ten during May and thirteen in June to give him twenty-eight home runs through sixty-nine games. He hit number thirty-eight on the last day of July.

The Yankees were in a battle with the Indians for the American League

3. Fifty-Nine Home Runs and Five Suspensions—1921 and 1922

pennant. Just a few games separated the two teams throughout the summer, with the Yanks never trailing by more than a few games. New York would occasionally take the top spot for a day or two, then would lose and fall back into second place.

The White Sox were struggling, as expected, due to the suspension of eight players, including the great Joe Jackson, for their part in fixing the 1919 World Series. In July, the entire nation watched as they went on trial for criminal conspiracy. On August 2, the jury delivered a not guilty verdict to set off a wild celebration in the courtroom. "The players had many friends in the court; it was most disgusting," wrote Taylor Spink. "Some of them treated the acquitted players as though they were returning heroes."

Bob Meusel was a powerful hitter and a good base runner, and possessed a great throwing arm, but displayed poor behavior off the field (National Baseball Hall of Fame, Cooperstown, New York).

The next day, Landis announced his verdict for the eight acquitted ballplayers: "Regardless of verdict of juries, no ballplayer that throws a ballgame, no player who entertains proposals or promises to throw a game, will ever play professional baseball."

The Yankees concluded August with a 17–9 win at Washington. In the win a twenty-four-year-old right-handed power-hitting outfielder Bob Meusel made three hits, including his seventh home run of the month.

Robert William Meusel had made an immediate impression as a rookie in 1920 when he stepped into the batting cage for the first time in Jacksonville, and belted balls to all directions of the distant outfield. "I'll bet he'll be one of the most talked about hitters in the country this season," predicting Miller Huggins. "He is one of those natural hitters with a perfect hitting swing."

Finding a spot for the talented rookie in the potent Yankees lineup was a problem. Meusel came to New York from the Vernon Tigers of the Pacific Coast League as a third baseman; when one of the veteran outfielders went out with an injury, Meusel filled in. He also received plenty of playing time at third base, and after a productive rookie season, he became an everyday starter in the New York outfield.

Meusel stood at 6'3", weighed 190, had good speed, and had a powerful throwing arm. One problem: he hung around a bad influence in Ruth. His poor behavior was not going to be tolerated by the Yankees, and that was mentioned in his 1921 contract. Offended by the clause, Meusel held out before finally deciding to sign.

A day after the lopsided win at Washington, Meusel socked his seventeenth home run of the season in another win that propelled the Yankees into first place. A day later, Meusel did it again, and then went 5-for-5 in another Yankees win.

The Yankees moved closer to the pennant after scoring thirty-eight runs in three games at Philadelphia, with Ruth hitting homers number fifty-three and fifty-four to tie his record. A week later, the Yankees scored thirty-four runs in three games with Meusel hitting three home runs, one with the bases full, to give him twenty-three for the year. On September 15, Ruth set the record when he connected at the Polo Grounds for his fifty-fifth home run.

As good as the Yanks were playing, they were unable to shake the Indians. In late September, with just one game separating the two teams, the Indians came to the Polo Grounds. Waite Hoyt struck out seven in the first game in a 4–2 New York win for the pitcher's eighteenth win of the season. After the Tribe took the second game, Meusel pounded out three hits, including his twenty-fourth home run, in a Yankees win. The next day, Ruth hit his fifty-seventh and fifty-eighth in another Yankees victory. He would homer in the last game of the season to set the new record at fifty-nine.

The subway World Series that McGraw had envisioned became a reality. The Giants and Yankees would meet in the last best-of-nine World Series. Like the Yankees, the Giants had spent most of the season in second place before streaking through September to take the pennant.

Mays and Hoyt pitched the American League champions to victories in the first two games. Ruth, making just one hit in the first two games, entertained the crowd by stealing second and third after his fourth walk of the series. While the fans went wild, Ruth looked at his elbow after swiping third and noticed he had sustained a severe cut during his display of speed.

In Game Three, the Giants rallied for eight in the seventh inning to break a 4–4 tie and win their first game of the series. Mays appeared to be on his game in Game Four until the Giants once again rallied for the lead. With a

3. *Fifty-Nine Home Runs and Five Suspensions—1921 and 1922*   27

Giants 4–1 lead in the last of the ninth, Ruth, disobeying the team doctor's order not to play, hit his first World Series home run to cut the lead to 4–2. However, Meusel fouled out and Pipp bounced back to the pitcher to end the game.

Hoyt was brilliant once again by pitching the Yankees to a 3–1 win in Game Five to reclaim the series lead for the Yanks. Meusel was the hitting star with an RBI double to score what proved to be the winning run. Ruth, once again ignoring his medical advice, scored from first on Mesuel's double, and then decided to listen to the doctor. He would retire for the remainder of the series. The Yankees, needing two more wins to become world champions, would have to do it without him.

Minus Ruth, the Yankees scored five runs in the first two innings in an 8–5 loss in Game Six. After that, the Yankees' bats went cold. They would score just one run to waste good pitching performances by Mays and Hoyt in Games Seven and Eight that resulted in a pair of one-run losses to lose the World Series.

Following the World Series, a now healthy Ruth intended to disregard baseball's bylaws by partaking in a barnstorming tour. He was slated to manage one of the teams and earn $25,000, a higher amount than his yearly salary. The rule would soon be changed, but at that time players who had participated in World Series were prohibited to barnstorm for fear that it would cheapen the World Series. It was a law that Judge Landis intended to uphold, and when he heard that Ruth and other Yankees had plans, he immediately phoned the players to clarify of the rule. Most of the Yankees dropped out when hearing from the Commissioner.

A day after the conclusion of the World Series, Landis was at the Commodore Hotel in New York with sportswriter Frederick Lieb when the phone rang in his room. It was Ruth, who had failed to return the Commissioner's previous calls, which annoyed Landis.

"Oh, you are, are you? That's fine," an angry Landis blurted into the phone. "But if you do, it will be the sorriest thing you've ever done in baseball." Landis slammed the phone onto the receiver "with such a bang that it nearly wrecked the instrument," then paced as he cussed up a storm. "Who does that big monkey think he is?" he asked. He paced and swore some more before saying, "It seems I have to show someone who is running the game."

Lieb left the judge and taxied to Huston's residence, where the Yankees co-owner was passed out on the floor after an evening of drinking with Harry Frazee. Lieb's rap on the door woke him. The sportswriter told him about the Landis-Ruth conversation, and Huston began to worry. If Ruth was to go on the trip there was no telling what the judge might do. "Aw, go tell that old guy to jump in the lake," Ruth told Huston. Ruth barnstormed, and Meusel, who did whatever Ruth did, joined him.

It was obvious that Ruth was going to get his. Knowing his punishment was going to be harsh, the Yankees sent someone to talk to Landis with the hopes of persuading him to go light with the penalty. Ed Barrow, having left the managerial post at Boston to become New York's business manager, drew the assignment.

"Well, what do you want?" Landis snapped when Barrow entered his Chicago office.

"I guess you know what," replied Barrow.

"Yes I do," said the judge.

The commissioner rose from behind his desk and led Barrow to his office window. They looked out at the street below where they saw two children. "I suppose they're saying to each other, 'That big white-haired so-in-so up in that office up there is the one who's keeping Babe Ruth out of the game.' But tell me: what would you do?"

"I'd suspend him too," said Barrow, who then headed to the door and traveled back to New York. The judge fined Ruth and Meusel their World Series bonus of $3,362 and suspended them through the first six weeks of the 1922 season.

Huggins believed he had solved the Yankees' problem with their lack of pitching depth that had been exposed during the 1921 World Series. Before October was over, he received two quality pitchers and a shortstop in a trade with Boston. The pitchers were "Bullet Joe" Bush, the author of the fork ball and a fifteen-game winner in seven of his eight full seasons, and "Sad Sam" Jones, a twenty-three game winner in 1921. The shortstop was Everett Scott, not as good as Peckinpaugh, especially in the field, but the man Huggins wanted for the job. Team captain Peckinpaugh was sent to Boston along with Jack Quinn and two other pitchers. The Yankees also took care of another weakness in centerfield by obtaining Whitey Witt from the A's.

As New York prepared for the season at the new spring training site in New Orleans, Ruppert and Huston talked to Ruth about a new contract, since his two-year contract had expired. The Babe played hardball, as usual, by declining a $40,000 per year deal. Fifty-thousand was offered. Ruth asked for fifty-two thousand. How come? He liked the idea of earning $1,000 per week. He was also rewarded the captaincy of the Yankees, a huge honor in those days.

Minus Ruth and Meusel, the Yankees got the season off to a good start, thanks to a strong pitching staff that hurled five shutouts. When Ruth and Meusel were back in the lineup on May 20, the two sluggers went hitless in an 8–2 loss to the Browns before 40,000 at the Polo Grounds, who had booed Ruth during his hitless day. The fans were louder during Ruth's one for five at

3. Fifty-Nine Home Runs and Five Suspensions—1921 and 1922

the plate the next day. The boo-birds continued into his third game of the season, and after Ruth caught a routine fly ball for an easy out late in the game, the crowd gave a sarcastic cheer. Ruth responded by mockingly tipping his cap. In the eighth inning, he hit his first home run of the season and looked at the ground as he trotted around the bases rather than acknowledge the cheers with a smile or a tip of his cap. Another hitless game dropped Ruth to 2 for 16 on the season. He did draw one walk, tried to steal second, and while he was heading back to the dugout after being thrown out, the booing was loud. The next game at the Polo Grounds, Ruth went 0-for-5; twice he grounded out with the bases loaded.

On May 25, before a weekday crowd of 10,000, Ruth finally got another hit. When he saw the centerfielder juggle the ball, he tried for second, but was thrown out. Ruth sprang to his feet with a handful of dirt and tossed it into the umpire's face. As expected, the arbitrator banished Ruth from the game. While storming his way back to the dugout to the hoots and catcalls of the home crowd, Ruth stopped to make a scornful bow. "Play ball, you big bum," yelled a fan. Ruth heard that. He charged the stand and jumped into the crowd. The fan hurriedly climbed over the seats until he was safely at the top aisle. Ruth shouted while shaking a fist at him. "Hit the big stiff!" another fan shouted. Ruth retreated and climbed to the top of the dugout roof. His face crimson, he issued a challenge: "Anyone who wants to fight, come on down to the field!" Nobody accepted the invitation.

Ruth leaped back onto the field and made the long walk to the clubhouse in centerfield to the sound of intense booing. He pointed at one more fan before disappearing.

After the game, Ruth, a little calmer, said he didn't mean to throw dirt at the umpire, "but I did mean to hit that bastard in the stands." That night Ban Johnson announced that Ruth would be suspended and fined. He also ordered that he be stripped of his captaincy. Everett Scott was named the Yankees' new captain.

Ruth began to hit in late May. He got eight hits in four games and hit his third home run on June 4. This time Ruth replied to the fans by tipping his cap as he smiled. All seemed fine and things appeared to be back to normal.

In Mid-June, the Yankees went into a slump and fell out of first place for the first time since the season's first week. In Cleveland, a play at second base that went against the slumping Yankees resulted in an argument. Ruth stormed in from the outfield to have his say, but his choice of words drew a game ejection. A report went to Ban Johnson that night. The league president read it, and then sent word to the umpires that Ruth was suspended for the third time this season.

Ruth exploded when hearing the news during batting practice the following day. He sought out the umpire and gave him an earful. "If you ever put me out of the game again I'll fix you so you'll never umpire again."

Umpire Bill Dinneen, a former pitcher, was a big man who was still in good shape, replied dismissively.

"You're yellow," Ruth told him.

"No one ever accuses me of being yellow," said Dinneen.

"If you don't like it, come under the stands," said Ruth.

That evening, Dinneen issued another report to Johnson, who added two more games to Ruth's suspension for his fourth suspension of the season.

The suspensions, the fans, the pennant pressure were getting to Ruth. Soon he was on his teammates. In late July, the Yankees traveled to St. Louis to meet the surprising Browns, who owned first place with a 1½-game lead over the second-place New Yorkers. Urban Shocker, once a Yankee, kept his curse over the Yanks by shutting them out in the first game of the series. In the second game, Pipp made a misplay, and he knew Ruth would have something to say. When Pipp stepped inside the dugout after the inning, he warned, "If that monkey says anything, I'll punch him right in that big nose."

Ruth entered the dugout. "For God's sakes, Pipp—"

Pow!

"Now stop that!" Huggins barked from the first base coach's box as Pipp and Ruth traded blows. Pipp landed most of the punches, connecting several times with Ruth's face as Ruth swung wildly. Yankees third baseman Frank Baker was hit by a few punches as he tried to push the two apart. When the two men were finally pried apart, Ruth said, "We'll settle this after the game."

"That's all right with me," answered Pipp.

The Yankees appeared to be heading for a collapse after that. The Browns scored five in the seventh to take a 6–3 lead. But led by two home runs by Ruth, the Yanks scored four in the eighth and four more in the ninth for an 11–6 win. "You birds ought to fight every day," laughed one of the Browns' coaches.

Ruth was in great spirits when he entered the victorious clubhouse. "I'm ready," Pipp told him.

"Oh, forget it," said Ruth.

The next day, Pipp made three hits including a home run in a Yankees win in extra innings. New York also took the final game to reclaim first place.

The Yankees got hot in August, winning 13 of 16 games. The Browns kept pace. After dropping three of four, New York won seven straight, yet were just 1½ games up on the Browns.

In late August, Ruth had another altercation with an umpire that resulted

3. Fifty-Nine Home Runs and Five Suspensions—1921 and 1922

in another ejection. Again, a report was sent to the league office. Again, Ruth was suspended, making it five in one season.

In September, Ruth made more headlines. Helen had been seen pushing a baby carriage outside the Ruth's summer residence, the Ansonia Hotel. When reporters began to question the hotel staff, they learned that the Ruths had been seen with a baby for the past month or two and Babe was very fond of it. "Oh, you found out about that," Ruth said when questioned in Cleveland on September 23.

> Yep, Dorothy is getting to be a big girl now. She weighed only two pounds when she came into the world, and for a while we weren't sure if the rascal would live.
>
> But when we put her in an incubator, she began to pick up right away, and now she is just as healthy as any other kid.

When asked where and when Dorothy was born, Ruth answered February 2, 1921, at the Presbyterian Hospital.

Mystified as to why the birth of Ruth's child had gone unreported for over a year, confused by the details supplied by the Ruths, and unable to find a birth record, the press assumed that Dorothy had been adopted (National Baseball Hall of Fame, Cooperstown, New York).

Back in New York, Helen became angry when reporters asked her if the baby was adopted. "I should say not," replied Helen. "That baby is mine, mine, mine!" She also mentioned that her baby was born with rickets, a disease caused by vitamin D deficiency and characterized by softening of the bones. When asked when and where Dorothy was born, Helen said June 7, 1921, at St. Vincent's. When told that her answer was different from her husband's, she said, "Obviously he confused it with his own birthday." She had no explanation about why he named a different hospital.

An investigation was made, but no records of the Ruth baby at St. Vincent's or Presbyterian were found. A check with New York City's Department of Health revealed nothing. "Don't you think that Dorothy is a dead image of her father?" Helen asked the sportswriters. "Her nose is a duplicate of my husband's. See how it turns up?"

The Yankees and Browns battled until the season's last day, when New York managed to win the pennant by one game, and once again would face the Giants in the World Series. Ruth hit thirty-five home runs in 110 games and drove in 99 runs. Meusel's home run production also fell to eight fewer than the year before, but he recovered from a slow start to hit .315. Joe Bush won twenty-six games, Bob Shawkey won twenty, and Hoyt won nineteen.

The 1922 World Series was a nightmare, for the Yankees and for Ruth. In a best-of-seven series, the Yankees salvaged one tie (Game Two was called due to darkness), and lost four. McGraw had planned for his pitchers to throw nothing but slow balls to Ruth while calling every pitch from the dugout. Ruth was humiliated by going two for seventeen. In Game Five, with the Giants on their way to another World Series win over their cross-town rivals, Ruth heard the taunts from the Giants bench. "Nice going, Two Head!" they yelled after he swung and missed and fell to a knee.

"Lay it over for him!" yelled McGraw. "He can't hit it even if you tell him what's coming!" A swing and a miss for strike two, followed by laughter from the Giants dugout. "Throw it in the dust!" yelled McGraw. Ruth swung and missed on a pitch in the dirt. It was that kind of series for him.

World Series participants were now eligible to barnstorm, and Ruth took advantage. When he returned to New York City, he isolated himself in his Ansonia Hotel apartment, but could not get away from the talk of the 1922 World Series. He saw the newspaper articles. "How did McGraw make you look so foolish?" a neighbor asked. Every time he set foot outside of his hotel, there were crowds, and one guy among the crowd kept asking if he could speak with him. Ruth kept waving him away.

Christy Walsh was a lawyer from California who came to New York with a career idea that would make fast money. He was twenty-nine years old, always wore double-breasted suits, and was a good talker. He held an advertising job for Maxwell-Chalmers automobiles in Detroit while learning to represent others by ghost-writing their stories, then selling the stories to newspapers. He wanted to do that for Babe Ruth.

One evening, Walsh was pondering an idea to meet Ruth as he sat alone at a delicatessen near the Ansonia, which secretly operated a bootlegging business, when the phone rang. He heard someone say, "Mr. Ruth for a case of bootlegger beer." This was Walsh's chance. Volunteering to make the delivery,

3. Fifty-Nine Home Runs and Five Suspensions—1921 and 1922

he got into Ruth's apartment. "Do you know who I am?" he asked while helping Ruth unpack and stock the beer bottles.

"Sure I know you," answered Ruth. "Ain't you been bringing our beer for the past two weeks?"

Walsh got down to business. He asked Ruth how much he was getting for his ghostwritten stories. "About five dollars each," answered Ruth, "What is it to you?"

Walsh guaranteed $1,000 in sixty days if Ruth hired him as his public relations manager. Ruth was intrigued. It was the start of a long-term business relationship. Walsh would come through as promised, and would become Ruth's business agent. He also offered to repair Ruth's damaged image that he had obtained during his turbulent 1922 season. With Ruth's approval, he planned a banquet at New York's Elks Club on November 15. Walsh invited sportswriters, politicians, and Broadway notables. State Senator Jimmy Walker (later to become the mayor of New York City) cut Ruth to pieces before the large gathering: "Babe Ruth is not only a great athlete, but also a great fool." Walker spoke about how Ruth let down his biggest and best fans: children, from the ones who play baseball in the empty lots, to the crippled children who were in hospitals.

Touched by hearing he had let down the children, Ruth began to sob. Walker put a hand on Ruth's shoulder as he concluded his speech by asking, "Will you not, for the kids of America, mend your ways? Will you not give back to those kids their great idol?"

Ruth got up and spoke to the crowd. "So help me, Jim, I will! I will go back to the farm in Sudbury and get in shape."

Feeling better, Ruth exited the banquet hall and was ready to travel to Home Plate Farm for the winter when he was handed a summons. A pregnant nineteen-year-old had filed a $50,000 maternity suit against him.

4

Miller Huggins

> "Let me tell you something. Huggins was a remarkable player. Despite the handicap of his size, he could bump into the big fellows and get away with it. He was as good as any second baseman that ever lived at making double plays"
>
> —Johnny Evers

The rookie's crooked smile and funny batting stance brought gales of laughter from his veteran teammates who couldn't decide if they should give him a toy bat and make him the mascot or give him a spanking and send him to school. "Pipe the new mascot," howled 6'5" Larry McLean, as he picked up the 5'6" rookie and held him high for others to see. "Why, kid, you're too little to play in the big leagues. We eat guys like you for breakfast. What's your name, Pint-Size?"

"I'm Miller Huggins," said the rookie.

"Well, I'm Larry McLean."

"Yeh, well, I'll be playing second base, and when you peg 'em down there, you better make them good, Big Boy," Huggins told the giant catcher.

Although scared at heart, Miller Huggins was too determined to listen to others remind him of his size and tell him he was too small to play major league baseball. He proved his point during his rookie season by ranging to his left to field a groundball and throwing to first base to get the out. An inning later, he scooted to his right for another grounder, and once again, he converted into an out. "Nice going, Mr. Little Everywhere," said McLean. He quickly earned the respect of his teammates, and the hometown fans who admired him for his hard work and using his size to his advantage. Huggins would make life difficult for opposing pitchers by crouching in the batter's box to make for an even smaller strike zone. Four times during his career he had led the National League in walks.

Baseball records indicate that Miller Huggins was born 1880; however,

4. Miller Huggins

Huggins penciled in March 27, 1878, on his 1918 draft registration card. He grew up in Cincinnati's Fourth Ward, one of the city's toughest neighborhoods, where he learned to fight his own battles. In spite of his size, he always held his own against the bigger kids.

His father, James Huggins, who came from England and worked his entire career in the groceries business, hoped his son would pursue a legal career that might lead to public office. His mother wanted him to become a minister—much like the kindly Dr. McClintock, the minister at the little parish church where the Hugginses worshipped. As a child, Miller dreamed about a life in the high seas—with a whole world of adventure lurking in each new unexpected corner. As Miller grew older, he began to consider professional baseball, a career that was against his dad's wishes. "Don't do it, Miller," his Dad would tell him. "That baseball is no business for a man. It's a kid's game. Stick to law, boy."

Huggins played shortstop and served as captain for his high school team. After graduating in 1897, he enrolled at the University of Cincinnati to study law. He continued to play baseball, and got his first taste of professional baseball with the Mansfield Haymakers of the Interstate League in the summer of 1899.

In 1902, Huggins graduated with a law degree, but bypassed a career in law for the game he loved. His dad was disappointed but never stood in his son's way. He knew he could always fall back on his law degree, although he would attempt to persuade him to practice law between baseball seasons. "Either I'm a lawyer or a ballplayer," Huggins told his dad. "You can't do both."

During a his three seasons at St. Paul of the American Association, Huggins hit .296, stole forty-eight bases one season, and was purchased by his hometown Cincinnati Reds. Never considered an outstanding hitter, Huggins once batted .292. In 1909, a sore arm limited him to fifty-seven games. Thinking that Huggins's career was declining, Cincinnati manager Clark Griffith traded him to the Cardinals, a move that was most unpopular among the Cincinnati diehards. One writer noted, "Cincinnati fans are so touchy over the deal that sent Huggins to the Cardinals that they will never forgive Griffith. Some think the proper thing would be to secure the return of Huggins and make him the manager in place of the man who traded him."

Huggins recovered from his injury during his first season with his new ball club and hit fifty-one points higher (.265) than the previous season, led the league in walks, scored over one hundred runs, and became a favorite among the St. Louis fans.

While his playing career was still active, Huggins was hired to manage the Cardinals by team owner Helene Robison Britton, who had inherited the

Cardinals when her uncle's will was revealed in 1911. The female owner selected Huggins to manage her team following a falling out with the team's current manager. Roger Bresnahan spoke to her like he would speak to any other owner. No man could talk to her that way, and she didn't hesitate to rid herself of Bresnahan and appoint Huggins as her team's skipper. "It's just like a woman to replace Bresnahan with the Little Shrimp," a sportswriter wrote. Another writer doubted that Huggins would be able to discipline the club as well as his predecessor, and perhaps he was right. The Cards finished last under the new manager's direction in 1913, but one season later, the Redbirds finished a surprising third. The astounded sportswriters tabbed Huggins as "The Little Miracle Worker of the West" following the Cardinals' successful season.

In 1915, Bob Connery, the one and only scout for the financially pressed Cardinals, discovered a prospect in a lower-tier minor league in Texas. After Huggins was informed, he went to team president Schular Britton (husband of the team's owner) and said, "Mr. Britton, I've got a chance to get a good infielder—a young fellow who can really pound that ball. How about it?"

"Sure, get him," replied Britton.

"But it will cost us $500 in cash," warned Huggins.

The team's president objected. Five hundred was money the Cards did not have. However, Huggins was persistent, and kept negotiating until he got the team president's approval to buy the youngster named Rogers Hornsby.

When Britton first saw the gawky, skinny, kid, who couldn't hit or field very well, he tabbed him as "Huggins's Folly" and added, "That rookie ought to be back on the farm."

By the end of the 1916 season, Mrs. Britton decided she wanted out of baseball. She called Huggins and her attorney to her home to tell them the news. "Gentlemen, I want the two of you to be the first to know in case you're interested in buying the club yourselves." Huggins was intrigued with the prospect of owning a team. He told his friend Bob Connery and contacted a friend in Cincinnati with the finances to back them. But before he could make an offer, the club was sold for $375,000. Huggins heard the news of the sale while managing the Cardinals through the 1917 spring training session. After the team got the season off to a good start, the team's new owner praised the manager before a room full of sportswriters. "But I need a man to run all the affairs as club president," the owner said. He asked the writers to cast their votes in the ballot box before leaving his office. And all the writers wrote the same name on their ballots.

Branch Rickey was the manager of the St. Louis Browns before becoming the team's business manager on the recommendation of American League President Ban Johnson to the Browns' new owner, Phil Ball. The two men were anything but a good match, and Ball's high voltage of adjectives never sat well with Rickey. When the Cardinals made their offer, he wasted no time in accepting.

It was reported that Huggins and Rickey shared mutual respect for one another as baseball men, although their philosophies differed. Nonetheless, Rickey believed that Huggins was a good manager. "There was never a sounder leader," he said of the St. Louis manager. He also knew of Huggins's desire to own a team, and his bitter disappointment when denied the opportunity to confer for the Cardinals. "He thought a certain club official had double crossed him by keeping him uniformed as to the progress of the negotiations," said Rickey. Following the 1917 season, Huggins told Rickey that he had a chance to manage a different club. Rickey told him he wanted him to stay. The Cardinals were still desperately in need of funds, but Rickey was able to offer $2,000 over his 1917 salary. Huggins declined. "He told me he wanted to get away, that he was out of sorts because he had been prevented from buying the club and that he could get $15,000 from another club," explained Rickey. "I told him if he could find such a club, I'd give him his release." When Huggins informed him he had landed with the Yankees, Rickey kept his promise.

Huggins left St. Louis on a good note. The 1917 Cardinals finished third, and once again, the manager was praised for his good work. "His record, considering he had very little money at his disposal, was remarkable."

The Little Miracle Worker of the West was in for an unpleasant surprise in the East. He got wind of the animosity between the two Yankees owners, and felt responsible. While in France during the 1918 season, Huston had plenty to say about Ruppert's managerial selection and having no say in the decision. He made charges of disloyalty by questioning the ethics in doing this while he was serving his country.

For Huggins, his first season at New York was enjoyable. The Yankees improved under his leadership by moving up two places in the standings (from sixth to fourth) and finished fifteen games closer to first place. The team batting average increased by eighteen points. The Yankees went from seventh to second in the league in runs scored. *New York Globe* sportswriter Sid Mercer was impressed enough with the revamped hitting attack to dust off an old nickname and apply it to the 1918 Yankees. The name he chose would go down as one of the greatest nicknames in sports history.

Murderers' Row was the name used for the block that housed the inmates on Death Row at New York's old Tombs Prison during the nineteenth century. The name had been applied to two other baseball teams before the Yankees: the 1903 Cleveland Indians and 1905 Yale University. Although it was applied to the 1918 Yankees, it would forever be associated with the New York Yankees dynasty during the next decade.

Life would never be the same for Huggins when Huston returned to New York in 1919. If Huston was resentful towards Ruppert, he was hostile with Huggins. He expressed his dissatisfaction of the managerial choice through his ties to the sportswriters, who made Huggins the scapegoat for the Yankees' shortcomings and credited the players, not the manager, for the team's successes. The players' respect for the manager began to dwindle to the point where discipline became a problem. When the manager tried, the players were unresponsive: "They had reason to believe that any shackles placed on them by Huggins would be struck off by Huston."

If Huggins had a peaceful moment in 1919, it was when the two owners coincided to battle the League President's ruling to null the Carl Mays trade. Due to lack of run support, Mays quit the Red Sox during a mid-season game. He had entered that game in Chicago with a respectable 2.47 season earned run average, yet had just five wins. "At that particular moment my whole world was falling down," Mays would later say. Less than two months before, he had whipped a baseball into the crowd in Philadelphia. The fans were celebrating a hometown rally by banging on the tin roof above the Red Sox dugout, creating a piercing dinging noise inside the dugout. Annoyed over the fans' jubilee, Mays stepped out of the dugout and heaved a ball at the crowd, striking a spectator on the head. Dazed but uninjured, the fan filed a complaint with the Philadelphia Police

Miller Huggins had no idea what he was in for when he accepted Ruppert's offer to manage the New York Yankees (National Baseball Hall of Fame, Cooperstown, New York).

Department, and a warrant followed for the pitcher's arrest. Luckily for Mays, the team was on the way to their next city when the police came looking for him.

In the Chicago game, the Red Sox and Mays owned a 4–0 lead when Boston catcher Wally Schang fired the ball toward second base in an attempt to catch a would-be stealer. The hurl struck the pitcher in the back of the head. After retiring the side, Mays dropped his glove and headed to the clubhouse. As he passed the Boston bench, he muttered, "I'll never pitch another ball for this ball club again!"

Mays refused to obey orders to return to the Red Sox, and demanded a trade. Ban Johnson stepped in and instructed all owners to back off for fear it may set a poor precedent among other players who were dissatisfied with their current team. All obeyed the League President except for the two colonels and Harry Frazee, who went through with a deal. Johnson retaliated by suspending Mays. "If necessary, we'll go to the courts," the two colonels shot back.

Ruppert and Huston obtained a temporary injunction to allow Mays to pitch. The injunction became permanent after the season, but Johnson fired one more shot by voiding New York's third-place finish and said the league would not pay their World Series share (received by the second, third, and fourth place teams as well as the World Series winners and losers). The colonels paid their players out of their own pocket. They were reimbursed at the December Baseball Winter Meetings when peace was made.

Rumors began to swirl around Huggins's dismissal during the tail end of the 1919 season. In *The Sporting News*, a photo of Wilbert Robinson appeared under a headline: "Picked to lead Yankees." The article accused Huggins of mishandling his pitchers and misdirecting his players. Much to Huston's dismay, Ruppert quickly signed his manager for another season.

Huggins must have known what he was in for in 1920. One problem would be dealing with Mays. "I was never on a club where a fellow was as disliked as much as Mays," said a Yankee player. Mays was moody, obstinate, unpredictable, and would often sail through a game for what looked like a sure win only to self-destruct and give up the lead in one inning. And there still remained an outstanding warrant for his arrest, meaning he would be unable to accompany the team when they played at Philadelphia (the warrant was finally dropped in mid-season).

The manager would also be dealing with Babe Ruth, another player who disliked advice. "Ruth could never accept managerial discipline," opined a New York sportswriter. "He does what he pleases." Ruth looked down on the little manager, and he often spoke behind his back. "You're too little to be around a ball club," Babe once roared to Huggins in the aisle of a club Pullman. "We're going to toss you off the train." Meusel grabbed the manager by the shoulders and Ruth grabbed his feet, but the plan was foiled when a black porter came to the manager's rescue. "You really wouldn't have tossed me off the train, would you?" Huggins asked Meusel the next day after his outfielder apologized for his actions. "Sure we would have," replied Meusel. "We would have thrown you off in a minute."

The job in New York left the manager second guessing his decision to leave St. Louis or even manage a ball club. He had already suffered from stress and anxiety, dental problems and other health issues prior to the New York job, perhaps the reason why he was a confirmend bachelor who lived with his sister. "Stick it out, Miller," Myrtle Huggins would tell her brother. "Don't let them say that you quit under fire." The "Mite Manager" hung in there, but it took a toll on his health. "Babe Ruth cost him about five years of his life," Myrtle would later say.

In October of 1920, Ed Barrow resigned as manager of the declining Boston Red Sox and accepted the offer to become the Yankees' new business manager. The position became available when the Yankees' longtime business manager Ed Sparrow had suddenly died in May of 1920. Oh great, Huggins must have thought. Here was another man in the organization who was against him, especially since Barrow had been hired by Huston. But to Huggins' amazement, the new business manager was behind him.

Realizing that Huggins was giving him the cold shoulder for a reason, Barrow broke the ice. "You're the manager, and you're going to get no interference or second guessing from me. Your job is to win, and part of my job is to see that you have the players to win with. You tell me what you want, and I'll make the deals." Huggins was stunned to hear this. "He looked at me like it was a new language," Barrow would later recall.

Nineteen twenty-one offered no less anxiety for Huggins. Rumors were constant about his impending dismissal. There was a claim by a player that Huggins was aloof and lacked warmth and the team needed a different kind of leader. "You can pat Moran but you can't kid Gleason," was the old schoolyard saying about the two managers of the teams in the 1919 World Series. Now there was another line to ridicule the Yankees manager: "You can't hug Miller."

If the Yankees players had another manager in mind, they found one in a teammate when Huggins was forced to take a leave of absence due to a boil that had formed on his cheek and needed to be lanced. Roger Peckinpaugh, the team's star shortstop, filled in.

Peckinpaugh was a good all-around player: a sweet fielder with a strong throwing arm and good hands, and he batted second for Murderers' Row. At age thirty, he had ten seasons of major league experience, and had once been called to temporarily fill in as New York's manager at the tail end of the 1914 season at the ripe age of twenty-three.

4. Miller Huggins

The Yanks won eight straight under their fill-in manager. "The club began to play as though it took some interest in the game." Peckinpaugh had proven to be a winner, someone the players liked, and was often referred to as a player's manager. There were reports that the players would meet with Huston to discuss the change of managers, but nothing happened.

September 19, with twelve games to go, the Yankees were tied for first with the Indians. All looked good after seven innings against Detroit at the Polo Grounds with the Yanks leading 4–0 behind the pitching of Mays. But the lead didn't hold. Mays, once again, collapsed during one inning. Huggins usually let Mays complete his games regardless of his lapses, but he had a change of heart this time and called on Bob Shawkey, which angered Mays.

Shawkey gave up a hit to Cobb and a triple to Bobby Veach. Huggins, eager to get a win to keep pace with the Indians, decided on another pitching change. Shawkey didn't argue with the decision, but expressed his dissatisfaction by heaving the ball before departing.

Hoyt gave up three hits before the inning finally ended in an eight-run rally off three Yankee pitchers for an 8–4 Detroit lead. The Tigers scored two more in the ninth inning for a 10–6 win.

That was the final straw for Huggins. Losing that game, facing the treatment of the press, hearing the catcalls from the fans, dealing with Huston, enduring the lack of respect among his players, Huggins decided enough was enough. He tendered his resignation; Ruppert refused to accept it.

The Yankees bounced back to take the last two games of the series. Nine games remained on the schedule, including four at home versus Cleveland in the very next series.

New York took two of two of the first three games with Cleveland to take a one-game lead. In the final game of the crucial series, Ruth blasted two home runs and a double for seven RBI to help erase a 3–0 deficit, and give New York an 8–7 lead after seven innings.

Believing that his three walks during the Indians' two-run seventh inning resulted because the home plate umpire was squeezing him, Hoyt asked his manager to remove him from the game; however, Huggins sent him out to pitch the top of the eighth. He managed to retire the first batter, then issued another walk. Peckinpaugh walked from his shortstop position to the mound, spoke with Hoyt, and then turned to the dugout to suggest a pitching change. Huggins sent his coach Charlie O'Leary to the mound to inform the pitcher that he was staying in. Hearing this, Peckinpaugh "scowled and said a lot of caustic things to nobody in particular."

After getting the second out of the inning, Hoyt was tagged for a double to put runners on second and third. Huggins then called on Mays, who recorded the last four outs of the game for a huge Yankees win. Five days later, Mays and the Yankees defeated the Athletics to clinch the American League pennant.

In Game Eight of the 1921 World Series, with the Yankees down 4 games to 3 to the Giants in the best-of-nine, and one game away from elimination, Waite Hoyt was the Yankees' starting pitcher. In the first inning, Giants runners were on first and second with one out when a ground ball to Peckinpaugh looked like a sure inning-ending double play. For Roger Peckinpaugh, who had handled forty-two chances in this series without a mishap, it seemed like a routine play. But this time he failed. The ball went through his legs and trickled into shallow left field. Then, for whatever reason, the star shortstop made no effort to retrieve the ball, thus allowing the runner on second to round third and head home for what would be the game's only run.

Peckinpaugh's days with the Yankees were over. The decision to trade him was considered surprising, especially to Peckinpaugh. "The fact that he made an error that possibly cost us a World Championship had no direct bearing on the decision Huggins and I reached that winter as we went over the club for 1922 and agreed to trade him," explained Barrow. "We agreed that Peckinpaugh was slowing up and we needed one better."

Life with the Yankees wasn't easier for Huggins in 1922. In addition to Ruth's five suspensions, he was dealing with the rowdiest team in baseball. In spring training at New Orleans, he made the mistake of cutting practices to once a day, leaving plenty of time for the players to enjoy their evenings. "Yankees training on Scotch," were the headlines. When Huggins saw that, he called for a team meeting. All but Mays appeared to understand his rules. The manager later fined the controversial hurler, leading to a shouting match in the streets of Norfolk.

The Yankees returned to their rowdy ways after the season had begun. It was almost too easy to find bootleg products in New York City with an estimated 32,000 speakeasies. Beer was just as easy to find when a team was on the road. "If a guy wanted it, he found it." Ruppert and Huston refused to look the other way and went through with an idea that would put an end to it.

In the team's hotel lobby in St. Louis, Wally Schang was approached by a friendly stranger named Kelly. "Oh sure, I remember you now," replied the catcher. The two struck up a conversation and became friendly enough for Schang to introduce him to his teammates, who also liked him, especially since he had beer packed in ice in the bathtub of his hotel room. "Like to play the horses?" asked Kelly. "See me tomorrow. I have some friends who own horses."

Kelly took their money, placed their bets, and they won. "Why not come to Chicago with us?" offered one of the Yankees. "All right," said Kelly after pondering the question. "I haven't got anything to do for the next few days, and I don't know a nicer bunch of fellows to be with."

From his box seat at Comiskey Park, Kelly invited the players to a party a friend was throwing. Later that evening, as the players were enjoying their steaks and beer, a photographer appeared. Kelly gathered the team for a photo, saying he wanted a team picture for a souvenir. The picture was taken, the photographer left and later reappeared with a print. While the players examined it, Kelly asked that each player sign his name beneath his picture in the photo. The players gladly obliged.

As Kelly continued to travel with the team, Babe Ruth became suspicious. "I'll bet you one hundred bucks that he's a detective," Ruth told a teammate.

"You're nuts!" Carl Mays replied. "But you got a bet."

Kelly said he would join the team in Boston, but then changed his plans. He said he had to go back to New York for business and mentioned he would see them back at the Polo Grounds.

In Boston, Huggins called for another team meeting. The players gathered in the clubhouse, sat down, and waited for the meeting to begin. They were surprised when Judge Landis entered, and with all the information: who was in the hotel room in St. Louis, who drank, who bet on the horses, and everything else. Then the judge pulled out the picture from Chicago: "Is there any of you who wishes to deny that this is his signature under his picture?"

Nobody replied.

Landis finished by giving a blistering lecture, and mentioned that Kelly had been hired by the team. "All right, sucker. I'll take cash or a check," Ruth said to Mays.

The next problem Huggins addressed was the fighting among his players. In addition to the Ruth-Pipp bout, Mays had a fight, two reserves had it out the next day, and Meusel and Schang tangled the same day of the Ruth-Pipp fight. A day later, Aaron Ward confronted a reserve. "I'm running a ball club, not a fight club," Huggins said. "Hereafter, if there is fighting you will pay for it in fines and suspensions." The fighting stopped.

Another dilemma was the ongoing lack of team discipline. Hoyt resented his manager's insistence that he pitch a certain way to a certain batter, but went along with his manager's decision. The strategy backfired and Hoyt lost the game, leading to a fiery argument on the bench between the pitcher and manager.

In Game Five of the 1922 World Series, with the Yankees on the brink of elimination, the game headed into the eighth inning with the score tied, 2–

2. The Giants put runners on second and third with two outs. Ross Youngs, a lefty batter, was due up. "Bullet Joe" Bush, a twenty-six-game winner in 1922, was pitching. He had lost Game One after losing a two-run lead in the bottom of the eighth in a 3–2 loss.

Huggins ordered his pitcher to intentionally walk Youngs. "What for, you stupid [expletive]!" protested Bush in a tone that was heard in the press box. Ignoring his manager, he pitched a strike. Huggins responded by restating his order, along with a few expletives of his own. Bush answered Huggins, but followed orders. The pitcher deliberately tossed a soft one to George Kelley, who singled to left center to score two runs for a 4–2 Giants lead. When the Yankees went down in order in the top of the ninth to end the series, Huston quickly left the Polo Grounds and headed to the Pressroom Bar at the Commodore Hotel without speaking a word. While seated at the bar, he pushed a row of cocktails aside before ending his silence. "Miller Huggins has managed his last game with the Yankees ball club. He's through! Through! Through!"

"I won't fire the man who brought us two pennants," Ruppert said in response to Huston's remarks.

Another disagreement brewed between the two owners as to which charity would receive the profits from the suspended second game of the 1922 World Series. "I'm through," Barrow told the two owners. "You brought me in here to run this club on a businesslike basis. How can I do that with you two quarreling all the time? Get someone else to try to work things out after you get through snarling them."

Ruppert greeted Barrow when he arrived at the Yankees' offices the next day. "Look, Ed, I'm sick of it too. If I buy out Huston, will you stay?" asked Ruppert.

"Yes," replied Barrow.

Huston couldn't argue that he was unhappy. Barrow stood with Ruppert and backed Huggins, making Huston the lone man in the organization. He agreed to sell his share and leave the Yankees on December 12.

Barrow sighed in relief when he heard the news. Huggins smiled back in Cincinnati as he stuffed tobacco into the bowl of his pipe. But before that date had arrived, Huston had a change of heart. He decided that he would continue as co-owner of the Yankees.

5

World Champions—1923

> "The Yankees are the champions.
> "The Yankees reached the journey's end, and a World's championship flag will fly in the Yankee Stadium next year."
> —*New York Times*

The name and story of a pregnant nineteen-year-old Long Island telephone operator named "Delores Dixon" began to appear in the New York newspapers. Her claim was she had been "automobiling" with Ruth four or five times per week during the previous summer and he assaulted her. Ruth, with Helen and Dorothy in New Orleans for spring training when the news became public, called the charge "blackmail." Helen stood by her husband. In April, Ruth's attorney presented a witness who would testify that the $50,000 paternity suit was a plot to extort money from Ruth. When learning the name of the key witness, the plaintiff dropped the lawsuit and Delores Dixon was never heard from again.

The dream stadium in the Bronx was christened on April 18, 1923. "I would give a year of my life if I could hit that first home run in the new park," said Ruth. "Yankee Stadium" was the first ballpark to be called a stadium. It comprised three decks that extended from behind home plate to both foul poles, and a single deck of wooden bleachers in the outfield to total the seating capacity at approximately 58,000. Above the stadium's top deck was a 15-foot-deep copper frieze that would forever be associated as the stadium. The stadium also had a quarter-mile red cinder running track surrounding the field, and a 15-foot-deep brick-lined vault beneath second base containing electrical connections for boxing events.

The first game (versus the Red Sox) was on a cold and windy day before an announced crowd of 74,217 (the exaggerated attendance would later be reduced to 62,200).

In his first at bat, Ruth lifted a harmless fly ball to leftfield for an easy out. In the bottom of the third, with the Yankees ahead 1–0, Ruth came to bat with two runners on base. "Be smart here, George, two men on," yelled Huggins from the dugout. With a 2–2 count, Red Sox hurler Howard Ehmke threw a slow ball. Ruth took two steps forward, swung, and lifted a long fly ball to right field. Ehmke, knowing he had surrendered Ruth's first home run in the new ball park, never looked. The Yankees went on to win, 4–1.

Ruppert and Huston resumed their buyout negotiation shortly before the 1923 season. The holdup had been a clause disagreement calling for Huston to stay out of baseball for ten years. With American League president Ban Johnson now pressing for Frazee to sell the Red Sox, Ruppert feared that Huston would buy and rebuild the franchise into a winner. But after careful consideration, Ruppert decided he could live without the clause for the sake of sole ownership of the Yankees. On April 18, the same day Yankee Stadium hosted its first ball game, the two men came to an agreement. They also agreed to withhold the news for five weeks "in order to allow Huston to receive his full share of the glory of Yankee Stadium."

"It was too good to refuse," said Huston, who received an estimated $1.25 million for his share. "I simply couldn't pass it by." He was now free of Ruppert, Huggins, and the Yankees, and he was unrestricted from buying a different team. However, he stayed away from the game until 1937 when he offered $1.7 million to buy the Dodgers. His offer was declined.

"It's all over now," Ruppert announced. "I am the sole owner of the Yankees, or at least I will be within another ten days." The deal went into effect on June 1, 1923.

The buyout and cost to build Yankee Stadium was an investment in the future for Ruppert. Since his brewery was now facing tough times due to the Volstead Act (his business turned to producing soda, syrup, and other products to stay afloat), the Yankees were his main source of income. He had Babe Ruth, the game's best drawing card, and a booming economy that would help keep the turnstiles clicking at Yankee Stadium.

The Yankees got off to a great start in the 1923 season. Winning their last 15 of 17 games in May to improve their record to 29–10, they were already seven games in front of the next best team. Leading the way was Wally Pipp, who hit safely in the last twenty-one games in May. Ruth, hungry to redeem himself for his troubled 1922 season, and win back the admiration of the fans, was off to a great start, hitting .341 with 11 home runs and 33 RBI by the end of May.

During the last week of May, the Yankees were in Washington to play the Senators. Before one of the games, Ruth and the Yankees were on the field taking batting practice when a friend of Ruth's named Jimmy Barton, a big

5. *World Champions—1923* 47

Evicted by their landlords in 1920, Ruppert and Huston constructed the greatest stadium of its time—Yankee Stadium (National Baseball Hall of Fame, Cooperstown, New York).

star on the stage who was in town to perform in the play *Dew Drop Inn,* called Ruth. His friend approached Barton's box, located behind the Yankees' dugout on the third base side, and took off his cap to say "hello" as he smiled. Barton introduced his guests, two young ladies from the cast he had invited to accompany him. Ruth appeared to pay little attention to the guests, or that's how it looked to one of the two, named Claire Hodgson. After talking briefly with Barton, he ducked into the dugout.

The next day, when Mrs. Hodgson arrived at the National Theater to perform in a matinee, Eddie Bennett, the midget batboy of the Yankees, was waiting with a note. With no idea what it was about, she read the note after Bennett handed it to her:

> I don't know what hotel you are at, so I'm sending you this note.
> Will you have dinner with me this evening?

The note was in elegant handwriting and signed by Babe Ruth.

"I wonder who wrote the note for him?" was the first thought that went through her mind. It wasn't that she did not believe that Ruth was capable of writing a note, but this was in beautiful handwriting, a talent that Ruth had obtained while at St. Mary's.

"Tell him I'll have dinner with him tonight, if I can bring my girlfriend," she told Bennett.

A short while later, Hodgson received a phone call backstage. "I'll be delighted to have you both," said Ruth in a "gruff" voice tone. He mentioned his hotel and suite number. "Aren't there any restaurants in Washington?" replied Hodgson.

"Lord, Miss Hodgson, I can't go into any restaurants. I get mobbed every time I try to eat in a restaurant," said Ruth. There was then a pause before Ruth began to laugh. "Don't worry. You and your girlfriend won't have anything to worry about. My suite will be lousy with people." Then with sadness, he added, "It always is."

Claire Hodgson stood 5'2", although she appeared taller, most likely because she often wore high heels. She was a sultry beauty with dark brown hair, lush red lips, piercing brown eyes, and a superb figure, and she was 5½ years younger than Ruth. She grew up in Gainesville and Athens, Georgia. Her dad, Colonel James Monroe Merrit, "was the very model of a Southern citizen lawyer." He taught at the University of Georgia while practicing law, and he had a client named Ty Cobb. He and his wife were "nice," and also "very, very strict," according to their daughter.

The catch of Athens, Georgia, was a wealthy thirty-three year-old widower and hotel owner named Frank Hodgson. One day, before celebrating her fifteenth birthday, Claire dropped off her school books at a grocery store and ran off with the town's most eligible bachelor. Less than two years later, she gave birth to a child, named Julia.

The marriage didn't work. "He just couldn't get home fast enough or often enough from that Elk Club and his friends." She became lonely and depressed, and began to think about fulfilling her dream as a model, an opportunity she believed was in New York City. There was an Uncle Joe Hodgson who sympathized with her, like most of the townspeople who felt badly for a child bride with a baby and an absentee husband. Uncle Joe controlled the family finances and affairs, and he believed that her getting away might bring her husband to his senses, but could hardly agree with going to New York City. "There isn't a decent woman in New York," he believed. Claire was persistent, and finally was able to convince him.

In November of 1920, along with her child and her twenty-year-old maid, Claire arrived in New York and checked into the only hotel whose name she knew—the Waldorf Astoria. When she arrived, she immediately went to see

5. World Champions—1923

Howard Chandler Christie, an artist she had sent a letter to that was written by her cousin who knew him.

The artist called Hodgson the following morning. "Be here by nine this morning," and she was hired as a model for ten dollars per day. The job led to other modeling opportunities and a three- to four-lines-per-play acting career. Claire loved every minute of it. Soon she saved enough money to move her family into an apartment.

In 1922, Frank Hodgson died, penniless. One year later, Claire lost her dad. Her mom moved in with her and her family, which made her extremely happy.

Claire and her friend, Bobbie Kane, arrived at Ruth's suite. It was jammed with "lousy people," most of whom were total strangers to Ruth. Before too long, Ruth and his guest sat away from the others and talked. He spoke about his spectacular 1920 and 1921 seasons before going into detail about his disappointing 1922 season. He worried that the fans didn't like him and he wouldn't win them back. "Thanks, keed," he said when a stranger handed him another drink.

"You know, you drink too much," said Mrs. Hodgson. "Drinking is not good for you."

"You sound like Miller Huggins," said Ruth.

Hodgson and her friend headed to the door. "So long, keed," Ruth said to his guest. "You know what?" Ruth said. "A lot newspaper guys and ballplayers have told me I should stop drinking, but you're the first dame who ever told me."

"You know, he's a very nice man, but he's really a child at heart," Hodgson said to her friend.

Ruth phoned the next day and asked Mrs. Hodgson to get two tickets for the show that evening. Delighted to have him as a guest, she paid for the tickets for Ruth and Yankees catcher Benny Bengough. Before leaving Washington, Ruth asked his friend when the Yankees and *Dew Drop Inn* would be in New York at the same time. She told him, but wondered if Ruth would ever call her again. He did. He called her almost every day. She would ask him for a report of his conduct, and he would tell her. He said he was behaving, eating right, and getting sleep. "I'm a working girl and need my sleep," she would say to end their long conversations. "It wouldn't be a bad idea if you went to bed, too."

Huggins and Ruppert received disturbing information following the 1922 season that a few of the World Series games were not on the level. The news was that Carl Mays was throwing games. Mays had always been mysterious in the sense that he would often cough up the lead in the late innings after cruising along. Now there was reason to believe that he was losing games on purpose. Sportswriter Fred Lieb claimed that he had been contacted by a man who said that Mays had been offered "a rather substantial sum if he had lost." The man said that, before the eighth inning of Game Four in the 1921 World Series, when Mays squandered a 2–0 lead, his wife had signaled by wiping a handkerchief across her face to indicate that the money had been handed over to her. Mays also lost in Game Seven, and there was speculation that he purposely lost in the 1922 World Series.

Lieb took his story to Landis, who hired a detective to investigate. The controversial pitcher was cleared of any wrongdoing, but that wasn't enough to convince Huggins. Mays, the highest-paid pitcher on the Yankees, would work in just twenty-three games in 1923 (and was waived to the Reds after the season). "What's wrong with me?" Mays asked a group of sportswriters. "Why won't Huggins pitch me?" Later, he addressed the question to his manager before a group of Boston sportswriters. "Hey, Hug! Why won't you let me pitch?"

"Why, Carl, you're still with this club?" asked the manager with sarcasm before turning and walking away.

On July 17, Huggins gave Mays a chance to pitch. Making his first start after an extended period of being inactive, Mays was rusty, and was rocked for 13 runs on 20 hits in a 13–0 loss. Huggins, showing no sympathy, kept him in for the entire game. "He told me he needed lots of work, so I gave it to him," the manager explained to the reporters.

"Carl, I want to tell you that in all my years in baseball, I've never seen anything so rotten as this," Everett Scott said to Mays. Late in the game, Scott decided he had played enough and withdrew. So did Wally Pipp. To finish the game in Pipp's place was a promising twenty-year-old who was playing in his just his sixth major league game.

On April 18, the day Ruth homered in the Yankees' first game at the new stadium, Yankees scout Paul Krichell watched Columbia University play Williams College at South Field on 115th and Broadway, and saw a sophomore pitcher strike out seventeen while smashing two hits. "I think I've seen another Babe Ruth," Krichell told Barrow. Two days later, the scout saw the collegian blast a 450-foot home run. A few weeks later, he witnessed another Ruthian-type home run.

One day in June, when the Yankees were taking batting practice at Yankee Stadium, Miller Huggins walked to the batting cage with a "broad-shouldered, good-looking kid walking behind him." "Let this youngster hit a few," said Huggins. The players stepped aside for the kid "who looked shy and awkward." The youngster grabbed one of Ruth's forty-eight-ounce bats. "Don't use that

5. World Champions—1923

one, son," said Ruth from behind the batting practice cage. "Go ahead," Ruth said on second thought. "You can't hurt it. I got others."

The collegian stepped into the batting cage with Ruth's bat and showed his nervousness by hitting a couple softly along the infield. Then he got hold of one and drove it into Ruth's favorite right field bleachers. He drove another one into the bleachers, and then another. Suddenly, Ruth was intrigued. Not many players had the power to drive them as far as he did. "Who was this powerful kid? His name was Lou Gehrig."

Ruth began to hit in July. He smacked ten homers during the month and added nearly forty points to his batting average to put him over .390. The Yankees continued to win and to maintain a league lead above ten games. The pitching staff had lots of depth, even with Mays riding the bench. Sad Sam Jones would lead the team with twenty-one wins, and four other hurlers registered 16 or more wins, including Joe Bush, and Herb Pennock, the latest steal from the Red Sox organization.

Fresh from Columbia University, Lou Gehrig put on an impressive hitting display in a batting practice session during his first visit to Yankee Stadium (National Baseball Hall of Fame, Cooperstown, New York).

The Yankees cruised through the home stretch of the season to capture their third consecutive pennant, finishing sixteen games ahead of the second-place Tigers. Also for the third straight year, they would meet their cross-town rivals in the World Series.

"Do you think you can win this time?" a writer asked Huggins.

"We ought to," replied Huggins. "We've got a better club and I think McGraw knows it. The only thing we've got to lick is psychology. The one thing the Giants have got to beat, and they may not realize it, is the law of averages."

The two teams split the first four games of the Series. In Game Two, at the Polo Grounds, Ruth hit two homers to show the sports world that this World Series was not going to be a repeat of the year before. After being shut out at Yankee Stadium by Art Nehf in Game Three, the Yanks bounced back to even the series with a 7–4 win that was highlighted by a six-run second. Meusel delivered the big blow in the rally with a two-run triple.

It was Meusel who starred in Game Five with three hits, and Dugan delivered four, including a home run, in a Yankees 8–1 win at Yankee Stadium to take a 3–2 lead in the series.

The series returned to the Polo Grounds for Game Six, where Ruth tagged Art Nehf for a first-inning home run on a 3–2 pitch to give the Yanks a 1–0 lead. However, Nehf was tougher on the Yankees than he was in Game Three. After serving up the long ball to Ruth, he retired all but two batters through the seventh inning. A hit in the second inning was erased on a double play, and he walked Ruth in the fourth before retiring the next eleven consecutive batters.

The Giants appeared to be in command with a 4–1 lead as the game headed into the top of the eighth. "And then, like a bolt of blue, it happened— a Yankees eighth inning which had its followers doing handsprings and making maniacal sounds in the stands."

Schang and Scott singled to bring the Yankees' game hit total to four, and a walk followed to load the bases. In a surprise move, Huggins sent a pitcher to bat for his leadoff man, Whitey Witt. "Bullet Joe" Bush, a fine hitting pitcher, stepped in, and he also walked to force in a run and cut the lead to 4–2. "By this time, McGraw was in a frenzy. Seeing Ol' Reliable Nehf walk two pinch-hitters on eighth pitches was worse than a shock; it was a catastrophe." McGraw went to his bullpen and called on Rosey Ryan, who walked Joe Dugan to force in another run to make it a 4–3 ball game.

Babe Ruth was now at the plate. Bases loaded, one out, this was a chance for him to become the hero of the 1923 World Series. "Never did the big Bambino try harder to break up a game. However, the Bambino was over-anxious and, after taking two furious lunges at Ryan's curves, struck out on a low pitch that hit home plate."

Bob Meusel followed by hitting a high bounder over the pitcher and into centerfield to score two to give the Yankees the lead. Dugan advanced from first to third, and when a Giants outfielder threw wildly in an attempt to get him at third base, "Jumping Joe" jumped up and scored for a 6–4 Yankee lead.

In the bottom of the ninth, with two outs and nobody on base, a ground ball to Yankees second baseman Aaron Ward resulted in the last out of the series. At last! The Yankees were world champions.

6

The Bellyache Heard Around the World—1925

"It is not remarkable that the stomach ache of Babe Ruth was felt around the world."—*New York Herald-Tribune*

Miller Huggins was looking forward to a future outside of baseball. "If I win the pennant this year, and if I land one more to make it five straight, then I'm done," he said prior to the 1924 season. He had always dreamed about going into business for himself since his playing days, when he considered investing in roller-skating rinks.

Although an American League or National League team had never won four consecutive pennants, the consensus was there would be another New York subway series in 1924. That was threatened, however, when both the Yankees and Giants encountered an unexpected challenger. The Giants' fight for the flag was against a surprise contender in the Brooklyn Dodgers. Wilbert Robinson had skillfully managed his Dodgers by shifting players to new positions and promoting others into the starting lineup. And with two of the league's finest pitchers in Dizzy Vance and Burleigh Grimes, Brooklyn, a second-division finisher in 1923, pressed McGraw's Giants into the final days of the season before finishing 1½ games behind their rivals. The Yankees, on the other hand, were unable to survive the surge of the Washington Senators.

Why did the Yankees fail to defend their crown with what most experts believed was the strongest roster in baseball? Each sportswriter offered a different reason:

"The World Champions of 1923 lost the pennant last year for one reason—overconfidence," one said. "They didn't perform the fundamentals," another opined. Also mentioned was the Yankees waited for the Senators to collapse rather than play to win. Washington won the pennant and went on to replace the Yankees as World Champions after stunning the Giants in the World Series.

Ruth followed his outstanding 1923 season with another great one in 1924. In 1923, he had led the league in home runs (41) and RBI (131), and posted the league's second best average (.393). In 1924, he won the batting title (.378), led the league in home runs (46), and finished eight RBI (121) away from winning the triple crown. He expected 1925 to be another great season, perhaps one that he would surpass his home run record, "or come dangerously close to it," Ruth predicted.

Most baseball experts believed the Senators had "lucked" their way to the world championship, and the Yanks would return to the top in 1925. The team's greatest antagonist and Ruth's biggest rival, Ty Cobb, agreed: "The Yankees are a great ball club, much better than they showed a good part of last year. That's the team I have to beat if I am going to win."

With the Yankees and Tigers in close contention during the '24 season, the Cobb-Ruth rivalry peaked in Detroit on June 12. Ruth had belted his fifteenth home run of the season and Meusel added four hits in a 10–4 Yankees win. Then trouble began when Ruth and another Yankee were plunked. New York shelled Cobb's starting pitcher the following day for a 6–2 third-inning lead. The Tigers' manager called on Bert Cole, the pitcher the Yankees had bombed the previous day, but this time Cole held the Yankees scoreless while the Tigers rallied to tie the game. In the seventh inning, New York rallied for four runs for a 10–6 lead before more trouble occurred when Ruth stiff-armed Cole on a play at first base. Two innings later, the hurler retaliated by pitching one that forced the home-run star to duck. After finishing his at bat with a weak pop out to the first baseman, Ruth was headed back to the dugout when he noticed centerfielder Cobb signal to his pitcher. Knowing the Detroit manager was up to something, he shouted a warning to the next batter, Bob Meusel. Sure enough, the first pitch hit the batter between the shoulder blades. Without hesitating, Meusel charged the mound as both teams emptied their dugouts. Ruth knew exactly where he wanted to go but was headed off before he could reach Cobb. After policemen took the field to restore order, Ruth and Meusel, both ejected from the game, gathered their belongings and were jeered by eighteen-thousand fans as they walked to the Yankees' clubhouse. When they reached the Tigers' dugout, which was where the entrance leading to the visiting cluhouse was located, they got into a shoving match with several Detroit players. Noticing two of their teammates outnumbered, the Yankees charged the Tigers' bench. Fans immediately began to spill onto the field. Aware that the angry crowd outnumbered the policemen, umpire Billy Evans acted by declaring the game completed.

As Meusel changed into his street clothes following the game, a member

6. The Bellyache Heard Around the World—1925

of the Tigers' ground crew entered the Yankees' clubhouse and approached him. "Cobb sent me," he told the Yankees' right-handed slugger. "He told me that if you think he's the kind of manager who would tell a pitcher to dust a batter off, he will be glad to meet you privately under the stands."

"Tell Cobb I will be right out," said Meusel.

"No, you don't," said Huggins. "Let things stand as they are."

"All right," said Meusel, "but I suppose I've got to tangle with the guy sometime and I want him to know that."

In late September, with New York trailing Washington by one game with one week remaining in the season, the Yankees traveled to Detroit needing to win to keep their fourth consecutive pennant hopes alive. The Tigers, heading for a third-place finish, and finishing six games behind Washington, took the first two games by identical 6–5 scores, which no doubt made Cobb happy. Detroit was ahead, 4–1, in the final game of the series when the Yankees threatened by loading the bases with one out in the top of the eighth. Huggins, wanting a pinch hitter, chose Lou Gehrig, who had enjoyed a fantastic season at Hartford of the Eastern League before joining the Yankees at the tail end of the season.

The manager's hunch was correct. Gehrig came through with a single to score two runs to cut the lead to one run. Being a bit too eager, Gehrig took a wide turn at first base and got trapped in a rundown. Cobb, coming in from centerfield to partake in the play, shouted an insult as he applied the tag on the runner. Gehrig replied and kept hollering when returning to the dugout to the point where the umpires told him to cool it. Ignoring their warnings, Gehrig was ejected from the game.

Shags Horan of the Yankees, a rarely used sub who was spending his only season in the majors, took exception to Cobb's actions. As he passed by the Tigers' dugout later in the game, he grabbed a handful of dirt and whipped it at Cobb. "I'll get you, Horan, next season!" shouted Cobb. "I'll get you on waivers and I'll send you to Toronto where they will make you play ball!"

The Tigers held on for a 4–3 win to put a dagger in the Yankees' pennant hopes. New York finished the season with nine fewer wins than in 1923 and two games behind Washington. "I wish them all the luck in the world against the Giants," said Huggins upon hearing the news that Washington had won in Boston to clinch the pennant.

Luck seemed to be with the Senators throughout the season and the World Series. In Game Seven a routine groundball took a sudden hop over the Giants' third baseman and rolled into left field to allow the winning run to score and make the Washington Senators world champions.

Could the Senators repeat in 1925? They almost didn't live to get the chance. During a spring training road trip, their overloaded bus was crossing a bridge when the planks of the structure cracked. The players heard the crack, then felt their bus drop and bounce several times. Projected girders beneath the planks had prevented the bus from plunging three hundred feet into the Santee River. The passengers, okay but shaken, we able to climb out of the bus. "I thought I was going to feed the fishes," said one of the coaches.

The Ruths headed to Home Plate Farm following the season hoping for a relaxing and secluded winter, during which Ruth would receive an occasional visit from members of the press. Before the press corps arrived, he made sure he had an ax in hand to demonstrate the art of chopping wood to stay in shape. "I used to chop the wood for him," according to Bert Haswell, who grew up on the farm next to Ruth's. "I'd do all the work and he'd sit there with a beer and talk to me." Fishing and hunting were Ruth's activities during his winter months. He rarely interacted with the community. When he did it was usually at the local grocery store to pick 2 or 3 pounds of hamburger. He would rush inside and head to the beginning of the line, explaining he was in a hurry and didn't have time to wait. The other customers didn't mind. After all, they were seeing Babe Ruth in person, and couldn't wait to go home to tell their families about it.

The winter following the 1924 season was far from what Ruth could have imagined. In December, all four hundred of his chickens had mysteriously died. For Ruth, who took great pride in his chicken farm, it was a devastating blow. Grieving the loss, he went inactive for the rest of the winter. He received more bad news when a bookie promised to expose him after he had failed to fulfill his promise to pay a racing debt by the end of January. "Okay, if that's the kind of guy you are, go ahead," said Ruth.

Ruth and Helen continued to quarrel during the winter: over the lack of time he spent with her and their child and other unresolved issues. All his difficulties, his inactiveness, and his appetite, caused him to balloon to between 240 and 250 pounds.

In February, Ruth traveled to his usual spring training preparation spot of Hot Springs, Arkansas. When a surprised sportswriter saw him, he warned his readers that Ruth looked "hog fat." While in Hot Springs, Ruth enjoyed the night life, continued to overeat, and began to have indigestion attacks that would hamper him throughout the spring.

Upon arriving in St. Petersburg, the new spring training site of the Yankees, Ruth was greeted with the news that his bookie had gone public. "Say it isn't true, Babe," pleaded teammate Whitey Witt. "Yes, I owe that money," said Ruth. "I made those bets last May. I lost seventy-five hundred dollars."

Seventy-five hundred was greater than a season's salary for several major

6. The Bellyache Heard Around the World—1925

league players in the mid–1920s, and led to the question about Ruth's financial status. "If Babe Ruth is broke, then Midas was a pauper and J.P. Morgan belongs in a bread line," someone said. Ruth was earning $52,000 a year with the Yankees, he had endorsements, and Christy Walsh had successfully invested his earnings in annuities. Ruth was far from financial ruin.

Al Lang, a longtime resident of St. Petersburg, the current president of the Florida State (baseball) League, and responsible for bringing the Yankees to the Sunshine City, escorted Ruth from the train depot to the Princess Martha Hotel, where the Babe received a grand reception from a packed lobby of tourists. The minute he entered the hotel's main area, the Scottish Highlander Band broke into the tune, "Hail to the Chief." A bellboy asked Ruth if he could carry the piece of luggage he was clasping to his chest. Ruth said no, explaining that he wanted to personally present it to his daughter, who was waiting with Helen in their suite on the top floor of the hotel.

When Ruth stepped into his suite, he set that special piece of luggage before his daughter and said, "This is yours." Dorothy's face lit up with joy when she saw a bull terrier puppy, and she responded by wrapping her arms around her father while showering his face with kisses. It was said that the puppy, cute as can be, had a face that indicated that he would grow to be an ugly brute with a pedigree.

The Princess Martha Hotel in St. Petersburg, Florida, served as the Yankees' spring training headquarters (St. Petersburg Museum of History).

Following breakfast in the hotel's dining room the next morning, Ruth headed over to Lake Crescent Park to inspect the grounds. It was raining and practice had been canceled, but when Ruth arrived he was greeted by a host of reporters who wanted to know what was up with his weight. He claimed to be at 225 pounds, "but I'll be down to 215 by opening day."

The sportswriters doubted that Ruth was telling the truth. "Just what our Babe weighs is somewhat of a mystery, but there is a suspicious bulge about his waistline and a fleshy squaring about his jaw that indicates a marvelous appetite and no food shortage during the drab winter days on the Sudbury farm," according to one sportswriter.

The skies cleared in time for the afternoon practice session. After Al Lang threw the "ceremonial pitch" to Huggins to welcome the 1925 spring training season, Ruth stepped into the batter's box for batting practice before fifteen hundred local citizens who were witnessing him bat for the first time. After taking a few practice swings, Ruth slightly bent his knees, lifted his bat over his left shoulder as he glared at the pitcher with an expression like he was going to hit the ball a country mile.

The first pitch came. Ruth took a hefty swing, and swish! A few groans were mixed with giggles after the batter had missed the ball by five feet. Ruth tugged his pants as he grinned in embarrassment, got ready for the next pitch, and swish! He missed again.

Ruth swung and missed five times before lifting a lazy pop up into the shallow outfield. A sportswriter shook his head at Ruth's unimpressive hitting display and began to write: "Ruth is old and fat and his best days are behind him." Unfazed over his poor hitting display and weight, Ruth appeared more interested in hitting the town with Helen. "Dog racing is a great sport," he announced. That evening he added to his debt at the local dog track. The next day, he complained about blisters on his hands and feet. A few days later, he sustained a finger injury and opted to rest for the remainder of the week. "Go out to the lot this morning and bag a few flies and run around a bit," Huggins suggested.

"Hug, I can't," Ruth told his manager. "My finger hurts like the dickens."

"Go out to the lot and run around a bit and bag flies," insisted Ruppert, who overheard the conversation.

Ruth had another excuse for staying away from the lot: he claimed there was an alligator in right field. He was right. The groundskeeper had warned the Yankees that he had seen a twelve-foot-long 'gator that morning. During the afternoon batting session, a rookie hopeful named Nick Cullop missed a catch on a fly ball. After the ball rolled up the embankment and stopped at the base of Lake Crescent, Cullop ran to fetch it. As he reached for the ball

6. The Bellyache Heard Around the World—1925

he heard a splash, and out of the corner of his eye he noticed something jump out of the water. When he looked and saw a man-sized gator with its eyes fixed on him, he ran for his life, jumped over the embankment far enough "to set a broad jumping record," and kept running until inside the safety of the Yankees' clubhouse. His teammates looked at the frightened rookie and asked what had happened. Cullop filled them in, then stepped on the scale and found that he had lost six pounds since the start of spring training. "Guess some fly balls over there would do the Babe some good," he said.

"Why didn't you come up with that ball?" Huggins teased Cullop upon hearing the story. "Don't you know that those balls cost money?"

"Yeh? If I came up with the ball that dog-gone alligator would have come up with Cullop," replied the rookie.

Ruth returned to work when the spring exhibition games began and started the preseason by making seven hits in his first sixteen at bats. He continued to behave in his wife's presence, but he missed the night life that he was unable to enjoy with his family around. "Why don't you blow out of here? You cramp my style," he had once told his wife during a previous spring, and perhaps he said it this spring. Heartbroken and disappointed with her husband's attitude, Helen headed back to New York City with her daughter.

The Yankees broke camp and left St. Petersburg to continue their exhibition season through the South. Ruth continued to neglect his health and would soon pay the price. His daily diet consisted of fried potatoes for breakfast, a half dozen hot dogs with carbonated soda for lunch, and a steak with gravy for dinner—usually eaten after eleven o'clock. Then there was the drinking into the wee hours of the following morning.

In spite of his poor diet and his indigestion problem, Ruth was averaging two hits per game. He went 4 for 5 with two home runs in Birmingham, which appeared to inspire his teammates into scoring runs. After the Yankees produced twenty-two runs in two games versus the Dodgers, the sportswriters were convinced that New York would return to the top of the American League. So were the confident Yankees, who were so sure that they would handle Washington, some were claiming that they had already won the pennant. "So I heard," said Bucky Harris, the twenty-eight-year-old second baseman and manager of the Senators when asked about the Yankees' prognostication. "You tell them that if they beat us, which they won't, they will beat a better team than the one they didn't beat the year before."

The Yankees impatiently waited aboard a train as Miller Huggins nervously paced the platform in Savannah, Georgia. Where was Babe Ruth? This was nothing new for the Yankees manager, who often wore out the rugs in hotel rooms across the American League during the early morning hours, wondering where Ruth could be.

Ruth and teammate Steve O'Neil finally arrived. They had hit the town the night before and decided to extend their party into the morning. A furious Miller Huggins had plenty to say. Ruth, never one to accept criticism, resented his manager's tone of voice and threatened to punch him. O'Neil held Ruth back, and was able to convince him to peacefully board the train.

The Babe received an ovation from over 5,000 fans in Atlanta when he came to bat. Hoping to see him hit a homer, the spectators booed their own pitcher after he threw three consecutive balls. "Don't walk him!" someone yelled. "Let him hit one!" Ruth swung and missed at the next three pitches. He then retired from the game with a stiff neck and a charley horse. He returned to the lineup the next day and belted a towering triple. That evening he became ill with the chills and a fever so severe that a doctor was summoned to the hotel at three o'clock in the morning. Ruth was expected to stay in Atlanta to recover, but twelve hours later he was on the field in Chattanooga. Just as the team's train was about to depart, the Yankees saw Ruth running to join them. "Sure I am going. Don't we play today?" He was wearing several sweaters, looked pale, and slept during the entire trip. He appeared to be unfit to play during the pregame drills, but he launched two mammoth homers in the game.

Following a stop in Knoxville, where Ruth knocked a boy out of a tree with a home run, the Yanks were traveling to Asheville, North Carolina, when Ruth complained about the chills, dizziness, and a stomachache. The train's route through the Smoky Mountains was curvy, and combined with the altitude, Ruth felt worse with each passing hour. The Yankees were cheered by the locals when they arrived. Ruth, although feeling extremely weak, responded by waving his hat. As he walked through the depot with his teammates, he began to experience more dizzy spells. When he reached the exit, he felt so light-headed that he staggered. He reached for a radiator with one hand to keep his balance as he covered his eyes with his other hand, and then he began to fall. O'Neil and Doc Woods (the team trainer) reacted in time to catch him. Ruth, weighing around 270 by now, was carried to a taxi and taken directly to his room at the Battery Park Hotel. A local physician named Charles Jordan was called. The doctor examined Ruth, and then made an announcement. The Babe was running a high fever and suffering from an intestinal attack. "All I can say about Ruth is unless he learns to use good judgment when he eats, his career as a ballplayer will be cut down by five to ten years," said Dr. Jordan. "From what I have heard, he shows no judgment when ordering food."

Dr. Jordan had heard it all when interviewing the Yankees about Ruth's eating habits. He immediately put his patient on a diet and said he would prescribe it to the ballplayer's New York physician. Ruth begged for more food and asked if he could continue to play. Both requests were denied.

"I will do your act today, Babe. I'll hit one for you," Meusel told his friend before to leaving for the ballpark. True to his word, he smacked one over the leftfield fence that was said to be the longest ever hit at that ballpark. "It was my longest ever," said Meusel, who went directly to Ruth's room upon returning to the hotel. He cracked the door, peeked into the darkness and said, "I tipped one for you today, Babe," then closed the door. Ruth, too weak to reply, managed to muster enough strength to smile.

The hotel guests watched in disbelief as Ruth groaned while leaning on the shoulder of Paul Krichell, the Yankees scout known for his discovery of Lou Gehrig, as they slowly moved through the lobby. He was running a 101 fever and was so weak, he needed assistance getting into a cab.

Ruth was heading back to New York. He would miss the remainder of the exhibition season, although it was believed that he would recover in time to play in the season opener. "Every bone hurts in my body," he said when he boarded the train. "I went everywhere in town, trying to find a size 48," said Krichell in reference to a pair of pajamas. "The best I could do was find a size 42." And in pink! Krichell slit the back of the top in order to make it fit. Ruth hardly cared. He needed rest, and all he could think about was sleeping.

The Yankees' next stop was Charlotte, North Carolina, where sacks of telegrams awaited from concerned fans sending Ruth their best wishes. After the game Huggins and eight of his players were aboard a bus that attempted to climb a steep hill. When the vehicle reached the top, the engine stalled and the bus began to roll backwards. The passengers quickly escaped through the windows, and as they lay on the dirt road, they watched in disbelief as the bus continued to roll until it crashed into a tree.

The news about Ruth's collapse was a hot topic from coast to coast. As people waited to hear more about the star's condition, Ruth and Krichell were heading northbound. When their train reached Salisbury, North Carolina, they learned that they had missed their connection to Washington, D.C. They were able to catch another train, but when the train they were booked on arrived in Washington without them, a rumor spread like wildfire that Babe Ruth had died. Upon hearing the news, the London newspapers stopped the presses and changed their headlines to the story about the ballplayer's passing.

Ruth and Krichell were informed when they had arrived Washington. Krichell immediately reported that the ballplayer was alive and well. Ruth sent a telegram to Helen in New York: "Meet me. The report that I am dead is a lie. Love."

When he boarded the train bound for New York, Ruth said he felt fine and fit for breakfast. Ignoring Doctor Jordan's prescribed diet, he ordered eggs with fried potatoes, and when it reached his infected intestines, the pain was so great that he was unable to hold it down.

As the train approached its final destination, Krichell escorted Ruth to the rest room after helping him dress. He left him to look for a comb. When he returned, he found Ruth unconscious on the bathroom floor. He had passed out and hit his head on the basin as he fell. Krichell ran for help and found a porter who was strong enough to help him carry Ruth's massive body to a berth. When the train finally reached New York, Mrs. Ruth, dressed in spring attire, was waiting on the platform with a family friend. She was unaware of what had happened, but sensed something was wrong after the last passenger stepped off the train with no sign of her husband. Her eyes filled as she rushed the train and smothered a cry. When she found her husband lying on a birth, he was still unconscious. His face was pasty and lifeless, his lips puffy and swollen.

A rollaway stretcher was ordered, but there was a problem: it could not be wheeled through the train's narrow aisle. The idea of the nearest window was ruled out since it was too small to get Ruth's huge body through it. Someone brainstormed and requested a screwdriver, which was used to remove the entire window frame. Ruth was then being placed on a stretcher and hoisted through the gap. He was carted to the baggage elevator, taken to the top floor, and wheeled to the street. As his wife and others in the party waited with Ruth for an ambulance, five hundred persons, wanting a closer look, were held back by several policemen.

Ruth regained consciousness and recognized his wife. "How do you feel?" Helen asked.

"Rotten," replied Ruth.

Helen began to weep.

"Helen," said Ruth.

Ruth's body suddenly underwent a series of convulsions, causing his arms and legs to lash out while he muttered incoherently. A hypodermic was immediately administered, and appeared to calm his body until he suddenly experienced another set of convulsions—this time so strong that his body almost stood up. As six men from his party attempted to keep his body on the stretcher, another hypodermic was given.

An ambulance had finally arrived, but with a problem—the steering was broken. Another ambulance was ordered. When this one arrived, and Ruth was placed inside, it was discovered that the sirens did not work. Without working sirens, the ambulance crept through traffic. Mrs. Ruth, in a front seat, turned to look at her husband as she wept, and looked in time to see her husband endure a third set of convulsions. He would have a fourth set when he arrived at St. Vincent's hospital.

Ruth was taken to room 19. As he lay in bed, Helen continued to cry at his bedside. "Cheer up," Ruth told her. "I'm all right." When Doctor King, the Yankees' team physician, assured her that he was okay, she smiled.

"I'm sick, I'm in agony, but I am not dead," said Ruth. "My head hurts and my eyes burn something fierce."

"The big fellow doesn't take care of himself," said Doctor King before a room full of newspapermen. "He lives an active life and eats heartily. He is subjected to colds, and when he gets them he pays no attention to them. The result is they settle and he becomes very sick." A reporter asked if Ruth kept late hours or if he dissipated in the winter. Everyone in the room laughed. "He's careless," Doctor King answered.

"He's resting now, and his condition is satisfactory," added the doctor. "If he passes, he might be out in two to three days. And he might be in the opening game of the season. Ruth is such a powerful fellow that he might recover overnight."

But Ruth would need more than a few days. On April 16, with the 1925 season underway, it was announced that the cause of the problem was an abscess in his stomach region that required surgery in order to be drained. The operation was set for the following morning. "That comes as a shock," said a disappointed Miller Huggins upon receiving the news in the New York dugout at Yankee Stadium. "We all felt that the Big Boy would help us in a week. Damn! That's tough luck."

7
Crash!—1925

"It isn't what you used to be; it's what you are today."—*Joe Dugan*

Clouds hovered over the Bronx on a chilly and overcast afternoon as over fifty thousand spectators filed into Yankee Stadium. Three bands on the field entertained the fans to carry on the tradition of opening day festivities, but much to the disappointment of the fans, the opening day excitement was minus a few things, the most notable being Babe Ruth. "I guess I'll have to take the doctor's advice," he said in disappointment. His consolation was he would get to hear the broadcast from his hospital bed.

Also missing was the raising of the championship banner. In 1922 and 1923, an American League Champions pennant was hoisted to the top of the centerfield flagpole. Last season, it was the World Champions pennant in honor of the Yankees' finally defeating the New York Giants for the world championship. Nobody was more confident than the manager that a banner would be part of next season's festivities. "We are ready for the bell to sound," Huggins said as he sipped his coffee at breakfast. "I'm more completely satisfied with my team this year than I have ever have been with any club I have managed."

Urban Shocker took the mound in a Yankees uniform for the first time since 1917. "I knew Shocker had the earmarks of a great pitcher. That's why I was able to use him in getting Pratt." In his first transaction as the Yankees manager, Huggins traded Shocker and four other players to the Browns for second baseman Del Pratt and a pitcher. "We finished third [in 1918] instead of sixth [in 1917]," said Huggins, believing that was largely due to Pratt's influence. At St. Louis, Shocker developed into a three-time twenty-game winner and earned the distinction of knowing Babe Ruth's batting weaknesses. "Not only will he win games for us, he'll be one less star pitcher I have to hit against," said Ruth. Huggins sent three pitchers to the Browns to get Shocker, including "Bullet Joe" Bush. "I'm no prophet, but I say Shocker will win twenty games for this team this year," said Huggins

Ben Pascal would be replacing Ruth in right field. He had failed to establish himself as a major league player after a trial with two other major league teams, but after a good season at Atlanta of the Southern Association in 1924, and a good showing with the Yankees at the tail end of last season, Pascal was in the big leagues to stay.

Batting in Ruth's number-three spot in the batting order would be centerfielder Earle Combs. "The greatest outfield prospect in a decade," someone called him. He was tabbed as a backup for Whitey Witt prior to spring training. That's until he hit .420 during the exhibition season to win the starting job. He could hit and field, and he showed great promise in 1924 by going 14 for 36 for New York after being purchased from Louisville of the American Association, and before a broken ankle ended his season. "He's fast, hits to all fields, and gets on base often," said Huggins.

Thirty-two-year-old Everett Scott, the captain of the Yankees, would enter the season as the record holder for playing in the most consecutive games. His record now stood at 1,291, but Scott said that he couldn't care less. "When I passed the one-thousand mark, I lost interest in the matter." He was only an average hitter, but Scott's pluses were his leadership and defense, although it was said that his fielding had slipped during the second half of the 1924 season. "A great weakness," a writer wrote about the Yankees' shortstop before the 1925 season. But if Scott proved to be an enigma in 1925, the Yankees claimed to have "the best fielding shortstop since [Rabbit] Maranville" in 5'7" rookie Paul "Pee Wee" Wanninger.

The excitement of a Yankees 5–1 opening day win increased Ruth's fever; nonetheless, he smiled when he heard the call on Paschal's homer. "They don't seem to miss me much," he said.

At 8:30 on the morning of April 17, Ruth was on the operating table. Dr. George Stewart made an incision that would leave a visible ripe scar for the rest of the 1925 season. The procedure was said to be quick, but painful.

The operation was called a complete success. It was over in twenty minutes, although the affects of the anesthetic lasted until noon. The report was Ruth was resting and his fever was dropping. He would be in the hospital for ten more days and begin to exercise in two weeks. The update the following day was he was feeling better. His spirits were lifted when he heard that the Yankees had defeated Boston, 6–3, before an unusually small Saturday afternoon crowd. "I guess we won't get bigger crowds until Ruth is back in the lineup," moaned Ruppert.

Phone calls were pouring in at St. Vincent's from fans wanting updates on Ruth's condition. Helen, Dorothy, and Ed Barrow were the only three permitted to see him. Helen and Dorothy were there every day. Impatient to get back on the field, Ruth became irritable. "It's easier to be in bed when you know you're not missing anything," he said. Helen, worried over her husband's health and attitude, developed a nervous condition. She spoke with Doctor King, and the physician recommended that she check into the hospital for better care. She took his advice and checked into St. Vincent's, where she was placed in a room two floors above her husband's.

The Yankees traveled to Washington for the yearly presidential home opener. As usual, the great Walter Johnson pitched before a sellout crowd that included President Coolidge. New York looked awful in a 10–1 defeat. "The Yankees have rarely looked worse than they did today," wrote James Harrison of the *New York Times*.

"Robbed by the umpires," Harrison wrote after the following day's loss in Washington. "I suspect Huggins' opinion of [umpire] Ormsby is not high." With a Washington runner on second, and with New York leading 1–0 in the bottom of the ninth, Ossie Bluege of the Senators laid down a bunt that was fielded by Pennock. The pitcher fired to third base in time for Dugan to place the tag on the runner. Bluege, meanwhile, rounded first and headed for second. Dugan's throw to the second baseman arrived before Bluege was within ten feet of the base. Yankees reserve second baseman Ernie Johnson put his mitt down and Bluege slid into it for the easy out. Umpire Ormsby, however, ruled that Bluege was safe. A walk and an error followed to load the bases. With the pitcher due up, Washington manager Bucky Harris called for a pinch hitter. The problem was he was out of reserves. He looked for Walter Johnson, a good hitting pitcher. It was then realized that Johnson was in the clubhouse and dressed in his street clothes. A messenger went to fetch him, and a delay followed as Johnson changed into his uniform. "Johnson is dressing," the messenger reported.

Huggins was livid. "Why in the hell don't you make them send up a pinch hitter?!" he yelled to Ormsby as he clinched a fist.

"Johnson is putting his stockings on," was the next report.

"We want to eat tonight!" Huggins yelled to Ormsby.

The came another report: "He's lacing his shoes."

Huggins grabbed Ormsby's wisk broom and heaved it down the third base line.

"Here comes Walter."

Johnson singled to centerfield to score two runs for a 2–1 Washington win. The Yankees were up in arms in their clubhouse following the game. "The hit should be null and void," announced Huggins. The Senators laughed upon hearing this in their clubhouse.

The Yanks lost by a run a day later in Washington. The Senators, the team the Yankees had to beat, had defeated New York in seven of the eight meetings. Two days later, they were hammered in Philadelphia, 8–0, and Huggins became concerned, especially over the lack of timely hitting. "Our left on base totals reads like the national census." The losing continued when they left nine on base in a 7–5 loss to the lowly Red Sox. "The Yankees have now plummeted to the depths of humiliation." They lost again the following day when Everett Scott, off to a poor start, whiffed on a groundball that allowed the winning run to tally. "I'm sticking with Scott," Huggins told the press. "I have no complaint about his effort." When asked about how soon he might switch to Wanninger, he replied, "I do not consider Wanninger experienced enough to stick in the infield regularly now that the campaign is on."

While New York was losing in Boston to make it eight defeats in nine games, Ruth held a press conference in his hospital room. It was the first time he had spoken to reporters since spring training. He was dressed in white pajamas. Roses in bunches were on each side of his bed. His room was spacious with a comfortable bed and a chair. He looked pale. "I don't know how long they will keep me here, but I don't think it will be for very long now."

"What's the trouble with you? Influenza or indigestion?" asked a writer.

"Influenza," answered Ruth. "The indigestion stuff is the bunk! Why, I never ate as much of three-quarters of the rest of the team."

"Collectively or individually?" asked a reporter. Everyone in the room laughed.

"I mean man against man," Ruth said.

"I never knew what pain was until this time," Ruth said in reference to his surgery. "I haven't been able to do anything except lie on my back, just like you see me now."

When the reporters left, Ruth stared at the window where the sun was streaming through on a bright day with an expression like a boy in a classroom looking out the window while daydreaming.

On May 6, Huggins spoke with his shortstop before the Yankees took the field against the Athletics. He informed him that he was going to the bench. Scott headed to the dugout without saying a word, tossed his mitt into the bench and took a seat. The longest consecutive-games streak in baseball history had concluded at 1,307. Little did anyone know that a greater one was about to begin for Lou Gehrig.

Scott was baffled, especially after getting two hits the day before in a Yankees win. His two-hit game broke a 0 for 18 drought, an indication in his mind that he was starting to hit. His manager felt otherwise.

Scott did say that his streak had lost its meaning after surpassing one thousand games, but this was an emotional time for him. He headed home to

Fort Wayne for a week on a leave of absence. The day he returned, he was used in his new role: pinch hitter.

New York lost, 6–2, in the rookie shortstop's first game. "Without Everett in the lineup, the Yankees look as strange as a man wearing a full dress suit without a collar." Wanninger looked good in the field. "He is young and has a natural appetite for ground balls. He nibbles 'em up as quick as Ruth of his pre-operation days used to nibble on a plate of pork chops." But while the press and Yankees scouts were high on Wanninger, the manager had little to say. When the Yankees traveled to St. Louis to meet the Browns, Huggins left the team to see a shortstop in St. Paul.

Miller Huggins's friendship with Bob Connery went back to the days when Huggins managed the financially handicapped St. Louis Cardinals and Connery served as the team's one and only scout. The former scout was now running the operations for the St. Paul Saints of the American Association. He invited his good friend to look at his shortstop and catcher. The Yankees manager liked what he saw in shortstop Mark Koenig, who was currently hitting .311. With Huggins in the crowd, he went 2 for 5, and the catcher, Pat Collins, hit one over the fence. Huggins told the *St. Paul Pioneer Press* that he believed Koenig would be a valuable addition to the Yankees following a season of experience in St. Paul. Before leaving to rejoin his club, he spoke with Connery about sending players from his current roster for Koenig. He also men-

Miller Huggins knew from the beginning that he had a great player in centerfielder Earle Combs (National Baseball Hall of Fame, Cooperstown, New York).

tioned that he liked Collins but needed more time to decide, and he also expressed interest in St. Paul outfielder Cedric Durst.

Babe Ruth was counting down the days until his release date of May 25. He praised the St. Vincent's staff for treating him "excellently," and said he was "anxious to get out." He was instructed to spend time at his Sudbury farm to recuperate before returning, but wanting to return to the diamond, he ruled that out. "All I need is a little more exercise to strengthen my legs. I still feel a little weak, but otherwise I'm in fine shape." He left the hospital one day and taxied to Yankee Stadium to take batting practice in privacy. Following the session he stepped on the scale in the Yankees' clubhouse and found that he had regained eight of the thirty pounds he had lost. "I go down south to lose weight and I get sick; I come back to get well and I lose weight. Then I get well and I find that I'm gaining weight. What I would like to know is what am I supposed to do in a case like that?"

The Yankees were off to a poor start with a record of 12–19 and already 10½ games out of first place. "The Yankees cannot possibly be this bad as the first few weeks of the season can indicate them to be," declared James Harrison. No, nobody could have imaged this, and now the natives were becoming restless.

On May 25, the Yankees trailed Boston, 3–2, in the bottom of the ninth during the first game of a double-header. With two outs and a runner in scoring position, Bob Meusel was cheered as he stepped to the plate. Three pitches down the middle and the Yankees slugger never took his bat off his shoulder. When strike three had ended the game, a chorus of boos rang throughout Yankee Stadium. "If he's a slugger, then I'm the reigning prince of Hindustan," said a disappointed fan. When Meusel stepped in for his first at bat in the nightcap, he received a Bronx cheer like no other hometown player ever had: "What an outburst of hoots and sepulchral moans." This time he came through by belting one to deep left-centerfield that split the two outfielders, and by the time the ball was sent back to the infield, Meusel had rounded the bases and crossed home plate while standing up. He was still hearing the boos the next day before he hit another inside-the-park homer, and the next day he continued his aggressive play by stealing home to earn the forgiveness of the fans.

Babe Ruth was finally discharged, although he would be leaving without Helen. It was confirmed that she had suffered a nervous breakdown, and reports were that her recovery was slower than expected.

The Yankees needed Ruth's big bat in their lineup. They were in seventh place with a 15–25 record, just 1½ games ahead of the last-place Red Sox, and currently on a four-game losing streak. They were last in the league in runs scored. Most of the starters were hitting under their lifetime averages, the most notable being Wally Pipp, batting just .242. Ford Frick of the *New York Evening Journal* believed the answer was to start Gehrig and the other youngsters to add more pep to the lineup.

The pitching was also underperforming. Waite Hoyt, averaging eighteen wins per season since coming to the Yankees, had yet to win a game. It took him fifty-two games into the Yankees' season to finally record his first win, and it wasn't easy. Against the Indians at Yankee Stadium, Hoyt took a 6–2 lead into the top of the eighth. After a Cleveland batter tagged him for a home run, and Tris Speaker followed with a single, the grandstand managers began to worry. "Take him out! Take him out!" they shouted. Hoyt responded by retiring the next six batters to record the win.

On June 1, Babe Ruth was back in the Yankees' starting lineup and was "in no condition to play." "The Big Bam looked pale and slightly thinner through the shoulders."

"He received a burst of applause when he came to bat for the first time," in the second inning against Walter Johnson. He hit a weak taper back to the pitcher for an easy out. In his next at bat, he swung and missed at the first pitch. The writers in the press box agreed that his swings were slow and not as sharp. Ruth swung at the next pitch and connected. The crowd jumped its feet as the ball sailed down the right field line, but curved and fell foul into the seats just two feet wide of the foul pole.

Ruth managed to coax a walk. Meusel followed by drilling one over the centerfielder's head. The crowd went wild as Ruth rounded second at a slow pace, then rounded third and headed home. The relay throw arrived to the catcher before Ruth was within ten feet of scoring. "In the good days he would have scored standing up."

Ruth remained on the ground after sliding. "The spirit was willing, but the flesh was weak and he became an easy out." As he slowly came to his feet, he announced, "The old dogs won't work fast."

In the fifth inning, Ruth sprinted back for a fly ball as he looked over his right shoulder. He leaped, got his glove on the ball, and fell to the ground. To his own amazement, he had made the catch, but he was gassed. As Ruth lay on the ground—exhausted—Combs came over to help him back on his feet.

Ruth grounded out in the sixth inning and then retired for the day. In the bottom of the eighth, with the Yankees trailing by three runs, Huggins lifted Wanninger for a pinch hitter. He sent in Lou Gehrig, who had appeared in just 11 season games as a pinch hitter and outfielder. Nobody could have imagined that Gehrig's plate appearance was history in the making. This was the first of a long string of consecutive games that would eventually eclipse Scott's record and last into the 1939 season.

The next day Huggins started his younger players, "just for luck," he said. "But the real reason is probably a deeper one than this casual explanation would indicate," according to Will Wedge of the *New York Sun*. "Something had to be done with the team to shake it out of the rut into which it had fallen."

Wedge continued, "Miller Huggins took his favorite lineup and shook it to pieces. Pipp, Ward, and Schang were given the opportunity to see what it is like to be on the outside looking in. Gehrig, [Howie] Shanks, and [Ben] Bengough were allowed to play. The three youngsters were full of pep, and they made the veterans look sick." The three newcomers had combined for seven hits, with Gehrig and Bengough making three apiece, in a Yankees 8–5 win over Washington. "The fans were sorry to see Wally go, but no tears were shed over Gehrig's three hits."

"Well, where have these guys been all season?" someone asked.

"From now on they'll be a hard outfit to beat," said Bucky Harris. "Believe me, I am glad we got a lot of games out of the way before the big fellow got back and before the young fellows got going. The Yankees are not yet out of the race."

Cobb and his Tigers made their first season appearance at Yankee Stadium in mid-June. Remembering the rivalry from the season before, the fans hooted Cobb all afternoon. Cobb and Ruth had made their peace while guests at the 1924 World Series. However, Cobb had new victim in mind, and Lou Gehrig, hearing it from the Detroit manager, suffered through an afternoon of miscues. He made two errors, and ran back for a pop fly in a way that distracted Ruth into dropping the ball. In the bottom of the ninth, a Detroit pitcher plunked Gehrig. On the next play, perhaps in retaliation, the rookie knocked down a Tigers infielder while trying to break up a double play. Both batter and runner were declared out when Gehrig was called for interference on the play. As he trotted back to the dugout, he was soundly booed by the hometown fans.

The booing was directed at all of the Yankees the next day during a 19–1 loss. "It was one of those games that you could fall asleep at any time and have no lifelong regrets." In the sixth inning, the Tigers scored 11 runs on 13 hits before the first out was recorded. Four Yankees pitchers passed seven batters in a forty-nine-minute inning. When Ruth caught a fly ball for the inning's first out, the crowd let out a sarcastic cheer. When the inning finally did end, the Tigers had scored 13 runs to present a problem for the scoreboard operators, since number 10 was the highest number in the Yankee scoreboard inventory. The operators improvised by posting a 7 and a 6.

On June 23, the contending Washington Senators came to town with a new player. "I guess some of you guys would like to be fired back to a championship outfit," said Everett Scott. One week before, Scott's playing days in New York ended when the Yankees sent him to Washington for a $4,000 waiver cost. It was a decision that Huggins never regretted. One month later, he pointed out that Scott's stats proved that he made no mistake. He also praised Wanninger for the first time: "He has improved wonderfully since replacing Scott, and he's hitting well. I prefer to lose with Pee Wee in there instead of Scott."

"You guys haven't a chance in the world. The season is almost half way over and you're 17½ games away [from first place]," a fan shouted at the Yankees in Boston. "Why, you're just a bum club going nowhere, and just playing out your schedule."

It wasn't about a lack of effort; the Yankees were simply having a bad season and fueling their own bad luck through unwise decisions and a failure to execute. In a loss to Cleveland, a pop fly to shallow centerfield was touched by three Yankees before the ball hit the ground to allow the batter to reach second base. After moving to third on an out, the runner scored ... on a sacrifice fly to the shortstop. "No club but the current Yankees could permit a play like that." With Aaron Ward on third base, Ruth on second, and with one out, Gehrig grounded back to the pitcher. Ward proceeded to get trapped in a rundown between third and home. After he was tagged out, Ruth got caught between the bases to complete a twin killing. "How two base runners with their eyes open in plain daylight could wander off the bags like pedestrians taking a stroll in the park will always remain a mystery."

"My boys are original. They know of ways of losing ballgames that the Red Sox never thought of," said Huggins, perhaps trying to keep his sanity during the turbulent season. "Tough," said Wally Schang when returning to the hotel after the Yankees blew a 5–1 lead in a loss to the Red Sox.

"Tough!" shouted Joe Dugan. "It's worse than that: it's impossible."

"Yeah, tougher than swimming in a river with an armful of eels," added Whitey Witt.

Never favored by the Yankee fans, Miller Huggins was now hearing more calls than ever for his dismissal. Fans were flooding the *New York Sun* mailbox with letters pleading for a managerial change. A rumor circulated that Huggins would resign under fire and Larry Stallings, the manager of the 1914 World Champion Boston Braves, would take over in 1926. "There is absolutely nothing to it," said Ed Barrow. "That's news to me," said Huggins.

On July 2, Wally Pipp entered the batting cage during batting practice.

Pitching was a prospect named Charley Cardwell, a current star hurler at Princeton University getting a look-over by the Yankees. The collegian threw an inside fast ball that hit Pipp squarely on the head. The batter fell heavily to the ground, then lay unconscious in the dirt. His teammates, running to his aid, picked him up and carried him to the clubhouse where he regained consciousness. Claiming he felt very nauseous, he was rushed to St. Vincent's, placed in room 14, and was said to be suffering from pain and shock. Later that evening, it was reported that he was feeling better.

Pipp would be in the hospital for over a week. When he returned he continued his role as Gehrig's backup and pinch hitter. Most speculated that he would retire after the season and become a coach in 1926. Never feeling bitter over his demotion, he taught Gehrig the finer points of playing first base. Pipp knew right from wrong, and he believed helping the rookie was the right thing to do.

In late June, Helen, now out of the hospital, quarreled with her husband once again, and this time it was the final straw. "I'm through," she told a player's wife, and before she headed back to the farm in Sudbury, she had phoned an attorney to discuss the conditions of a separation. When a "For Sale" sign appeared in front of Home Plate Farm, a reporter asked Ruth about it on a day the slugger was in a foul mood. "The farm has become a nuisance," answered Ruth. "I'm there only in the winter and for a few days in the summer. Mrs. Ruth is in New York with me at the same time, and there is nobody to look after the farm." Helen had asked Babe for a separation and a payment of $100,000. Ruth told her to get lost, but by end of the summer the two would legally separate on the grounds of incompatibility, and Ruth would owe $100,000 to be paid to her in four installments from October 1925 through October 1928. Dorothy was placed in Helen's custody.

On June 27, in Boston, Ruth batted twice before taking himself out of the game when he twisted an ankle while running out a grounder. "It feels like somebody sticking me with a pin," he said. "I guess a little piece of bone got chipped off. Doc Woods thinks so. I've got the ankle all taped up." He did not play in the nightcap. The next day, his ankles badly swollen, he headed back to New York and checked into St. Vincent's, which led to speculation that Ruth's season was over. "I may be laid up for a while, but I won't be out of baseball for the rest of the season, I hope," Ruth said.

Ruth was also complaining of exhaustion. "My bats feel heavy. I can't swing them the way I used to."

FORD FRICK: "When do you think he will be in shape?"
HUGGINS: "I don't think he will be in shape all season."

FRICK: "Will you use him in the lineup?"
HUGGINS: "Oh yes. We'll give him another rest and then use him from time to time."

Ruth returned to the lineup three days later.

Huggins was beginning to lose patience. Ruth had returned to his poor habits of overeating, drinking, and ignoring curfew. His manager could tolerate that when the Yankees were winning and Ruth was producing league-leading statistics, but in 1925 his team was in seventh place and Ruth was having his worst season. In mid–July, with his batting average at just .265, and with nine home runs in eighty-one games, it was evident that his poor season and attitude were affecting the team. The Yankees were sixth in the league in runs scored, the fielding was struggling, Joe Dugan had injured his knee, Aaron Ward was having a tough season at second base, and Pee-Wee Wanninger was failing to cover the ground as hoped.

The pitching staff was also struggling. Hoyt, Shocker, and Shawkey were all having poor seasons. Pennock, the only hurler on the staff who allowed fewer hits than innings pitched and an ERA under 3.00, was frustrated with the team's season and their lack of run support. He had lost nine one-run games, three by a score of 1–0. "I have practically made up my mind to retire from baseball after the season," he announced. "Business considerations and my future interest demand it." His goal was to devote his full time to breeding silver foxes. "This is one of the great young industries of the country, yet comparatively little exploited." Pennock owned thirty-three foxes at a value of $4,500. "I've been pitching professionally for twelve years now. It's time to think about another business that I can stick to permanently."

The Yankees' woes continued with a 5–13 record during their second trip out west. "In the first game there was no fire to the Yankees game, not even heat. There was no dash, not even a walk."

The manager's troubles with Ruth continued to the point where Huggins had just about reached his limit. Ruth continued to violate his curfew, and even went as far as to neglect to return to the team's hotel in Chicago. "I was visiting the homes of some personal friends," Ruth would later say. "The next day, Huggins plastered a $1,000 fine." By that time the Yankees had already hired a detective to trail him. According to the detective's report, those personal friends were at six residences registered to six different females.

During the last game of the series in Chicago, Ruth made an unwise decision by ducking out of the way to allow centerfielder Earle Combs to make the catch on a routine fly ball that Ruth clearly should have had, and the ball fell to the ground for a hit. At the plate during that same game, he failed to run on a dropped third strike.

HUGGINS: "Guess you want to go back to New York ahead of time?"
RUTH: "Don't care if I do, the way we're going."
HUGGINS: "You don't need to play anymore."

And Huggins sent in a replacement.

"Can you imagine that guy talking to me like that!" snorted Ruth.

When the team arrived back in New York following their disappointing road trip, Huggins told Ruth to forget the fine.

With the 1925 season a complete washout, Huggins began to talk about 1926. "New York is not patient with ball teams. Delivery must be immediate. I intend to go into the market for two real boxmen [pitchers], a seasoned backstop [catcher], and a well-developed second baseman. I cannot show my goods at this time, but I expect to have what I am after at training camp next season."

Huggins did mention that he had two good pitching prospects in the minors, one being a former Red Sox hurler, George Pipgras. He also reminded the writers that Koenig would be a Yankee in '26, although the deal had yet to be completed.

The Yankees' scouts were traveling the country searching for shortstops. In late July, Paul Krichell sealed a deal for $12,000 with Hartford of the Eastern League for a brash nineteen-year-old shortstop named Leo Durocher. The Cubs had made a $10,000 offer for him, and Worster manager Casey Stengel had also expressed interest. But Koenig and Durocher were small in comparison to a shortstop being watched in Salt Lake City of the Pacific Coast League who was being valued as a "$100,000 beauty."

With the team's future to be invested in youngsters, Huggins began to release his veterans. He started with Witt, then O'Neill, and said this was only the beginning. Next to go were pitcher Alex Ferguson and outfielder Bobby Veach. The two were informed when they had arrived back at the team's hotel in Detroit emptyhanded after fishing on a day off. Mark Roth, the team's traveling secretary, and Yankees coach Charley O'Leary broke the news, and the two veterans reacted in a sarcastic manner. "Oh, goody, goody. Let's give three cheers and a tiger for dear Mr. Huggins," they sang as they danced.

The Yankees were 41–55 and twenty-two games away from first place when July concluded. Things did not improve in August, especially for Ruth, who went into his worst slump of the season by going 7 for 45 from August 2 to August 16. The Yankees headed out west for the third and final time in 1925. Once again, the Yankees were pounded. They dropped seven of eight before entering their last series game at Chicago.

The final game at Chicago started like the Yanks were finally going to win. In the top of the first, New York scored three times. In that inning, with runners on first and second, Ruth went against his manager's order by bunting to move the runners up a base. Paschal followed with a single to score the two runners, but the lead didn't hold. Wanninger's fielding slump continued with two errors, leading to four Chicago runs.

With the Yanks trailing by a run in the do-or-die ninth, Meusel and Combs were on base with nobody out when Ruth was given the bunt sign. He saw the signal, ignored it, and drilled one that was earmarked for a hit to right field. Chicago first baseman Earl Sheely leaped high to knock the line drive to the ground, recovered in time to throw to second to nip Combs, and then, to everyone's surprise, shortstop Ike Davis made a return threw to Sheely in time to complete the double play. Was Ruth running on the play?

In the dugout, Huggins was seething. Once again, Ruth had crossed him. As the manager and ballplayer exchanged angry words when Ruth returned to the dugout, Gehrig hit a fly ball for the last out of the game to complete another Yankees loss.

Following the loss, Huggins sat by himself on the train ride to St. Louis. What was on his mind? What was he going to do about Ruth? In St. Louis, Ruth once again missed curfew before the first game, which New York lost, 1–0, for their seventh consecutive defeat. That same day, Huggins placed a long-distance call to the Yankees' office. He spoke to Barrow and told him he planned to finally take action on Ruth. "Will you get Colonel Ruppert's backing on this?" Huggins asked.

"Ruppert's backing isn't necessary," Barrow said into the phone. "If that's what you want to do, go ahead. You've got my backing."

The next day, the Yankees were on the field for batting practice before the second game of the series, all except for Ruth, who had once again missed curfew the night before and had now failed to be at the ballpark on time. With his team on the field, Huggins sat on a bench as he smoked his pipe in the deserted clubhouse while waiting for Ruth to arrive. He had something important to tell him.

8

Suspension—1925

"Ruth has been a bad boy this season and I'm going to stand firmly behind Huggins on the matter."—Jacob Ruppert

Babe Ruth burst through the entrance of the Yankees' clubhouse at Sportsman's Park. As he walked to his locker with his overcoat over his shoulder and his necktie astray, he noticed his manager smoking a pipe while seated on a bench. "Sorry, Hug, I had some business to attend to," Ruth told him as he walked by. His manager made no reply. When Ruth reached his locker, he took off his jacket and hung it. "No use putting on that uniform," Huggins said, "You are not playing."

Ruth looked at his manager's expressionless face and frowned. "Now what's the matter?" he asked.

"You know very well what's the matter," replied Huggins. "I'm sorry, but this is the finish. You're fined five thousand dollars and suspended indefinitely. You're to go back to New York on the five o'clock train. Mark Roth [the Yankees' traveling secretary] has your ticket."

"Five thousand dollars?" Ruth asked in disbelief. "Five thousand dollars! Who the hell do you think you are?" Ruth shouted obscenities and warned his manager he "would never get away with this." "I'll never play another game for you, you little—! I'll go to New York and see Jake. You don't think he will stand for this, do you?"

"Do as you please," replied Huggins, who then stood up, turned and headed for the walkway leading to the field. Ruth grabbed his jacket, slammed his way to the clubhouse door, and traveled back to the Buckingham Hotel to pack and check out. A hotel employee later claimed that he appeared calm and never expressed the slightest trace of anger. From there Ruth headed to the west side of town to visit a friend. A phone call was placed to the residence, where it was reported that he had left and was heading back to New York City. But Ruth decided on a different plan. He would head to Chicago to file a complaint with Judge Landis. "I just want him to understand things." After arriving in the Windy City, he was told that Landis was vacationing at his summer home in Burt Lake, Michigan. "Then I will see Jake [Ruppert]," Ruth said.

The commissioner knew nothing of Ruth's suspension and fine until a reporter had called.

> LANDIS: "How do you know he wants to see me?"
> REPORTER: "He said so."
> LANDIS: "Where is he?"
> REPORTER: "At the Congress Hotel."
> LANDIS: "He can come up here, for I will be here for two or three days yet. He can get a train at 5:30 p.m. for Burt Lake."

Ban Johnson heard the story and responded: "I will back Huggins to the finish. Ruth has the mind of a fifteen year-old boy. Drinking and staying out all night will not be tolerated."

At Chicago's Congress Hotel, Ruth left word at the front desk not to be disturbed until 10:00 a.m. the next morning. Sportswriters began to congregate outside his door several minutes before that time. At the exact hour, someone firmly knocked on the door. Ruth cracked the door. "Holy smokes," he said in surprise. "I thought it was the bellboy. Wait a minute."

A few minutes later, Ruth opened the door and invited his guests to step into his suite. He was dressed in a bathrobe and he was holding a suit which he wanted pressed. He laid down the suit, took a seat, and gave his side of the story:

> If Huggins is the manager [in 1926], I am through with the Yankees. Either he quits or I quit, regardless of my contract, which expires next year.
> Huggins is making me the "goat" for the rotten showing of the team.
> The fine is a joke. Why, I know of guys killing people, and bootleggers, who don't get that tough of a fine. I haven't killed anybody.
> Can you imagine a fellow who hit about .240 when he was playing ball trying to tell players who have .350 averages how to hit the ball?
> The truth to the matter is that Huggins is incompetent. He had a wonderful team under him in the past and it virtually managed itself. Last year we lost the pennant to Washington when we should've won by fifteen games. That was Huggins's fault. He did not get the most out of his team.
> If Huggins is a baseball manager, I can swim the English Channel, and I am not much of a swimmer.

Ruth defended his decision to disobey Huggins in Chicago, "because I thought it was the proper play." He admitted to breaking curfew on several occasions, and on the recent trip to St. Louis. "Anyway, it's too hot to sleep in St. Louis," Ruth said, then laughed at his answer.

8. Suspension—1925

Ruth didn't stop. He spoke about his manager's unsuccessful transactions, especially the Peckinpaugh trade. "He was afraid that Peckinpaugh would get his job. Peck ran the club for a while during Huggins's absence. He succeeded. We played our heads off for him. Peck's award was he was traded. Washington would not have won the pennant without him last season."

A sportswriter showed Ruth the quote in the local paper by Ban Johnson. Ruth responded with a smile. "Well, what do you think of it?" the writer asked.

"Looks like Ban is always right," Ruth replied.

Reached for comment, Huggins said: "I appreciate the contrary of being given the opportunity to defend myself, but I do not intend to engage in any argument with Ruth on the subject. I am really not interested in what he has to say now or in where he has gone."

The Yankees manager mentioned the reason for disciplinary action was due to misconduct off the field. "Of course it means drinking," he said when asked. "And it means a lot of other things. There are various kinds of misconduct. I have tried to overlook Ruth's behavior for a while, but I have decided to take summary of action to bring the big fellow to his senses."

SPORTSWRITER: "Will the five-thousand-dollar fine be in cash?"
HUGGINS: "What a question [laughs along with the other sportswriters]. Ruth will feel at once in his pocketbook that he has been disciplined."
RUTH: "He charges me with excessive drinking. That's a lie. I never trained so faithfully in my life as I have this year."
RUPPERT: "Anything Miller Huggins says goes with me. Huggins is running this club, not Ruth. Ruth can quit if he wants to. Huggins, despite of what Ruth says, is not to be blamed for this season. He can remain as manager of this team as long as he cares to. I have said that before. As long as he is the manager, his decisions will be backed to the limit."
BARROW: "Find us a customer, someone who will take Ruth's contract and his upkeep, care, and trouble and we might talk business [says with a laugh]. Can you think of any club owner who would want to undertake that job?"
SPORTSWRITER: "If Ruth comes back here and says he's sorry and wishes to get back into the game again, what will be the decision of the Yankees club?"
BARROW: "That will be up to Huggins."
HUGGINS: "When I think that Ruth has learned his lesson, when I think he is ready to do the right thing, and in my opinion, he is sincere, I will reinstate him."

The Yankees arrived back in New York City at 11:00 p.m. following the most difficult road trip of their disappointing season, which concluded with four wins and eleven losses to put them twenty-two games under five hundred. When he stepped off the train, Huggins was surrounded by reporters who asked about Ruth's remarks in Chicago. The manager replied that he did not care, and added that he had nothing else to say until after he met with Ruppert.

Three thousand fans, including a group of pressmen, were at Grand Central Station to greet Ruth upon his arrival from Chicago. There was a roar among the other passengers who were unaware that they were riding with a celebrity. Father Joseph Quinn of Scranton, Pennsylvania, an old friend of Ruth's dating back to his days at St. Mary's, was there to greet him. "Leave him alone," Quinn said to the press. "He wants to see his wife first. She has been ill, as you know."

"Come to the [Concourse] hotel, boys, later on, and perhaps I will have something to see then," Ruth said unenthusiastically.

The press continued to ask questions as they walked along with Ruth and Father Quinn while they headed to the exit: "Are you going to quit the Yankees?" "What was the reason for suspension?" "Did Mrs. Ruth file for separation?" Ruth ignored the questions.

"What about you and Mrs. Hodgson? Are you going to see her?" Mrs. Claire Hodgson! The cat was now out of the bag, or was it when the model and actress was pictured on the back page of the *Chicago Tribune* the day before with a sentence claiming her to be a pretty female admirer of the Babe's?

> FORD FRICK: "The Bambino is going to have to explain about the rumors linking his name with that of the charming Mrs. Claire Hodgson of 315 West Seventy-Ninth Street."
> HELEN RUTH: "I know absolutely nothing about those affairs. I don't care to talk for publication now. However, I do intend to discuss these matters with my husband when he returns."

Ruth was greeted by a crowd of reporters who followed him into his suite inside the Concourse Hotel. Helen was there, appearing to be worn out to the point where she was on the verge of another nervous breakdown. "She couldn't cope," Yankees pitcher Bob Shawkey said. "She couldn't stand all the talk about all those women." She had a large bandage around her left ring finger, the result of an infection that caused the digit to swell enough to require her wedding ring to be sawed off.

Babe and Helen excused themselves from the newsmen and headed into the privacy of their bedroom for a long talk. When they reappeared, the sportswriters asked if the two could pose for photos. Ruth took a seat on a bed with Helen seated in his lap. She began to weep and his eyes began to fill. Perhaps to save face, Ruth turned and stared out the window for several minutes before facing the reporters again.

Ruth left for the Yankee Stadium offices to chat with Ruppert. He then left for Yankee Stadium to talk to Huggins. He admitted he had overreacted and was wrong. In his heart he knew he wanted to be a Yankee, and now he wanted to get back on the diamond.

Ruppert: "I have heard both sides, and Huggins is handling the matter. I won't go over his head. I told Ruth that the matter was his to settle with his manager." He added: "Ruth is not running the Yankees, and he won't be traded or sold, but he can retire from baseball if he wishes to."

Ruth arrived at the Yankee Stadium clubhouse and spoke with a few teammates before spotting Huggins. This would be the first time they would speak since the manager had informed him about his suspension in St. Louis.

"Hello, Miller," said Ruth.

Huggins responded. The two, surrounded by reporters, edged off to one side for privacy, but the writers stepped with them. With their pens and notepads ready, the writers looked at the two men, waiting for one to speak up.

"Well, what do I do?" Ruth asked his manager.

"Babe, I can't see you today," replied Huggins. "I can't see you tomorrow. I will call you on the phone when I am ready to see you."

Ruth stopped by the clubhouse the next day, hoping that his manager would let him suit up. When he arrived, he looked to Huggins's small office on the right side. Noticing the door was closed, he gave a light knock. Huggins emerged with his pipe in his mouth. "May I put on a uniform?" Ruth asked.

"Not today. Call me Friday afternoon," said Huggins, who then closed the door.

Ruth spoke to his teammates for a few minutes. He then sat down at a card table and began to play a game of solitaire. While he focused on his game, the other players left the clubhouse. Huggins emerged from his office, walked by without saying a word, "and soon Ruth was all alone, thinking over his mistakes."

The experience may have reminded Ruth of the pain of feeling all alone. Going back to the dinner hour on Ruth's first day at St. Mary's from twenty-three years before, he always remembered that intense lonely feeling when he visualized his family gathered around the dinner able and his chair being empty. He sobbed that night while in bed when he heard a voice ask, "What's the matter, Babe?" He looked up and saw the six-foot-six frame of Brother Matthias. (In his book, *Playing the Game*, Ruth claimed that to be the first time he heard the name, although he told other stories about how the name originated.)

Ruth paid a visit to Yankee Stadium the next day when the Yankees were idle. He stepped onto the playing field and looked around the deserted stadium where he had once starred. He noticed the Yankee Stadium groundskeeper, Rick Schmenk, working in the outfield. Ruth walked over to say hello. The two spoke for a few minutes before Ruth departed.

"Hello, is this you, Hug?" Ruth asked through the telephone on Friday afternoon. "Well, I'm ready to play. What's the verdict?"

"I'm not ready to talk to you yet," Huggins told him. "When I am ready I'll call you."

"Gosh, I'll go stale," Ruth said.

Huggins told the press: "The main thing is that Ruth must convince me in his assertion that from now on he will behave. That's why I am in no hurry to reinstate him."

On Saturday, Ruth got a phone call from his manager. They met at the stadium and had a long talk. Ruth apologized. Huggins allowed him put on a uniform and practice, but would not let him play. He instructed him to meet the team at the train station the next day.

"Well, Hug, I'm here," Ruth said at Grand Central Station.

"Yes, I see," said Huggins. "I've decided to accept your apology and lift the suspension. You will not play today, but you can accompany the team to Boston. The five-thousand-dollar fine stands."

"All right, Hug. I'll be there," Ruth said as he smiled.

At Boston, Ruth was the first one dressed and on the field. He was happy to be back, but his day would end on a sour note when he learned his bull terrier broke loose from his Sudbury farm and attacked a neighbor's prize-winning cow. The press joked that Ruth's dog would be "fined five thousand dog bones," but the neighbor found no humor in losing a prize-winning cow, and intended to sue Ruth for $1,000. "They come in bunches like bananas," Ruth said. "Well, this luck can't last forever."

In his second day after returning to the lineup, Ruth pounded out four hits in a double-header sweep at Boston. When he blasted one over the right center field fence, the Boston fans, who had soundly booed him during the Yankees' previous visit, stood up and cheered. Ruth smiled as he rounded the bases, and when he got to the dugout, Huggins greeted him with a smile. The next day Ruth went four for four with two doubles to give him nine hits in eighteen at bats since his return.

In Philadelphia, Murderers' Row became the fifth team in baseball history to hit three consecutive home runs. It happened in the fourth inning when Meusel blasted his twenty-eighth of the season into the left field seats; Ruth followed with one that landed on a residence rooftop in right field; Gehrig hit one through an open window of a nearby home.

Mark Koenig was now a member of the New York Yankees. He had joined the team in Boston, played his first game as a late-inning substitution, and got his first major league hit when he started the next game. The scouting report said he was a good fielder but not much on hitting; however, he looked to be

The Yankees manager's relationship with his best player changed forever after taking action in August 1925 (National Baseball Hall of Fame, Cooperstown, New York).

good all around in his first starting assignment. "Koenig hits well, looks good, and was tidy in the field, barring a couple low throws that Gehrig had to excavate." Huggins was impressed, and believed he would take care of a huge problem. "It has been a shame the way balls have traveled through our infield for hits that should have been easy outs."

The Yankees were now playing winning baseball and put together a five-game winning streak during a home stand. In win number five, Ruth leaned into a slow ball and knocked it for a home run. One week later, Ruth would hit one in dramatic fashion.

Trailing 5–2 in the bottom of the ninth, the now rarely used Wally Pipp came up as a pinch batter and walked. Combs and Koenig followed with singles to load the bases for Ruth. After taking two inside pitches, he drilled a long one into the seats for a foul ball. Then after taking another ball, he belted one into the right field bleachers for the second game-ending grand slam of his career. The crowd stormed the field, forcing Ruth to fight his way through the mob to get to home plate to record the winning run.

The Yankees finished seventh to conclude their worst season "since the unhappy days of Frank Chance," and somewhere Roger Peckinpaugh smiled as he looked to the heavens. Not only did the thirty-four-year-old shortstop help the Senators win another pennant, he enjoyed his best season, resulting in his naming as the league's MVP. "It seems like poetic justice and I feel repaid many times over for the anxiety and disgust caused me by the raw New York deal," he said. "I think Mrs. Peckinpaugh takes an even keener delight in my honors. It tickled her to death when I was voted 'most valuable player.' 'I guess that will show them something,' she said to me."

Maybe someone should have warned the Peckinpaughs to knock on wood. In the 1925 World Series, the veteran shortstop committed a record eight errors in the Senators' loss to the Pirates in seven games.

The good news for the Yankees was they were 19–13 following Ruth's suspension. They had a good core of young players. Lou Gehrig pounded out twenty round-trippers and improved tremendously during the course of the season. "His progress has been amazing this year." Earle Combs hit .342, and produced a seventeen-game hitting streak during the last month of the season. Koenig looked good, proved to be a lot better than Wanninger, and was tabbed as the Yankees' shortstop of the future.

Meusel led the league in home runs (33) and RBI (138). Ruth had his worst season as a Yankee, but finished strong by hitting .346 with ten home runs following his suspension. Although there were a few bright spots, for all practical purposes 1925 was a year that Babe Ruth and the Yankees preferred to forget.

9

Comeback Season—1926

"Babe Ruth not only will stage a comeback next season, but also will enjoy one of his greatest years he has had on the diamond."
—Artie McGovern

"Losing your pep? Well, don't. Build up a strong and healthy body at our gym, and make a new man of yourself. Leading physicians recommend us."

Located on the fourth floor of the Liggitt Building, at 41 East 42nd Street, was an 11,640-square-foot gymnasium owned and operated by Artie McGovern. Marshall Field and Jack Dempsey were among his well-known clientele, and now Babe Ruth. Christy Walsh had introduced Ruth to McGovern in the fall of 1925, and the trainer wasted little time in putting his new patient to work. The workouts, plus a meatless and sugar-free diet, helped Ruth lose thirteen pounds in one month. When the sessions began, "Ruth weighed 254," according to McGovern, "his blood pressure was low and his pulse was high. He was a total loss as any patient I have ever seen under my care. The slightest exertion left him short of breath. His muscles were soft and flabby."

The sessions consisted of riding a stationary bike for several minutes followed by the rowing machines, stomach crunches, leg lifts, a series of leg exercises, and working with the medicine ball. When the time came for Ruth to report to St. Petersburg, he was in the best shape of his career.

The Sunshine City was growing. A total of 682,000 permits were granted in 1925 and thirty-five million dollars had been invested in building homes, apartments, and tall buildings. Trucks rumbled through the streets with bricks to build new roads. New York businessmen were buying up the properties, including Colonel Ruppert and his real estate business partner, Miller Huggins. The Yankees skipper purchased a house in St. Petersburg, located within walking distance of Lake Crescent Park.

Colonel Ruppert arrived in St. Petersburg by seaboard with four distin-

Babe Ruth with Artie McGovern. Christy Walsh had introduced Ruth to the trainer following the 1925 season and McGovern whipped Ruth back into tip-top shape through a daily series of calisthenics and by placing him on a diet (National Baseball Hall of Fame, Cooperstown, New York).

guished friends. "Let's go get breakfast, fellows," he said. His companions followed him to the dining room in the Princess Martha Hotel. As the Yankees players passed by after checking in at the front desk, they stopped in to say hello to the boss.

"Well, vacation has ended," said Babe Ruth at breakfast in the dining room. "Goodbye golf, goodbye doggies, goodbye song and laughter. Today I go back to work."

"Yes," echoed a waitress. "Goodbye to everything. I started work this morning."

Ruth was the first player to arrive at Lake Crescent Park. He was first to put on a uniform and step onto the field. "It's the first time since he joined the Yankees that he was first in anything except the dining room." He was also first to step in the batting cage. As he got ready to take a few cuts, the writers whispered about his waistline. Ruth was forty-four pounds lighter, thanks to working with McGovern.

9. Comeback Season—1926

Hoping to impress the reporters and spectators, Ruth over-swung, missed the first pitch, lost his grip on the bat, and fell to a knee. As he slowly got back on his feet to the sound of hoarse laugher, he shouted to his manager, "Hey, Hug, this guy his hooking 'em. Make him quit it." Huggins, laughing along with the others, made no reply. Ruth missed the next pitch, and missed for a third time before tagging one to the base of Lake Crescent.

Next in the cage was the rookie shortstop from Salt Lake City who had been tabbed as the $100,000 beauty. "He's a sure bet," said Paul Krichell, "he can't miss."

"He has a wonderful arm, and he can run like a sprinter," said Yankees scout Eddie Herr.

Tony Lazzeri's credentials were a baseball scout's dream, although there was a condition: he was epileptic, and that kept other major league teams away. It also discounted his projected $100,000 price tag. To be safe, Barrow instructed a scout to head to the ballplayer's hometown of San Francisco to investigate his medical history. The news was good, including that no other family members were affected by epilepsy. The Yankees also hired a doctor to examine Lazzeri. When convinced that all was okay, New York finalized the deal for $65,000. However, their worst nightmare occurred when Lazzeri suffered a seizure on the train trip to St. Petersburg. He would recover, but Barrow would watch him carefully, always fearing that he might suffer a breakdown on the field.

"At 190 pounds, he's built more like a fullback than an infielder," a writer said upon seeing the rookie for the first time. He was powerfully built with wide shoulders that he attributed to his job of pounding rivets at the Keystone Broiler Works in San Francisco.

Known at Salt Lake City as "Poosh 'em up Tony," Lazzeri did what Babe Ruth had yet to do: hit sixty home runs in a season. He also drove in over two hundred runs and hit .355 in 197 games during the 1925 season (back then, the Pacific Coast League scheduled over two hundred games per season). "Ever since I was a kid I wanted to be a big league player," said Lazzeri. "Somehow the game was always fascinating to me." His other dream was to save enough through professional baseball to finance a trip to Italy.

Like Lazerri, Koenig was born and raised in San Francisco, and lived through the famous quake that devastated the city in 1906. "My folks often told me about it," said Koenig, who was two years old at the time:

> We were living in the crowded downtown section and in the fire that followed the earthquake, our house burned down and we had to flee to Golden Gate Park and camp out in a tent.
> They tell me that I took to the park at once and I grew big and strong in the

fresh air of the outdoors. So when things settled down my father decided to get a house right near the park so I could have a handy place to play. I practically lived at Golden Gate Park from then on. I was playing ball there before I was six. That's where I learned the game.

The Yankees sold Pee Wee Wanninger to St. Paul and sent Wally Pipp to Cincinnati in a waiver deal to make room for the two rookie infielders. Aaron Ward would ride the Yankees bench along with Mike Gazella, a minor leaguer the last two seasons following a brief stint with the Yanks in 1923. With two highly touted rookie shortstops, what was Higgins going to do to place them in the starting lineup? Aware that Lazzeri played some second base in the minors, the manger announced he would play him at second and Koenig at shortstop.

The 1926 Yankees infield was projected to be a liability with a rookie double play combination and starting third baseman Joe Dugan returning from knee surgery, but nobody questioned the team's decision to go with Lou Gehrig at first base. Left to right: Lou Gehrig, Tony Lazzeri, Mark Koenig, and Joe Dugan (National Baseball Hall of Fame, Cooperstown, New York).

9. Comeback Season—1926

To town came a well-known sportswriter named Westbrook Pegler, the author of a syndicated column which appeared in sports sections from coast to coast. An old friend of Colonel Huston's, he arrived with a ready barb to jab into Huggins and the Yankees. When asked how he liked St. Petersburg, he replied, "Like it better than the Czar. The whiskers then were black and fuzzy. Now they're white and wavy."

"Is there anything I can do for you to make your stay more pleasant, Mr. Pegler?"

"Yes, there is," answered Pegler. "See if you can fix it so they'll let me bet on the mechanical rabbit at the dog races."

The Yankees started the exhibition season like they had begun their dismal 1925 season. In their first exhibition game, the veterans suffered an embarrassing 18–6 defeat at the hands of their rookies. Hopefully, that game, and the events from the following day, would not be an omen of what was to come in 1926. The next day Lou Gehrig, Paul Krichell, Doc Woods, Urban Shocker, and Benny Bengough went fishing. They launched their boat on the beach property owned by Ruppert, and traveled twenty-three miles off-shore hoping to catch amberjacks and bass. When they dropped anchor, they discounted water at the bottom of the boat until it became higher. When the water reached eight inches, they began to bail and wave their hats and coats, hoping to get the attention of one of the other crafts. A big launch close by came to their rescue. By that time the wind had picked up, making for a difficult trip to shore, and caused the Yankees to become seasick.

When the exhibition season resumed, the Yankees looked awful in a 6–1 loss to the Braves. "The Hugman looked as bad this afternoon as any club could look in their first game, and at a later hour nobody could think of a single alibi." But if anyone said that things could get worse, they were right. The next game resulted in an 18–2 defeat to the Braves. "It was like one of those games where the fat men play the thin men at the annual picnic and clambake." After two shutout defeats at the hands of their rookies, people began to guess that 1926 would be worse than 1925. "I am not much of a baseball historian but I do remember that in 1919, when the Reds won the World Series, they didn't win a game during the spring trip," said Ruppert. "On paper the Yankees look like a fourth place team at the very least."

Untimely poor hitting, errors, and base running mistakes continued in another loss to the Braves. During the game, National League umpire Frank Wilson called "a rather sour strike on Lazzeri." After the rookie told the arbitrator that he disagreed, Wilson explained the call and finished by calling Lazzeri "a busher." O'Leary, hearing the remark from the coaches' box, bolted down the third baseline to protest, and was tossed out of the game. Huggins stormed out the dugout to partake in the argument, and he was ejected. After ball four was called, Lazzeri took a few steps towards first, turned to say something, and Wilson told him to join his coach and manager. "I'm not a man for a few words," Lazerri told Ford Frick after the game, "but in our league we don't let fresh umpires get our goat. I'm a peaceful chap—but I won't be imposed on."

"A few more words and I would have socked that guy [Wilson] right in the nose," said Ruth.

Before the Yankees could cool off, more fuel was added to the fire when Westbrook Pegler's syndicated column appeared in sports sections from coast to coast. His uncomplimentary preseason preview of the Yankees, titled, "If Huggins had a ball team and could manage—he might," expressed his opinion about the Yankees and their manager:

> If Miller Huggins knew how to manage a ball team, he might manage a pretty good ball team if he had a team to manage.
> One of the Yankees was complaining about the matter today. "Who can this guy [Huggins] lick?" he inquired. "He can't even lick Eddie Bennett who handles the bats."
> They aren't a ball team; they're just a lot of ball players who think their manager is a sap.

The Yankees were appalled by the article. "That made us fighting mad," Ruth would later recall. But there was more to come.

New York Sun sportswriter Will Wedge suggested a game between the Yankees and the Princess Martha bellboys, and another New York sportswriter mentioned a fund to buy Joe Dugan a motorized wheelchair.

Huggins, deeply hurt by the articles, never did have a problem with criticism, but he drew the line with ridicule. "I feel sometimes I would like to take the newspapermen, one by one, out in the middle of the diamond and try to whip them," he said. "In all the years I've directed the New York team, I have never had a bunch of fellows who have worked harder for me. They are out at the park before ten in the morning and stay until four in the afternoon. Some of them don't even take time to go to the hotel for lunch."

Nobody was working harder than Joe Dugan. The twenty-nine-year-old third baseman was making a comeback after his 1925 season had ended with a knee injury. Following the season, he underwent what was described as a "dangerous operation" since the cartilage would be sewed back to the knee. The operation was declared a success, and Dugan was expected to make a full recovery.

Ruth was working hard and obeying curfew. "The big fellow has come to his senses and has worked himself into splendid physical condition," said Ruppert. "I have not seen him look so good at this time of year since he first arrived here from Boston. He firmly believes that we are going to finish first. His confidence is contagious."

Was Ruth too confident? "There's no doubt about it, the Yankees are going to win the pennant," said Ruth. "Their only competition will come from the Athletics." When asked about the two-time league champions, he replied that the Senators would be lucky to finish fourth. "They had a few old fellows who happened to come through for them last season."

Following their conclusion of their training session at St. Petersburg, the Yanks packed for a tour through the South to play twelve exhibition games against the Dodgers. A bulletin was posted for the Yankees players in the lobby of the Princess Martha:

> Yankees Baseball Club Bulletin
> Depart Friday Night, March 26th. Next town—Waycross, GA.
> Train leaves at 9 p.m. Have baggage ready to be taken to the bus which leaves at 8:15 p.m. We will arrive in Waycross at 7:30 a.m.
> Will stop at the Phoenix Hotel where the players will dress before going to the ballpark. Game time is 3:00 p.m.
> Special Notice: Don't forget all personal trunks must be packed and ready to leave rooms at 10 a.m. Thursday, March 25th.

Mark Roth withdrew $2,800 in crisp bills for the players' meal money. No longer would they sign the checks in the hotel dining rooms. The prediction was the money wouldn't last until reaching New York.

Wilbert Robinson said his Dodgers were ready for the Yankees, and he was going to shoot his four starting pitchers at the Yankees.

"Meanwhile, what does he think my batters will do?" asked Huggins. "Four of my eight regulars are batting over .300 and Gehrig is just below that mark."

Huggins must have meant that Gehrig was due. At Waycross, the first baseman clubbed two home runs, and Koenig hit one in a 7–3 win. In Birmingham, Combs hit for the cycle while Ruth, Meusel and Lazzeri all homered in a 10–2 win over the Dodgers. The next scheduled game was rained out. As Robinson watched the rain fall from his hotel room window, he said, "Well, there is one way I am sure to stop the Yankees from hitting home runs against my club. I am sick and tired of looking at home runs."

As the Yankees were checking into the Andrew Jackson Hotel on their next stop, a teammate explained to Ruth that Nashville was the hometown of "Old Hickory" Andrew Jackson. "He must have been a considerable citizen to have a bat named after him," replied an impressed Babe Ruth. At Nashville, the Yankees won again, 11–4, with Lazzeri belting a grand slam and Gehrig tagging his fourth homer of the series. "The Brooklyn Dodgers outfielders are getting dizzy turning around to watch home runs pop over fences."

The Yanks continued their onslaught by tagging the Dodgers' hurlers for nine runs in one inning en route to their sixth straight win over Brooklyn. Through six games, they were hitting .350 with 63 hits for 114 total bases, and they were just warming up. In the next contest, they scored nine times in the first three innings to make Robinson a firm believer. "The Yankees have the greatest hitting club ever assembled. No pitching can stand up to such relentless batting."

New York scored thirty runs in the next two games to make it 9–0 versus the Dodgers. "There seems to be nothing that the Yankees cannot do. It wouldn't surprise me if some of them can swim the English Channel." In Richmond, Meusel hit "a screamer" that flew over the centerfield wall and plunged into the Jones River. Koenig, who continued to impress, also hit a home run. When the series moved to Yankee Stadium, Koenig and Lazzeri were welcomed with a loud ovation. In the last game of the series, Koenig popped three hits and Lazzeri hit his fifth home run. Koenig finished with four home runs, hit safely in eighteen consecutive games, and piled up a .407 batting average. For his outstanding work, he was rewarded with the leadoff spot in the batting order. Combs would bat second, Gehrig, after hitting .382 during the spring, would be third, followed by Ruth, Meusel, Lazzeri, Dugan, and (new team catcher) Pat Collins.

The Yankees completed their twelve-game series sweep over Brooklyn, and then headed to Boston to begin the season. "No, I don't want to predict that," said Huggins when someone asked if he wanted to predict the Yankees to win the pennant. "I'd rather see them predict us to finish lower. That would give the boys an incentive for battling in this race."

As they warmed up before their first game of the season on a cold day at Fenway Park, a few of Ruth's teammates asked him about his claim to speak almost fluent Spanish, something he said he had picked up when he had visited Cuba and the Havana Racetrack. His teammates wanted proof. "Sad Sam" Jones suggested that he communicate in Spanish with Red Sox Cuban infielder Mike Herrera. With all the confidence in the world, Ruth led his teammates to the Red Sox dugout, where he found Herrera seated on the bench. After Ruth had delivered a few lines of his best Spanish, Herrera looked at him with a blank expression before answering: "You have to excuse me; I do not speak the English very well."

Koenig began the 1926 campaign with a bunt single, Combs walked, and Gehrig bunted for another hit to load the bases. Ruth's ground ball

9. Comeback Season—1926

was booted to allow one run to score, Meusel's ground-out scored another run, and then Gehrig and Ruth followed by executing a double seal for a 3–0 lead. Lazzeri walked, Dugan singled, and Ruth scored on Collins's hit. New York increased their lead to 11–1, but that did not sew up the game. Boston rallied to make it interesting before the Yankees held on for a 12–11 win.

"This is the hardest hitting club I ever had," Huggins said after the Yankees scored seven runs, but lost by one in their second game of the season. "That might look like a broad statement, but every man in the lineup can slug." His team had scored 19 runs on 26 hits through the first two games, but on a not-so-good note his hurlers gave up as many hits and runs, and the fielders had already committed seven errors. "I'm not so worried about the pitchers. If we continue to hit, and develop strength at short and second, we'll go far."

The Yankees faced Walter Johnson in Washington a week after the great pitcher hurled a fifteen-inning complete-game shutout over Philadelphia on opening day. In the first inning, Ruth tagged a fastball for his first home run of the season. "People who were taking the afternoon constitutional saw the stranger in the sky and thought it was an army dirigible." New York shelled the Big Train in three innings en route to an 18–5 win in what was Ruth's best day in a long time. He had driven home six runs on five hits, including two doubles, and "smoked two through the infield that the infielders never saw."

A Wednesday crowd of forty thousand came to Yankee Stadium for the home opener versus Boston on a warm afternoon. "It was warm enough to take off your overcoat without freezing to death." In the bottom of the fourth, with New York still trailing 4–0, Ruth singled, and perhaps trying to get something going, he took off for second and made it safely. The next five New York batters singled, and Combs made it six straight hits with a home run to cap a six-run inning. Meusel added a home run in the eighth in an 8–5 New York win.

Following a loss, Ruth homered in the next two games, both resulting in a Yankees win to up their record to 7–3. The Athletics, favored to win the pennant by almost every expert, came to town, and although Ruth did not homer in the three-game series, the Yanks outscored the A's, 18–4, to sweep the series.

Not only were the Yankees hitting, their pitching was outstanding, and their fielding was coming around. Ruth made the best defensive play of the series against the A's when he fielded a base hit and fired in time to the plate to cut down the runner. Lazzeri also turned in a great defensive play in the series when he leaped high enough "to break the World's standing high jump record," to take away a sure base hit. And Meusel, rearing back and throwing with stunning power to the plate in time to nail a would-be scorer, showed why his throwing arm was said to be the best of his era. "It was one of the gamest throws of the decade," declared Harrison.

"It looks like now that the only thing that can stop the Yankees is another amendment to the Constitution." The Yankees were 12–3 through April, with fifteen home runs and averaging seven runs per game. The winning streak reached eight before Lefty Grove cooled them off in an 8–3 Athletics win. Grove had struck out five Yankees in the first five innings, causing Philadelphia fans to ask, "How did those birds ever win eight straight?" The A's swept the series to prove the Yanks were human after all, and with two losses at home to Detroit, New York dropped to second place. In the ninth inning against Detroit, Gehrig faced Earl Whitehill with two outs and New York down by two when Gehrig complained to home plate umpire Bill McGowan that the first pitch had hit his hand. "Let's see that hand," shouted Whitehill. Gehrig turned and headed towards the pitcher. McGowan quickly moved in front of the angry batter and gave him a "brisk shove in the chest" while ordering him to take his base. "Come under the stands after the game and I'll attend to you," Gehrig said.

"I'll be there on the dot," promised Whitehill.

Confusion has reigned through the years as to what happened next. A sportswriter gave his account when speaking to eyewitnesses. His story was the two ballplayers did square off. Babe Ruth intervened by pulling Gehrig away, but pulled so hard that he swung Gerhig into a concrete pole, and both Yankees fell to the ground. Just then Cobb came walking by. He looked down and appeared confused when he saw the two Yankees on the floor. Fred Merkle, a Yankees coach who was standing by, accused Cobb of trying to kick Ruth. Both Ruth and Gehrig got up, and hearing that the Tigers' manager was going to boot Ruth, demanded an explanation. Cobb said that he was not going to do such a thing. When Ruth and Gehrig were convinced that he was telling the truth, everyone peacefully went to their respective clubhouses.

The next day, Cobb and Gehrig were asked about their ongoing feud. Both denied there were any hard feelings. "We've always been good friends and the first thing he did when he saw me this season was to congratulate me on winning the first base job," explained Gehrig.

On the day of the Gehrig-Whitehill confrontation, an American explorer named Richard Byrd took off from Spitsbergen, Norway, with a crew of three on an expedition to fly over the North Pole. His plane was powered by a new Wright-Whirlwind radial engine, an invention that was expected to make a revolutionary impact on aviation by greatly increasing the chances for a successful transatlantic airplane flight. Bird's accomplished mission served as the dress rehearsal for the Orteig prize.

In 1919, hotel owner and air enthusiast Raymond Orteig offered a $25,000 prize for the first person to complete a transatlantic flight from New York to Paris or vice versa. His offer had expired before anyone dared to try. He renewed the offer in 1925, and in September 1926, Rene Fonck, a French flying ace, attempted the feat in "a huge modern looking four engine plane" along with three crewmen. As the plane moved down the runway, the landing gear dropped from the bottom and scraped along the ground. The aircraft swerved to one side, rolling off the end runway, and burst into flames. Fonck and one crew member escaped. The other two crewmen had perished.

The New York bats heated up again and propelled the Yanks back into first place. "All the Yankees need now is good pitching," said Huggins, who seemed confident, especially in his two rookies. "Lazzeri is a fine fielder and Koenig fills the bill at shortstop, even though he is inclined to be erratic. Both youngsters will get better as they go along."

New York Times sportswriter James Harrison wanted to see more before he was convinced that they could hit major league pitching. He went along with the manager's assessment of Lazzeri as a good fielder, "better than Ward." He believed that Koenig was not quite as steady as Everett Scott, "but he can cover more ground." At the plate, both rookies showed they needed time to adjust to major league pitching. Lazzeri was batting just .247 and Koenig .230; however, Lazzeri showed the awesome power he possessed when he belted one of the farthest home runs seen at Yankee Stadium. The ball traveled into deep center field, landed on the cedar track, took a high bounce, and kept rolling.

"Ruth went hitless for the first time in a week. Someone will pay." There were no more questions about Ruth making a comeback. By mid–May, he had ten home runs to temporarily place him ahead of his 1921 pace. Against the Browns, Ruth tagged a fast ball for a home run. "Getting hold of a straight one [fastball], Ruth crushed it a dozen rows of the top of the Yankee Stadium bleachers." Later in the game, Ruth hit one that landed within six rows from the top. In the next series, Ruth hit one that was called the farthest ever at Fenway Park and one of the top three or four of his career. "It would have gone over the stand at Yankee Stadium." New York swept the five-game series from Boston to increase their winning streak to sixteen. They were 30–7, already 8½ games ahead of the next best team.

"The Yankees must be stopped or the pennant will be a joke," warned Connie Mack. In front of forty thousand in the Bronx, Lefty Grove struck out nine in a 2–1 Athletics win to snap the winning streak. "You can't hit what you can't see. Grove's fastball comes hopping in like a kangaroo, and his curve had blind staggers." Gehrig whiffed three times, and when he came to the plate with two men on base in the seventh inning, the crowd shouted for a pinch-hitter. In the nightcap, the Yankees trailed by two with a runner on third and Ruth on second with one out. The runner on third scored on an infield ground-out, and Ruth, always aggressive on the base paths, rounded third and kept running. He plowed into the catcher as the ball arrived and was called out to end the game. As he walked to the dugout, A's third baseman Jimmy Dykes, bothered by Ruth's rugged play, trailed him before putting a hand on his shoulder and making a comment. Ruth yelled back. Several fans responded by running onto the field. No punches were thrown.

By the end of May, Ruth was batting .380 with a league-high sixteen home runs and fifty-one runs scored. Herb Pennock, back with the Yankees after deciding that his fox-breeding business could wait, had won eight of nine decisions. Hoyt had seven wins, Shocker six wins, and Joe Dugan was red-hot until his injured finger was placed in a splint. "Out a week," he said, "but I left the boys a good batting mark to shoot at." Dugan was leading the league with a .414 batting average.

At Detroit, the Yanks swept a four-game series to make their season record 39–14 for a .736 win percentage. Aware that maintaining that pace for an entire season was unrealistic, Harrison warned, "The Yankees at some point or another are due for a slump."

Long lines extended at the ticket windows at Comiskey Park. The last time the White Sox were content was back in the days of Shoeless Joe Jackson. Their 1926 team was surprisingly in second place, although 9½ games behind the Yankees. There was a very distinguished guest for the third game of the series in Cardinal Joseph O'Donnell. He received a warm welcome from 32,000 fans as he entered a decorated box beside the Chicago dugout. Ruth was the first to greet him. He knelt and kissed the ring on the Cardinal's right hand. He then spoke to His Eminence for a minute, then knelt and kissed his hand a second time. With the Cardinal watching, Ruth knocked two hits and drove in two runs in a 6–5 Yankees win.

Following the series in Chicago, Ruth showed up at the train station wearing a floral-pattern shirt while dragging a huge yellow portmanteau as a group of Yankees players watched. "Look at the Babe," one of them said before they burst out laughing. They laughed louder when a porter struggled to carry his baggage onto the train. Ruth got his ticket from the conductor and immediately complained: "I never slept on an upper berth in my life."

"Don't worry, Mr. Ruth," said the conductor. "I'll fix you with a lower in a minute."

9. Comeback Season—1926

The Yankees arrived in Boston at 7 the next morning. Ruth, walking with Pat Collins, exited the train station. "Can you tell me how to get to the Brunswick Hotel?" he asked a cab driver. "My charley horse needs exercise." Ruth handed the cabdriver a tip for giving him walking directions. While heading to the hotel, Ruth, very confident of winning the pennant, began to talk about the National League pennant race. "What's the matter with those Giants?" No reply from Collins. "Do you think the Cards have a chance? What a break that would be in the World Series," he said in reference to the players' World Series share. "You can't crowd much money into that small St. Louis park. And those white shirt guys in the centerfield bleachers waving their newspapers. It's like looking at a checkerboard to bat against that background."

Rogers Hornsby, once called Huggins's Folly, led the National League in hitting the last six consecutive seasons, finishing over .400 in three of those six seasons. It was said that Huggins made him into a great hitter by changing his batting style. "I did nothing of the kind," insisted Huggins. "I simply changed a bad habit that someone was trying to teach him. One day I noticed him in batting practice trying to take a chop swing at the ball." Hornsby told his manager that someone had advised him to do that. "Well, suppose you cut that out and take a free sock at the ball," Huggins said. "Hit it the way it seems most natural to you."

Like Huggins in his first season as manager, Hornsby was playing second base and managing the Cardinals, and through his leadership St. Louis trailed only the Reds in the National League.

When the two ball players arrived at the hotel, Ruth was told the rooms were not ready. "What the hell," he said to Collins. "Let's eat." After a breakfast of nippers and tea, Ruth checked with the front desk, and was told the rooms were still not ready. "Put my bags someplace," he told a bellhop as he handed him a tip.

"We'll have you fixed up with a room, the first one, Mr. Ruth."

Ruth and Collins took a seat on a couch in the lobby and talked about something other than the National League pennant race. An elderly lady, the only other person seated in the lobby, quickly became annoyed by their presence. Ruth pulled out a flat round tin cup of Copenhagen from his vest pocket while talking about his visit to Cuba. He took a pinch and put it in his left nostril with his left thumb. "He fanned," one bellhop said to another. "No, he crossed up the snuff," the other replied.

The Babe said he was unable to remember which year he was down in Cuba, but mentioned that he enjoyed his time there, and got a kick of the natives pronouncing his name "Baby Root."

By this time, the elderly lady had heard enough. Not interested in Cuba, or fearing that Ruth might make a devastating sneeze, she got up and walked away. "This damn charley horse," Ruth complained. "Never have I had a worse one."

It was rumored that when the Yanks visited Boston, Ruth would receive a visit from his wife and daughter at the Yankees' hotel. Helen and Dorothy were still living on the Sudbury farm until the upkeep became too much for a single mom who suffered from health problems and was trying to raise a child. The farm was finally sold, and Helen moved back to Boston to be closer to her family. She rented a two-bedroom apartment in the Back Bay area for $60 per month. Wanting to save money, she later downgraded to a one-bedroom. According to the other building tenants, Helen was aloof, quiet, modest, but friendly, and enjoyed associating with jazz musicians.

When the Yankees were in New York, Ruth was spending much of his time at Claire Hodgson's apartment on West 79th Street. "The Babe liked my mother. He hunted and fished with my brothers," said Claire. And he was wild about her daughter, Julia.

The Yankees finished their road trip at 12–8 and remained 9½ games ahead with the season approaching its halfway point. The road trip was costly, however, when Meusel caught a spike while sliding and sustained a leg injury that put him on crutches. It was a big loss for the Yankees. Meusel was hitting .365 with nine homers.

At Philadelphia, the Yankees faced Grove and lost, 2–1. Grove stuck out ten, including Ruth twice and Gazella four times, to give him thirty-six in three starts against the Yankees.

"How did you like what Grove did to your boys?" a writer asked Huggins.

"Didn't like it at all, but I admit that Grove was outstanding," replied the Yankees manager. "I'm still blinking from Grove's speed and I was no nearer to the plate than the dugout. He is the fastest pitcher in the league at the present."

Huggins recalled that the Yankees were very interested in buying Grove when he was hurling for the Baltimore Orioles. "Jack Dunn seemed unreasonable to meet. Grove was considered a gamble back then because of his wildness. I suspect [A's catcher] Mickey Cochrane got credit for settling Grove and teaching him to cut the corners in big league style." Credit actually belonged to A's coach Kid Gleason for tutoring Grove and instructing him to count to fifteen in between deliveries. When Grove complained that was too long, the count was reduced to ten.

Asked about comparing Grove's speed to Walter Johnson's, Huggins said that Grove had more now, "but not as much as Johnson had a number of years ago. I think Wild Bill Donovan and Pete Alexander were faster in their primes than Grove."

A week later, the Yanks faced Grove in Philadelphia. Bob Shawkey matched Grove in every inning, and in fact led 1–0 after six innings. In the seventh frame, Shawkey retired the first two batters before Grove came to the plate and hit a routine grounder to Koenig. Hoping to preserve his energy to pitch, Grove stopped in the base paths, yet Koenig threw the ball by Gehrig. A walk and a double followed to tie the game, 1–1. An inning later, Koenig dropped a routine popup that resulted in another unearned run, and a 2–1 Yankees loss.

In the next game, Huggins shifted Lazzeri to shortstop, started Ward at second base, and sent Koenig to the bench. "I'm losing too many ball games," Huggins explained. "If I have a better double play combination I must find it now." A sportswriter mentioned that Koenig had started like a whirlwind, like the Yankees, but was now cracking under pressure and making mistakes in key situations. "He may not last the season."

Would the Yankees' lead last? People were now predicting their demise. "The Yankees will crack," warned Washington Senators president Clark Griffith. "Like all clubs, good or bad, they will have their unlucky spells," said Roger Peckinpaugh. "The injury to Meusel may be the first in a long series."

10

Yankee Pride—1926

"You may say a lot of uncomplimentary things about the Yankees, but their gameness is unquestioned."—James R. Harrison, *New York Times* sportswriter

"What's the matter with the Yankees?"

"Nothing," replied Huggins.

Yankee fans began to worry when their team lost nine of fourteen, yet they were still ahead of the next best team by seven games. "A few key injuries and some bad baseball; the injured are coming back. I hope the bad baseball doesn't," said the manager.

"What about Koenig?"

"He was in a slump and worrying too much," according to Huggins. "The worse he got, the more he worried, and the more he worried, the worse he got. The only sensible thing to do was to take him out of the lineup for a rest. He agreed with me that the rest would probably help."

Koenig's fielding difficulties continued when he returned to the lineup. In the seventh inning of a tie game against the Browns, with one out and a runner on first, he booted a routine grounder that should have been a twin killing. The miscue led to a four-run inning and another Yankees loss.

New York dropped another one before they got hot again. After rallying for four runs in the bottom of the eighth for a 5–4 win, they scored twenty-four in their next two victories. In the first of those two wins, Gehrig hit one of the farthest home runs ever seen at Yankee Stadium when he sent a fly ball to straight-away centerfield that cleared the cedar track and crashed against the wall. Not to be outdone, Ruth smacked a 3–2 pitch over the track for a grand slam.

At Chicago, with the game tied 1–1 in the top of the eighth, Ruth responded to the booing from 20,000 fans by sending one over the twelve-foot wire fence and into the wooden bleachers in centerfield. It was said to be the longest home run at Comiskey Park. "The crowd could hardly believe its eyes." In the bottom of the ninth, Koenig made another error to allow Chicago to load the bases with nobody out, but this time the rookie redeemed himself when he gloved a hard grounder and threw to home in time to get the runner for one out. Jones struck out the next batter, and the final out came on a groundball for New York's tenth straight win.

The winning streak was snapped at eleven; however, the Yanks salvaged the last two games against the now second-place Indians at Cleveland to increase their lead to eleven games with less than one-third of the season remaining. "If the Indians can't gain on the Hugman at home, their chances of winning the pennant must be considered slightly slimmer than Mr. Ruth's chances for getting the presidential nomination."

Detroit was the next stop, and that meant court for Babe Ruth for a fishing violation from the previous trip when he and a friend were arrested in a small Michigan town for fishing a few days prior to the official opening of the fishing season. "I engineered the whole party," Ruth's friend told the judge, "and I caught all the fish. Ruth isn't guilty. He isn't a good enough fisherman." Ruth felt otherwise: "I didn't catch any fish, but I was fishing. I guess I'm guilty." Ruth paid the $15 fine. His friend was fined $35. In the game that afternoon, Ruth smacked his thirty-sixth home run and Lazzeri hit his fifteenth to help build a 9–4 Yankees lead. With two outs in the ninth, an easy pop fly looked like the end for Detroit, but Koenig dropped it. The Tigers capitalized to score four runs to cut the lead to one before Ruth caught a fly ball for the final out.

Before a double-header at Washington, a stranger claiming to be a friend of Ruth's entered the Yankees clubhouse. He pretended to dry his hands as he stood at the sink when suddenly a diamond ring scooted across the floor. Doc Woods became suspicious and seized the man. When he checked his towel, he found jewelry and money belonging to the players. Woods and a few others took the law into their own hands by giving the stranger an old-fashioned thrashing. There were additional fireworks during the game when Hoyt gave way to four runs on seven hits in less than three innings, and Huggins signaled to the bullpen. Upset over getting the hook, Hoyt winged the ball against the backstop. Huggins, unwilling to tolerate angry behavior since reading Ruth the riot act the previous season, informed the angry pitcher that his extra pitch would cost $200. Hoyt redeemed himself two days later by pitching the win. The Yankees finished their road trip at 11–8, and still owned a comfortable lead of 8½ games with forty to play.

Pitcher Dutch Ruether made his Yankees debut as a pinch-hitter on August 31. "I'm not what I would call a good hitter," he said, "but I will say for myself that I usually go down swinging." Ruether, a left-handed pitcher, was obtained from the Senators for a player to be named later. He received his first starting assignment the next day against Lefty Grove, and the thirty-four-year-old veteran responded by retiring the A's in the first inning. Grove appeared to be nervous, according to Harrison, and he immediately gave up two runs. When he issued three consecutive walks to load the bases for Ruth in the bottom of the second, Mack made a pitching change. Ruth greeted the new pitcher with a two-run hit. In the ninth inning, with New York ahead 6–2, Simmons tripled, and Koenig dropped a popup, but no harm was done. Huggins called on Shawkey, who retired the side for a Yankees win.

Koenig continued to struggle. He muffed a double-play ball for an error in a 7–2 loss and booted another one a few days later in the ninth inning. A grounder to Lazzeri on the following play should have been a double play, but Koenig dropped the second baseman's toss. The Yankees held on to win, but poor Koenig walked off the field shaking his head.

In an exhibition game at Baltimore against the Orioles, with Ruth playing first base, Koenig made another error. Following the inning, Ruth made a comment to Koenig in the Yankees dugout, and the rookie responded by swinging. Ruth grabbed the shortstop's wrists and told him to calm down. After the altercation, Koenig refused to speak to Ruth until they shook hands on the last day of the season.

Bob Shawkey pitched a four-hit shutout over the Red Sox in the last game of the season at Yankee Stadium. The Yankees would play their last seventeen games on the road, including six at Cleveland, with a comfortable eight-game lead. Their first stop was Detroit. "I don't think we got good enough pitching [this season]," said Cobb. The Tigers never seemed to. With first base open late in the first game, and with Detroit clinging to a one-run lead, Cobb elected to pitch to Ruth, and the Babe rocketed one to centerfield "with terrific speed" that cleared the wall by two to three feet for a three-run homer, Ruth's forty-second, to give New York a 9–8 win.

Ruth's behavior this season was like night and day compared to the season before. He had worked hard to regain his superstar status, beginning with his grueling workouts with Artie McGovern, and through spring training. He was leading the league in home runs and RBI, and was batting .375. Nobody was happier for him than his manager. "Babe, I admire a man who can win over a lot of tough opponents; but even more a man who can win over himself," said Huggins.

"That fine, Hug," said Ruth. "Do I get the fine back?"

"No," replied Huggins.

The Tigers took the next two games to cut the Yankees' lead to 5½ games. Next was Cleveland for a six-game series against the red-hot Indians; winners

In 1926, Babe Ruth led the league in home runs (47) and RBI (153) and came within six batting average points (he hit .372) of winning the triple crown (National Baseball Hall of Fame, Cooperstown, New York).

of fourteen of their last nineteen games, the Tribe had awakened their pennant hopes.

A day after Fonck's plane crash, a twenty-four-year-old airmail pilot named Charles Lindbergh was working his daily airmail route from St. Louis to the Chicago suburb of Maywood with scheduled stops in Springfield and Peoria. The skies were clear when the pilot left Peoria, but while he was en route to Maywood, a heavy fog descended upon the night to minimize visibility. The Maywood ground crew turned on the searchlights and burned a drum of gasoline to help the pilot locate the field. Unable to find a break in the fog, Lindbergh circled until using his last drop of fuel. Following the emergency procedure, he leaped from the plane at five thousand feet. After falling one hundred feet, he pulled the ripcord of his parachute. As he floated to the ground, he heard the plane's engine restart, apparently due to residual fuel. The machine came with three hundred yards of the pilot as it zigzagged through the sky before crashing to the ground.

After he safely landed, Lindbergh traveled two miles to retrieve the mailbags from the wreckage. Determined to complete his route, he was on a train with the mailbags by 3:00 a.m.

Whether his misadventure in the sky had influenced him is unknown, but shortly after, Lindbergh decided to compete for the Ortig prize. With just $2,000 in his savings account, he knew he would need investors to raise $15,000 needed to build a plane. Soliciting the St. Louis community, he found backers who knew he would bring honor to their city if he won the prize.

When he secured the funds, Lindbergh wrote several airplane manufacturers, including a small company in San Diego that specialized in building monoplanes. Noting that Fonck had used huge aircraft with crewmen, Lindbergh opted to use a lightweight plane in a solo flight, an alternative that would be scorned by the press. A solo transatlantic flight meant over one full day without sleep.

Lindbergh received an acceptance letter from Ryan Airlines. He traveled to San Diego to overlook the construction of a single-engine plane made of lightweight materials, and included a Wright Whirlwind engine.

The excitement and competition of the race for the Ortig prize began to heat up. Richard Byrd was considered the favorite to win when he announced his entry, and even after he broke his wrist when his plane crashed during a test flight. Another failed test flight attempt resulted in a more devastating outcome when two pilots lost their lives in their test trial in Hampton, Virginia.

Lindbergh's plane was named the *Spirit of St. Louis* in honor of the city of the businessmen who had backed him. When his aircraft was completed,

10. Yankee Pride—1926

tested, and ready to be flown east, he heard that two experienced pilots had taken off in Paris. Fearful of their reputation, and upon learning that their plane had been spotted over the Newfoundland coast, Lindbergh began to study maps of the Pacific. But following their sighting, the two flyers were never seen or heard from again.

Huggins attempted to inspire his team with a pep talk before the first game in Cleveland: "Beat those fellows today, that's all I ask. Just beat them today." Barrow also made an attempt to influence the squad by sending Huggins the Westbrook Pegler article from March with instructions to pin it on the clubhouse bulletin board "to let those fellows know what one sportswriter thinks of them."

Twenty-two thousand fans jammed into little League Park and cheered Cleveland to a 4–1 lead after five innings. In the sixth, Ben Pascal delivered a two-run pinch single to cap a four-run rally for a Yankees win. Koenig was spectacular in the field by handling sixteen chances without an error, just one shy of the American League single-game record. Unaware that he had a chance to set a new record, he let Mike Gazella take a grounder late in the game. "If I had I known, I would have knocked Mike out of the way," Koenig said with a smile.

Things got nerve-racking when New York scored only two runs on nine hits in three consecutive losses to the Indians. With a miracle on the minds of the Indians' fans, 27,000 turned out for the fifth game of the series. The overflow crowd sat on the grass in left and right field, leaving a small opening to the centerfield wall. With a distance of just 290 feet from home plate to the right field fence, the crowd reduced right field into the shortest of all major league parks. "The result was an absurd condition to play, which resulted in measly pop flies that became two baggers." The Yankees failed to capitalize on six walks. They made only four hits and lost 3–1. Their lead was now down to 2½ and Tris Speaker let them know. While the Indians manager-centerfielder received an intentional pass from Shocker in the seventh inning, he began to chide the Yankees hurler. Huggins charged out of the dugout and went nose-to-nose with Speaker. As two umpires pulled the Yankees manger away, he was razzed by the Cleveland fans.

A record home crowd of 31,000 was on hand for the final game of the series. Once again, the Yankees manager gave his team another simple pregame speech: "We're playing rotten ball. We're horrible. Beat those fellows anyhow." Hoping for more run production, Huggins changed his batting order by placing Ruth and Meusel in their familiar number three and four spots, Gehrig fifth, and Combs first.

With the Yanks ahead 5–3 in the seventh, Ruth hit a long drive between the two outfield crowds that dropped into deep centerfield. He rounded the bases for a home run, his forty-third of the season. After Meusel fouled out, Gehrig parked one over the right field wall to ice a Yankees win. New York left town with a 3½ game lead, and with eight games remaining.

For Huggins and the Yankees, clinching the pennant wasn't going to be easy. New York dropped three of four in Chicago to reduce their lead to two games. The next stop was St. Louis to close out the season. They arrived in time to see the city celebrate the Cardinals' first pennant in team history after a 6–4 win at the Polo Grounds. Factory whistles and fire truck sirens blasted throughout the city. Automobile horns sounded. An avalanche of shredded newspaper floated from all twenty floors of the Railway Exchange Building. Across the Mississippi in the town of East St. Louis, fire trucks rambled down the road with firemen announcing that the Cardinals had done it.

With the attention focused on the Cardinals, few cared about the Browns and Babe Ruth. Fewer than 2,000 turned out for a double-header at Sportsman's Park, with New York a sweep away from clinching the pennant. In the first game, Ruth hit one over the right field roof and landed it on the boulevard for a grand slam in a 10–2 Yankees win.

Back in New York, Ruppert was a guest at the Polo Grounds, where he spent more time watching the out of town scoreboard than the Cardinals and Giants as he rubbed his cat's ring—the only piece of jewelry he allowed himself to wear. "I believe it's good luck. I've worn it all year."

Back in St. Louis, Ruth made a long run for a foul ball. The ball hit the ground and Ruth stepped on it, causing him to twist his ankle. No chance was he going to leave this game. He hobbled back into position and continued to play. In the third inning, Gehrig homered, his fifteenth of 1926, to give New York a 3–0 lead. Two innings later, Ruth doubled between two outfielders for another run. In the next inning, Ruth got hold of one and sent it over the right field roof "with yards to spare" for an 8–1 Yankees lead. Later, he blasted another one, his forty-seventh of the season.

The final score was posted at the out-of-town scoreboard at the Polo Grounds: New York 10, St. Louis 4. "It took more than luck," Ruppert said. "It took all my prayers and hopes to win the pennant. We had a great team and manager. There is no better manager in the business."

"It's nothing," Ruth told concerned reporters as he hobbled from the clubhouse. "It will be all right when the series starts. It's just got to be."

11

The 1926 World Series

"He [Pete Alexander] had a curveball that did a lot of queer things." —Tony Lazzeri

Eleven-year-old Johnny Sylvester of Essex Falls, New Jersey, was fading. In late September, his parents were told that their son was in danger of dying. When the 1926 World Series began, Johnny's doctors believed he had one week to live. The child, an avid baseball fan, was asked by his parents if there was anything they could do to make him happy. His answer was a used game ball from the World Series.

In the summer of 1926, Horace Sylvester took his wife and four children to a rented home in Bay City, New Jersey. One day before dusk, Johnny and his friends were riding their horses to the stable when Johnny's horse stepped into a hole and tumbled. While quickly climbing to its hoofs, the horse accidentally booted the child on the head. The injury would eventually develop into osteomyelitis—an infection of a bone or bone marrow.

Horace approached George Buckly, the vice-president of the First National Bank, and told him about his son's condition and wish. "Horace, we will not only get the ball, but we will get it signed by the players," said Buckly, and he immediately dispatched telegrams explaining the story.

The crowd began lining up at the Yankee Stadium ticket window on the eve of Game One. They made themselves as comfortable as possible by sitting on boxes or in reclining positions on improvised pillows of newspapers. Albert Aiken, thirty-eight years old, was the first one in line at ten o'clock the night before. He was followed by two twenty-year-olds from Georgia. "They seem a bit out of their class," said Aiken when looking them over. "They seem like nice boys but they are up against tough competition." Next in line were a couple from Passaic, New Jersey, followed by Mrs. J.W. Eldridge of Raton, New Mexico, who had motored east for a sports vacation. Her first stop was Philadelphia to see the Dempsey-Tunney fight. She expressed her disappointed about Dempsey's loss. "I would like to see St. Louis win," she said.

By 8:30, as those who lined up got drenched by the rain, there were over two thousand customers in line. At 9:00, automobiles with license plates representing twenty-five states filled every stadium lot. When the gates opened at 9:30, thirty minutes earlier than announced, the line had extended down 161st Street.

Subway and surface car lines discharged loads of new customers. Traffic around the stadium was heavy. Hoping to alleviate the congestion, policemen set up check stations a block away for motorists to show their tickets. The fans, so content to have tickets, failed to notice Babe Ruth drive by in his bright yellow automobile.

"Hello, kid!" Ruth said enthusiastically as he entered the Yankees clubhouse at 10:40. He was well-dressed, wearing a brown suit verging on a plum shade, with a natty brown silk shirt. "Ho-hum, another day of work," Ruth said before dropping onto his tiny stool before his locker. "What the hell?" he said when he noticed a pile of yellow envelopes at the bottom of his locker. "More requests for tickets, I suppose." He opened a few before tossing them aside. "Only wires of congratulations from friends.

"I feel pretty good, but I got to have the trainer tape me up a bit. Where is Doc Woods?" He scanned the locker room until he sought out the Yankees trainer. "Hey Doc, come here and hitch my left knee. It's kind of wobbly."

One block from the stadium a policeman stopped a cab at a checkpoint and asked to see tickets. When the passengers failed present them, he refused to let the cab pass. "Why, I'm Rogers Hornsby," said one of the passengers.

"And I'm President Coolidge," replied the officer.

"You flatfoot!" hollered the other passenger. "I'm a St. Louis pitcher."

"St. Louis has no pitchers," said the officer.

Lou Gehrig happened to be passing by while walking to the stadium. He stepped over to verify that the passengers were Rogers Hornsby and Pete Alexander. The cab was then permitted to proceed.

"Will it rain?" was asked before the game was about to start. Graham McNamee and Phil Carlin were ready at the microphones to announce the game to fifteen million people tuned in through twenty-three different radio stations throughout America. American League umpire Bill Dineen adjusted his chest protector, and then put on his mask. "We are just about ready to go," McNamee said into the microphone. Herb Pennock went into his windup, threw his first pitch of the game for a strike, and the 1926 World Series was underway.

Both pitchers appeared nervous; both gave up a run in the first inning.

Ruth was greeted with cheers in his first at bat. The cheers turned to boos when he walked. He was on first base in the third inning when Meusel grounded back to the pitcher. Ruth slid hard into the second base bag, and remained on the ground after the play. "Babe is the color of a nice red brick house," McNamee announced. Two of the St. Louis infielders and the pitcher surrounded Ruth while Doc Woods stepped onto the field with a needle and lots of thread. The trainer took plenty of sod from the field to patch Ruth's pants. "Trousers or no trousers, we will have a World Series."

In the sixth inning, Ruth spread his hands on his bat and shortened his swing. The ball rolled through the left side of the infield for Ruth's first hit of the series. Meusel followed with a sacrifice and Gehrig singled to right. Ruth ran hard, rounded third, and as he came into home to score, McNamee's description of the play was drowned out by the roar of the crowd.

Pennock held the Cards in check for the rest of the game in a 2–1 Yankees win. "The credit goes to Pennock," Huggins announced in the happy Yankees clubhouse. "He deserves all the praise for pulling us through."

The weather was warmer for Game Two. The sun was bright and the temperature was expected to reach the seventies. Thirty-nine year-old Pete Alexander, Hornsby's starting pitcher choice, seemed tense when he began the bottom of the first by walking Combs on four pitches. Koenig hit a grounder that Alexander managed to tip and slow down to allow the shortstop to field the ball, step on second, and fire to first to compete the double play. Alexander showed no fear of Ruth by throwing three over the plate for a strikeout.

Meusel began the bottom of the third with a single, Gehrig bunted, and Lazzerri tagged an Alexander pitch for a hit to score Meusel for the first run of the game. Dugan followed with a hit to advance Lazzeri to third, and with two strikes on Shocker, the base runners attempted a double steal. O'Farrell called a pitchout and threw the ball down to second base. St. Louis shortstop Tommy Thevenow immediately made a return throw to trap Lazzeri in a rundown. Alexander, taking part in the play, threw past the fielder to allow Lazzeri to score for a 2–0 lead.

The Cards roared back with two in the top of the fourth to tie the game, 2–2. In the bottom of the fourth, Alexander gave up a hit to Combs. "Alex will never last," a writer said, but the veteran pitcher got out of the inning without damage, and then struck out the side in the next inning. Through six innings, he had struck out nine, just three away from the record.

Urban Shocker, fulfilling his dream by pitching in his first World Series, had retired twenty-two in a row before tiring in the seventh. Two hits put runners on the corners, and then Cardinals outfielder Billy Southworth drilled one. As Ruth ran back to the fence, a writer jumped to his feet while shouting,

"Get in there! Get in there!" Ruth leaped, extended his arm to the fullest, but wasn't even close. The ball landed in the crowd for a 5–2 Cardinals lead.

In the top of the ninth, Thevenow popped one down the right field line. Ruth ran at full speed, got his hands on the ball, but was unable to hold it. As the ball rolled into the corner, Ruth had no idea where to look. He had completely lost sight of the ball, and by the time he found it, Therevenow had circled the bases for a 6–2 lead.

"We couldn't hit Alexander. That's all there's to it," Huggins said after the game. He remained confident in his club and said he was satisfied that things were "going smoothly" and his team was playing "a nice, steady game."

"We'll win the series, I'm sure of it," Ruppert said with a smile as he sat in Huggins's office. "It was a great game and the series is going to be a hard-fought one, I believe."

As the two teams showered and dressed into their street clothes, a fleet of limousines awaited them. With a police motorcycle escort, they were hurried to Grand Central Station. After the Yankees boarded their train, they headed to the dining car, then to the club car after dinner. As the train headed westward, Huggins sat by himself as he gazed out of a window while others were in their sleepers, playing poker, or joined Huggins by looking into the night.

HUGGINS: "Well, well."
FRANK GRAHAM (*New York Sun* sportswriter): "What about?"
HUGGINS: "What about what?"
GRAHAM: "The game?"
HUGGINS (shrugs his shoulders): "There is nothing much to say. They hit better than we did in Saturday's game. Alexander is a great pitcher. I said he would give us trouble. Shocker pitched a fair game. He didn't mean to pitch wrong to Southworth. He gave him a slow ball that he meant to keep low, but it stayed high."
GRAHAM: "Who will you pitch tomorrow?"
HUGGINS: "Probably Ruether."
GRAHAM: "Anything more?"
HUGGINS: "No. Except baseball is a funny game."
GRAHAM: "Then why aren't you laughing?"
    No reply.
RUTH: "Still a great pitcher. That Alexander looks as good as eleven years ago, when he pitched to us in Boston [in the 1915 World Series]."
GRAHAM: "Where did the ball go that Thevenow hit?"
RUTH: "Into that little gully just in front of the stand. I saw it hit the stand an lost sight of it. None of those guys out there [spectators in the bleachers] told me where it was. I had to look for myself."
KOENIG (puts down his book): "How does it feel to be in the World Series? Elegant."
GRAHAM: "You're bearing up nobly under the storm."

11. The 1926 World Series

KOENIG: "On the level, when the game begins, it's just a ball game. Just like any other ballgame you play during the season. You just go out there and play ball."

The Yankees' train trip to St. Louis took twenty-three hours and twenty-five minutes. They arrived thirty-five minutes ahead of schedule, and encountered a huge crowd to greet the Cardinals. Five minutes later, the crowd went wild when their hometown team appeared.

The Sportsman's Park field was soggy following nine consecutive days of rain. It drizzled during batting practice before the sun finally appeared, and the rain stopped. The crowd began to cheer when the band played "It Ain't Gonna Rain No More."

They said Jesse Haines hadn't a chance to win, but he managed to shut out the Yankees through the first three innings. Ruether did the same to the Cards, although he worked out of a jam in each inning. In the top of the fourth, Ruth singled and moved to second on a ground-out. As Gehrig stepped in, it began to rain harder, to the point that the game was delayed for over an hour. While the two teams sat in their dugouts to wait out the rain, two husky policemen entered the dugouts with shining new baseballs. "It's for a sick kid," they explained. "Scratch your names here, will you?"

Fifteen St. Louis Cardinals signed one baseball. One player wrote a message: "To Johnny Sylvester: Hoping soon that you will be batting 1.000 percent in good health."

Koenig, Meusel, Pennock, Collins, and Ruth signed the other ball. They also included a message: "To Johnny Sylvester: We're glad to know that you knocked the bug for a home run."

Babe Ruth wrote his message: "I'll knock a home run for you in Wednesday's game."

The two baseballs were packaged and hurried to Lambert Field in time for the 3:30 airmail flight for Maywood. Had it missed that flight it would have been on Lindbergh's route the following morning. The package made it in time to be placed on the evening's airmail flight to New York City.

When play resumed, Haines worked out of the jam by getting Gehrig to pop out and catching Lazzeri on a ground-out. St. Louis went to work in the bottom of the inning by putting two runners on with just one out. A groundball to Lazzeri looked like an inning-ending double play, but Koenig, who was slow in covering second base, made a poor off-balance relay that skipped by Gehrig to allow the first run of the game to score. Haines followed by hitting the first pitch into the right field bleachers for a two-run homer. St. Louis added one more, and Haines completed the shutout in a 4–0 win.

"It's the same old story, but I have to say it," said Huggins, "we're not hitting." The manager remained confident; he even predicted that his team would start hitting in Game Four. "We're going to start tomorrow."

"I can't see the Cardinals as a ball club, no matter if they licked us today," said Ruth as he looked beneath a bench for his shoes. "They have been lucky, that's all."

Fans across the country were unable to tune in to Game Four due to trouble with the phone lines. As fans waited impatiently by their radios, engineers frantically worked to reroute the lines.

Babe Ruth stepped in for his first at bat. He swung at the first pitch, a fastball by Cardinals pitcher Flint Rehm, and sent a drive to deep right field. There was no question that the ball had home run distance. But would it stay fair? The fans were unsure when the ball fell into the bleachers, but when they saw Ruth trotting around the bases, they broke into a cheer. The home run was the first extra-base hit by the Yankees in the series.

After Hoyt took the mound to throw his warmup tosses in the bottom of the inning, the radio reception returned, and Graham McNamee summarized the top of the first. A mixture of cheers and boos greeted the Babe as he stepped in for his second at bat in the third inning with the game tied, 1–1. Rhem threw a waist-high slow ball. Ruth swung, and this time there was no doubt about it. The ball disappeared over the right centerfield grandstand roof and took a bounce on Grand Avenue before crashing through the Well's Motor Car store window.

Ruth came to the plate in the fifth in a tie game. This time there was nobody out and a runner on second. St. Louis lefty pitcher Art Reinhart wisely pitched around Ruth for a walk. The next two Yankees also walked to force in a run for a one-run Yankees lead. New York added two more before the end of the inning for a 7–4 lead.

New York still owned a three-run lead when Ruth came to the plate in the top of the sixth with a runner on first and one out. The St. Louis outfield responded by shifting far to the right. "The Babe is waving that wand over the plate," McNamee said. "It looks like a toothpick, he's so big."

Ruth got hold of another one. "Oh, what a shot!" McNamee shouted as he watched the ball sail into centerfield. The crowd watched open-mouthed as the ball cleared the twenty-foot-high centerfield wall and dropped into the second half of the bleachers, around 450 feet away from home plate. "That's a World Series record—three home-runs in one World Series game—and what a home run!" The crowd, still in awe, remained silent until Ruth rounded third base. Then they broke into a cheer.

In his final plate appearance of the day, Ruth took four consecutive for

11. The 1926 World Series

a walk. The disappointed fans, hoping to see Ruth sock another one, began to boo their own pitcher.

"I said we would start hitting, didn't I?" Huggins said to the writers following the Yankees' 10–5 win to even the series at two games apiece. "Well, we started today and we won't stop. He added, "I look to see the boys keep the hitting up in the next three games. If we do, we can't miss on winning the championship."

Ruth agreed. "I don't think there is anything that can stop us."

As Ruth changed into his street clothes, he whistled the 1926 summer hit song, "Bye-bye Blackbird." "Boy, was that a darling," Ruth said about his third home run. "I guess I had a pretty fair day today, didn't I?" After exiting the clubhouse, he was hounded by autograph seekers. A fan approached him with all three of his home-run balls and asked if he could sign them. As usual, Ruth obliged, and he signed them "no. 1, 2, and 3," in the order they were hit.

That evening, Horace Sylvester came home with a gift for Johnny. When he had arrived at his Wall Street office to start his workday, the package was on his desk. The boy untied the strings, opened the box, and was amazed to find two signed baseballs. He looked very closely at Ruth's signature and home run message. He asked if Ruth had homered, then learned that his hero had hit three when his Dad showed him the headlines of the evening paper. That night, Johnny slept with a signed baseball in each hand. His temperature was taken the next morning, and the good news was his fever had declined by two degrees.

Two days later, Johnny got another gift when a signed football arrived at the Sylvesters' residence with a note. The ball was signed by Red Grange. The note promised a touchdown in his first game of the season.

Would Ruth hit one, two, or three more in Game Five? He received a loud ovation in his first at bat. After taking a strike and turning away from an inside pitch, Ruth grounded out. As he took his place in field after the inning, he was jeered by the fans in the bleachers. In his second at bat, Ruth looked at four slow balls for a walk. St. Louis starting pitcher Bill Sherdel got out of the inning to keep the game scoreless.

In the bottom of the inning, Ruth barely missed on a shoestring catch. Combs, alertly backing up the play, held the runner to a double. A hit followed to score the first run of the game. The next batter hit one down the line. Ruth, running hard, reached out, bounced into the barrier, but managed to hold on for the catch. The fans responded by applauding his effort.

Sherdel had not allowed a Yankees hit since the second inning. He began the top of the sixth with what appeared to be a strikeout. Certain that he swung and missed for strike three, Pennock headed back to the dugout until he heard home plate umpire Bill Dineen, ruling a ball on the previous pitch, call him to the plate.

On the next pitch, Pennock lifted a routine fly ball to leftfield. When Chick Hafey was unable to locate the ball in the sunny sky, the play resulted in a double. Following a walk, Koenig singled to score Pennock to tie the score.

Ruth was up next with two runners on base and nobody out. With a ball and a strike, Sherdel's next pitch was called a ball. Unhappy with the call, the hurler began to bark at the umpire. The following pitch was closer to the plate. "Ball," ruled Dineen. St. Louis catcher Bob O'Farell argued while the Cardinals complained from the dugout. Ruth swung and missed the next two pitches, both slow balls, for a strikeout.

Meusel followed with a long fly out to right field. Gehrig walked to load the bases, much to the dismay of the Cards. "It was low," Dineen told the St. Louis bench when they grumbled on ball four.

Lazzeri belted one to right field. Southworth ran back, and then stopped as if he had conceded a grand slam. Realizing the wind was going to keep the ball in play, he stepped back to the wall to make the catch to end the inning.

St. Louis got another run in the seventh to take a 2–1 lead on O'Farrell's third hit of the game. In the eighth inning, Sherdel retired Ruth and the Yankees to preserve the lead.

In the top of the ninth, Gehrig hit a Texas-leaguer barely out of the shortstop's reach, and hustled to second for a double. The next batter, Tony Lazzeri pulled his bat back after he squared to bunt. Hornsby charged in from his position to complain, and got the call for strike one. Huggins came onto the field and pointed to the scoreboard to show that ball one had already been added, therefore, the umpire's original call should stand. The arbitrator disagreed.

Lazzeri laid down a bunt on the next pitch, ran hard, and beat the throw to put runners on first and third with nobody out.

Dugan, the batter due up, took a few practice swings before hearing Huggins calling him back to the dugout. Disappointed to bow to a pinch hitter, the Yankees' third baseman tossed his bat and headed to the New York clubhouse entrance in the St. Louis dugout.

Paschal was sent up to bat for the Yankees' third baseman. Hornsby instructed his infielders to move in and his outfielders to play deep. The pinch batter dropped a hit into shallow left centerfield to score Gehrig and tie the game, 2–2.

Ruth, zero for three on the day, came to the plate in the top of the tenth with the game still tied. With a runner on second and nobody out, Huggins ordered his best hitter to bunt. After fouling on two sacrifice attempts, the writers in the press box scratched their heads. Why would Huggins have Ruth bunt?

Ruth walked to put runners on first and second. Meusel moved the runners along with a sacrifice, and Gehrig was purposely walked to load the bases for Lazzeri. Following a St. Louis huddle at the pitcher's mound, Lazzeri lifted the first pitch into left field. As Hafey camped under the ball, Koenig, on third base, prepared to run after the catch. "Now watch the play," McNamee announced about the anticipated play at the plate, but there was no play. Koenig easily scored to give the Yankees their first lead of the day.

When Pennock induced the final batter to ground out, the Yankees were heading home with a three-games-to-two series lead. "You can't beat a fighting spirit like that," Huggins said about his team. "We have them on the run now." The manager was informed about a brass band and a gala reception to greet the Yankees when they returned home. "Nothing doing," said Huggins. "Let's wait until the title is clinched before we begin to celebrate victory."

"I have to say it, but ordinary pop ups that that anybody could have caught were allowed to go for two-base hits," said a disappointed Rogers Hornsby, sounding more upset than the day before when complaining how miserable his pitching was. "I had a bunch of fine fellows out there this afternoon," he said loud enough for his players to hear. "The final score should have been 2–1 in our favor."

On the twenty-one hour and twenty-minute train trip covering 1,051 miles to New York City, Hornsby changed his tune. "We kicked the game away from Sherdel. Every break went against us. But that will change. We have to merely fight harder to win, but we will win." When asked if he would use Alexander in Game Six, he replied, "Of course I will use Alexander." Alexander was confident and so were the Cardinals. He had warmed up before Game Five and said he felt fine. "We're just one game behind, that's all," he said. "We are no worse off than we were after the first game—just one game behind."

"Alexander has a world of speed today," warned Graham McNamee when the veteran struck out Koenig on three pitches. He then threw three consecutive balls to Ruth, much to the disenchantment of the fans. He finally got a strike over, and then got Ruth to ground out to end the inning.

The Cards were getting plenty of hitting and good fielding to support the pitcher. Before Alexander took the hill in the last of the first, the Cards owned a 3–0 lead. A five-run seventh made it 9–1. Alexander went on to strike out six in a complete-game win. Ten–2 was the final score, and there would be a seventh game for the third consecutive World Series. "They can't beat us now," a player shouted in the happy Cards dressing room. "We'll win tomorrow."

"Alexander stopped them and won, just like I said he would," said Hornsby.

"We didn't hit," Huggins said with some sadness, but he did express confidence in a win the following day.

Hornsby was going to send Jesse Haines to the mound in Game Seven. If he encountered trouble during the game, he would call on Alexander. He told his star pitcher to be ready. To be sure, Alexander made no plans to drink that night, "but some 'friends' got hold of him and thought they were doing him a favor by buying him a drink. Well, you are doing Alex no favors by buying him a drink, because he just couldn't stop," St. Louis catcher Bob O'Farrell would say in later years.

It was drinking that made Alexander available to the Cardinals during the 1926 season. Unwilling to tolerate the hurler's drinking problem, plus his disregard for team rules, Cubs manager Joe McCarthy waived the veteran pitcher. Cards coach Bill Killefer, a former teammate and Cubs manager, suggested to Hornsby to claim him, and Alexander won nine games for the Cardinals.

The weather for Game Seven was cold, damp, and rainy. An anticipated huge crowd turned into a disappointing attendance of fewer than forty thousand. Scalpers, surprised by the lighter than expected turnout, dropped their prices to $3.50 per ticket, and eventually to a buck.

In Essx Falls, New Jersey, Johnny Sylvester listened to the game while gripping one of his signed baseballs. "This is the way Alex holds them," he explained to his mom, who smiled. His doctor said the baseballs—"so gloriously inscribed"—had saved the boy's life. Mrs. Sylvester agreed.

Babe Ruth walked in his first at bat, and made a nice running grab in deep right field in the second inning, "one of the best catches of the series." In the third inning, he hit one over the right field fence to give New York a 1–0 lead.

Hoyt got Hornsby on a come-backer to the mound for the first out of the fourth inning. A hit and a muffed grounder by Koenig for his fourth error of the series put two runners on base. The next batter, Chick Hafey, lifted a two strike pitch into leftfield. Koenig ran back. Meusel ran forward. Thinking Koenig had it, Meusel slowed up until noticing that Koenig was looking for him to make the play. He then charged, but was too late. The ball fell for a hit to load the bases.

Another pop fly, again with two strikes, caused confusion among the New York outfielders. Combs had the best chance to make the catch, and to make a throw to the plate; however, Meusel called him off. "Oh, Meusel," said McNamee. Meusel had dropped the ball. A run scored and the bases remained loaded. With strike two, Thevenow sliced one to right field that scored two more for a 3–1 St. Louis lead.

Lazzeri struck out for the second time to begin the Yankees' sixth. Two hits followed to produce the Yankees' second run and reduce the deficit to one. The Yankees threatened in the bottom of the seventh when Combs singled, Koenig sacrificed, and Ruth was intentionally walked—his tenth pass of the series. As he trotted to first base, he turned to yell encouraging words to Meusel. The big outfielder hit into a force play at second base for the second out of the inning. Gehrig followed with a walk to load the bases.

Bases loaded, two outs, and New York trailing, 3–2. "Poosh-em up Tony! Poosh-em up Tony!" the crowed began to chant for the next batter, Tony Lazzeri. The St. Louis infield huddled at the mound, and then the players in the conference looked into left field. Leftfielder Chick Hafey responded by jogging towards the Cardinals bullpen to deliver a message. "Then from around the corner of the bleachers, while fumbling at the buttons of his scarlet jacket, came a tall, burly figure with a slouchy walk. He walked like a man in no hurry to go anywhere in particular and in no hurry to get there." The crowd was uncertain as to which hurler Hornsby had selected until a "ghostly figure" moved closer to the infield, and the name "Alexander" rang out among the spectators.

Walking slowly was the thirty-nine-year-old pitcher's plan. He looked at Lazzeri, and believing he was eager to get to the plate and clear the bases, he stared at the rookie until they locked eyes. "Like a fighter who fidgets in the corner while his rival looks nervously at him, I could see I had his goat," said Alexander. "His clubs thrashed the air somewhat faster as I glared at him." Wanting to increase the pressure on Lazzeri, Alexander turned his slow trot into a walk when he reached the infield.

Hornsby was the first to greet the pitcher. "Can you do this, Alex?" asked Hornsby as he looked into eyes to be sure he was alert and sober. "I can try," said Alexander as he took off his jacket and handed it to first baseman Jim Bottomley, who delivered it to the St. Louis bench.

"Alexander now pitching for St. Louis," the stadium announcer shouted into his megaphone.

Alexander, Hornsby, and O'Farrell talked strategy until they came to a decision to pitch low and away to Lazzeri.

Lazzeri dug into the batter's box, and readied himself for the first offering.

"Alexander's arm goes up. Here's the pitch."

The first pitch, a curveball, was low and outside for ball one. The next pitch was a fastball that skimmed the outside corner for a strike. Lazzeri swung at Alexander's next pitch, and connected. The crowd roared as the ball sailed down the leftfield line. O'Farrell, seeing the ball curving foul from his position behind the plate, added a little body English to make sure.

What was Alexander doing? O'Farrell called time and headed to the pitcher's mound. "I thought we were going to pitch him low and outside?" he asked.

"He'll never get another one like that!" Alexander promised.

O'Farrell returned to his position, Lazzeri dug in, and Alexander threw a low sweeping curve. Lazzeri swung and missed for strike three. As Alexander sauntered towards the dugout without even a slight smile, the appreciative home crowd put their alliances aside to applaud the pitcher's effort. While his teammates patted him on the back, he took his jacket from the batboy.

After the Cardinals failed to score in their half of the eighth, Alexander went back to work, and remaining poised, he sent the Yankees down in order. Eager to end the series, the Cards quickly went out in the top of the

Bottom of the seventh, bases loaded, two outs in a one-run game, Tony Lazzeri swings and misses at a pitch by Pete Alexander (National Baseball Hall of Fame, Cooperstown, New York).

11. The 1926 World Series

Babe Ruth tosses his bat after taking ball four with two outs in the bottom of the ninth of a one-run game. On the next pitch, Ruth attempted to steal (National Baseball Hall of Fame, Cooperstown, New York).

ninth. The game was now squarely on the shoulders of Alexander. He would face the top of the New York lineup in the ninth inning, and that meant Babe Ruth.

"The Yanks must score or the Championship will go to St. Louis."

Alexander, working slowly, threw two strikes past Combs before the outfielder bounced one to the third baseman for out number one. Against Koenig, the hurler got two strikes by, and then got another ground-out for out number two. Now came Babe Ruth, and luckily with the bases empty, although that seemed make little difference to Alexander, who said he had no problem with Ruth at anytime the day before.

After throwing a ball, Alexander threw a strike and a foul ball. The Yankees were now down to their last strike.

The pitcher missed on the next three pitches. "What's wrong with that?" he yelled to home plate umpire George Hildebrand after ball four.

"It was just that far outside," replied the umpire while spacing his two index fingers to show the hurler.

"If it were that close, I'd think you'd give an old geezer like me the break," said Alexander.

Meusel was the next batter, followed by Gehrig. The day before, Meusel had tagged Alexander for two extra-base hits. Alexander said he had meant to place the ball inside on the Yankees slugger, but the balls he threw did not break properly.

The first pitch to Meusel was exactly where the pitcher wanted it. Meusel swung and missed, and then O'Farrell suddenly stood upright and heaved the ball to Hornsby at second base. Surprisingly, Ruth broke for second, later reasoning that the way Alexander was going, the Yankees would never get two consecutive hits; therefore he believed he needed to get into scoring position.

Hornsby received his catcher's perfect throw before Ruth had attempted to slide. When Ruth finally hit the dirt he slid into Hornsby's waiting glove. The umpire, hunched over to get his best view of the play, made a sweeping motion to signal that Ruth was the final out of the 1926 World Series.

12

Babe Ruth, the Legend—1927

> "Nobody worked harder to win the championship last season than Babe and I know he intends to keep up his fine work."
> —Miller Huggins

"Two gentlemen to see Mr. Johnny," announced the maid at the Sylvester residence. The two men were escorted upstairs to Johnny's bedroom, and when they entered, the boy's eyes enlarged as if he could not believe what he was seeing. "Hello, Johnny," Babe Ruth said in a loud voice.

"Gosh," Johnny said. Ruth asked the boy how he was doing as he shook his hand. "F-f-fine," answered Johnny.

Johnny's hero handed him a baseball that was inscribed "the last ball used in the first game of the World Series: Yankees 2 Cardinals 1." Under the team names were the names of the starting pitchers: Pennock and Sherdel.

After nearly a half hour, Ruth said he was two hours late for an obligation he had committed to. He promised to see Johnny again, then said, "Good-bye, Johnny." The boy, his eyes still wide, nodded as he continued to stare at his idol. Johnny's little hand disappeared into the ballplayer's huge palm as the two shook hands. A few minutes later, he heard the sound of Ruth's car slowly fading away. "Gee, Mother," he said. "I couldn't say anything. If he were here now, I'd ask a pile of things."

"Johnny's a fine looking boy," Ruth said. "I was glad I went to see him. He's coming along fine. He's going to get well."

When Johnny fell asleep that night, he dreamed about playing baseball with Babe Ruth. The next morning, he held a press conference at his bedside with his friends and a syndicate reporter. "I am already counting the days until I can get up," he said.

A few days later, Johnny received a signed tennis racket and personal letter from Bill Tilden. Unpublicized was Lou Gehrig's kind gesture of sending

Ruth promised young Johnny Sylvester a home run but delivered three. Here he is seen smacking one for Johnny in Game Four of the World Series (National Baseball Hall of Fame, Cooperstown, New York).

a baseball with a note claiming the ball was in play for the last out of the 1926 World Series.

Johnny was back in school by the end of October. When Essex Falls held its first annual pet show, his silver rabbits won first prize. In December, Ruth sent Johnny a letter to wish him a Merry Christmas and a Happy New Year. "You and I have a lot to remember about the 1926 World Series," he wrote, "and when the Yanks win the championship next year I hope you will be there with me in person at the stadium to help us win another pennant."

In an unsurprising move, Ty Cobb resigned as manager of the Tigers. "I want to settle down for a while. That's my reason for my getting out as manager," explained Cobb, whose temperament had made him unpopular with his players. "I want to be traded if Cobb is the manager next year [1927]," said Tigers pitcher Earl Whitehill.

Cobb also said he had "swung his last bat in a baseball game." "I am going to be forty on December 18. I don't want to be one of those who fades or has to be pushed out."

On November 28, the sports world was baffled to learn that Tris Speaker resigned as manager of the Indians. Why? The Tribe had a strong finish in 1926 and challenged the Yankees down the season's homestretch. "The Indians finished second last season and I can step out now without questioning my actions," said Speaker. Like Cobb, Speaker said he was retiring as a player as well.

Five of the eight American League teams made managerial changes after the 1926 season. In the National League, Rogers Hornsby, due to philosophical differences with the St. Louis ownership, was traded to the Giants for second baseman Frank Frisch. Outraged about the transaction, Cardinals fans voiced their protest in an unsuccessful attempt to reverse the decision.

Baseball writers became suspicious over the resignations of Cobb and Speaker. Judge Landis and other baseball officials said they had nothing to say but could not stonewall forever. On December 20, the United Press International reported "a baseball scandal which may surpass all previous exposes."

Dutch Leonard, a former teammate of Speaker's in Boston, and a pitcher for Cobb's Tigers, claimed that in September of 1919, when he was with Detroit, he had met with Speaker and Cobb beneath the stands at Navin Field to talk about fixing a game so the Tigers could win and finish in third place in order to receive a share of the World Series spoils for their high finish. Leonard sent a letter to Ban Johnson, claiming it had been sent by Cobb after the season. The letter mentioned bets, but failed to mention what they were for. Detroit won that game, 9–5. Cobb got a hit, Speaker hit two triples, Leonard didn't play, and nobody recalled seeing anything out of the ordinary.

Leonard had jumped to an outlaw league in 1922 due to a contract dispute with the Tigers. He was reinstated in 1924 and pitched with the Tigers. In 1925, Cobb sent him to Vernon of the Pacific Coast League, despite the pitcher's objections. According to a former player who had visited him in California, Leonard expressed a desire to get even with Cobb and mentioned that he had something he could use against him.

American League president Ban Johnson, resenting Landis from the time he had taken charge of the World Series during his first season as commissioner in 1921, took the matter into his own hands by secretly ordering the two managers to resign and retire. When Landis was informed, he stepped in.

"There are two fellows going out of the game absolutely clean," Cobb said without a trace of anger in his voice. "I know I am and I think the same for Speaker." He also made a plea to the baseball world: "Friends and fans, please believe me when I say I am innocent."

Fans throughout the country sided with the two ballplayers, believing their claims of innocence and that they were getting "a dirty deal." One unnamed American League source said, "Ty Cobb and Tris Speaker never again will play ball or manage in the American League." It was known that the unidentified person was Ban Johnson. The American League president had more to say, including that he had confidential evidence to prove the two ballplayers were guilty.

The American League owners found that Johnson had no evidence. They also learned that he was ill, under the care of a physician, and had been instructed to get rest. During the 1927 season, the owners were able to persuade the American League president to retire in order to take care of his health.

Landis met with Cobb's and Speaker's attorneys behind closed doors. The commissioner may have already made his decision, but just in case, the two lawyers presented a list of affairs among ballplayers and owners and promised to go public if their clients were banned. On January 26, 1927, Landis announced the reinstatement of the two ballplayers. They were free to sign with any team they desired. "I am mighty glad that Commissioner Landis has cleared Cobb and myself," said a relieved Tris Speaker.

The sweepstakes for the two ballplayers began. Several offers were made, except from their former teams. "It wouldn't be good for baseball," said a Cleveland Indians official. Cobb was pitched by new Browns manager Dan Howley to come to St. Louis, but the man he wanted to be with was Connie Mack and the Philadelphia Athletics. "Yes, I want Ty Cobb," admitted Mack. "I will make every effort to secure his services." The two met and came to an agreement. Cobb signed a one-year deal for a base salary of $60,000, plus incentives. "This will be my last year in baseball," Cobb told reporters. "Naturally, I would like to play for a pennant contender and get one more fling at the [World] Series."

The Yankees expressed interest in signing Speaker for $25,000. Speaker was interested until he learned that Huggins was unwilling to guarantee steady employment, unlike the Washington Senators, who promised the starting centerfield job. "I was determined to get Speaker," said Clark Griffith. "And it would have taken a neat pile to get him from me." The word was he had received a $50,000 contract, plus a $10,000 bonus for the 1927 season (although it was later mentioned that his base pay in Washington was $25,000).

With the Cobb and Speaker case now completed, the focus shifted to Babe Ruth and his new contract. His five-year contract for $52,000 per season had expired after the 1926 season. Following his great comeback season, he talked about $100,000 per season for two years. "There's nothing else to say," said Ruth. "Either I get it or I don't." He made noises about partnering with Artie McGovern to open up gyms throughout the country. "The bitching between Ruppert and Ruth should not be taken seriously," a New York sportswriter told his concerned readers. "The Yankees need Ruth and Ruth needs the Yankees."

Ruth was in Los Angeles during the winter for the filming of his next

12. Babe Ruth, the Legend—1927

movie, *Babe Comes Home*. McGovern was also there to whip his client into shape for the 1927 season. One morning McGovern woke him after he had overslept with little time to make it to the set on time for the day's filming. "You're crazy," Ruth told his trainer. "I can't get out there in a few minutes in my car."

McGovern insisted that he would, then told him, "But you're not going in your car. You're going to run out there," and Ruth ran five miles to work.

"Ruth is in perfect condition," McGovern said before he and Ruth headed back to the East Coast. "He has ten good years of baseball left in his system if he takes care of himself."

Before departing Los Angles, Ruth visited an old friend. "He and I had met in 1921, and over the years we watched each other reap glory and publicity," said former heavyweight champion Jack Dempsey. "Walking in the house, he stopped by the kitchen to fortify himself before coming out back to see me."

Dempsey had retired from boxing after 1923 to make movies, endorse products, and travel. He also added to his income by putting on the gloves once in a while to perform in exhibition bouts. In 1926, he reentered the ring to defend his title against a super heavyweight named Gene Tunney. "It's a bad match, as I see it," Babe Ruth said a day before the bout. "I still think he's a great fighter and I doubt that Tunney could beat him," added Huggins. The fight took place in Philadelphia on September 23, and Tunney won in a ten-round decision.

DEMPSEY: "No, Babe, I know when I'm through."
RUTH: "All right then, sit on your ass and feel sorry for yourself. You know, pal, it's guys like us who just can't back off the spotlight. We're the ones who got to go to bat, trying for those friggin' home runs until we grind ourselves into the ground."
DEMPSEY: "Babe, it's different. You ain't lost nothin'."
RUTH: "Oh, no? Every time I walk up to home plate I'm at zero. Zero. You know what that means?"
DEMPSEY: "Babe, I don't know if I still got it, see?"
RUTH: "Well, damn it! You won't know until you get out there and try."

A sign hung at Grand Central Station to welcome the Babe back to New York City. "Babe Ruth Comes Home" was marked in red letters on a sign. As Ruth walked through the terminal, there were shouts of, "Get your one hundred thousand, Babe! Get your one hundred thousand!" Ruth waved his hat to two thousand fans when he appeared through the forty-second street exit. He headed to McGovern's gymnasium, where he was greeted by reporters wanting to know if he would take less than $100,000 per season. "I'll have to see Ruppert," he told them. "I hate like the devil to have to quit baseball, but I have other propositions I could earn money at."

Inside McGovern's office, he called Ruppert to confirm their meeting. He then called the Hotel Almanac to reserve a suite.

RUTH: "This is Babe Ruth."
HOTEL OPERATOR: "Who?"
RUTH: "Ruth! Ruth! Babe Ruth!"
HOTEL OPERATOR: "Who?"
RUTH: "Babe Ruth. Didn't you ever hear of me?"
HOTEL OPERATOR: "Oh, Ruth—yes, I think I've heard of you."

On his way to the meeting, Ruth stopped at the St. Vincent's Hospital to visit Helen, who had suffered another nervous breakdown. When asked how she was doing, Ruth said, "Nicely."

Helen had another man in her life, a prominent Boston dentist named Edward Kinder. They began to date, and soon were living together. With the proceeds made from the sale of Home Plate Farm, Helen helped Dr. Kinder finance the purchase of a two-story home at Forty-five Quincy Street in the Boston suburb of Watertown. After a sun porch was added, Dr. Kinder, Helen, and Dorothy moved in on May 31, 1927.

Dr. Kinder was a quiet man who took little time to entertain Dorothy, although others remembered him being very kind to her. The child accepted the dentist as a friend, because he never pushed himself upon her as a new dad.

At 1:00, Ruth arrived at Ruppert's Brewery. The two men entered the Yankees owner's office and began their meeting. At 1:55, Ruppert opened the door and asked twenty sportswriters to step inside.

In St. Petersburg, Huggins was tracked down by a host of sportswriters in the lobby of the Princess Martha Hotel. He was wearing a windbreaker and a paisley shawl to stay warm during unseasonably cold weather. "May we say you are delighted beyond words, Mr. Huggins?" asked a sportswriter.

"Delighted because I beat O'Leary and Krichell at pinochles?" Huggins replied. "Why should I be delighted about that? Those birds ain't such-a-much to beat."

"No, no, we mean aren't you delighted about Ruth signing?" a writer clarified. "You know, Babe Ruth, one of your outfielders."

"So he signed, did he? Well, well. What a blow to an art. How can the movies spare him?" Huggins said as he winked.

Someone mentioned the details of the three-year contract for $70,000 per season. The Yankees manager, making $20,000 a season, was amazed. "When I was playing ball I never dreamed there was such a sum of money as $70,000. I thought only real estate agents dared to talk of such figures.

12. Babe Ruth, the Legend—1927

"It's a big gamble," said Ruppert in reference to a three-year deal, "but I'm convinced that Ruth won't make me sorry." Ruppert told Ruth that if he dropped his demands, he would offer three years. Ruth liked the sound of that and agreed to a total of $210,000 for the next three seasons.

Several Yankees were unsigned when spring training began. Pennock had yet to sign, and was once again talking about trading baseball for breeding foxes. "I'll get what I asked for from Colonel Ruppert, or I will quit the Yankees. I haven't had a ball in my hand since last year and I don't care whether I pitch another game or not." Combs, Shocker, and Meusel were also holding out, which gave someone an idea for the 1927 Yankees motto: "To hold or not to hold." Huggins laid down the law that all holdouts were prohibited from signing meal checks. "There are lots of trains heading back to St. Louis," the manager warned Shocker (who lived in St. Louis). The next day, he signed his contract, and eventually the others signed.

Ruth received his most enthusiastic greeting at the train depot since the Yanks had been training in St. Petersburg. Two hours later, he was on the links at the Jungle Club. The several spectators watching cheered as if he had hit a home run after he clubbed his first drive for 365 yards. He had a great front nine with a score of thirty-eight, but his game fell apart in the back nine, and he finished with a disappointing score of ninety-two.

The next day he was at Lake Crescent Park for his first practice. "Overall, he looks fit," someone said. "Up with the sun and to bed with the chickens," Ruth said when asked about his California trip before heading to the batting cage. He belted the first offering for a long ride. "Well, I kissed that one," he said with a smile as he watched a batboy ride a bike to go fetch the ball.

St. Petersburg was packed with tourists to the tune of 125,000. There were 70,000 hotel guests registered. The city's population, less than 15,000 in 1920, was now over 35,000. The *St. Petersburg Times* circulation grew from 3,137 to 10,570 during that same period. Tourists and residents were buzzing over the opening of a new baseball movie, *Slide, Kelly, Slide*. The picture would be playing at New York City's Embassy Theater the following week. Making a cameo appearance were Bob Meusel and Tony Lazzeri. "The gamest sports movie ever screened," opined a writer of the *St. Petersburg Times*. "There is good photography, and clear titles make it a real gem."

There were six newcomers to the Yankees in 1927, the most interesting being Wilcy "Cy" Moore. A rookie soon to turn thirty, he had won thirty games for a lower-tier minor league team in 1926. "He can't pitch," insisted Yankees scout Bob Gilks after scouting Moore. "And anyway, he says he's thirty, but must be forty."

"I don't care," Barrow told him. "Anybody who can win that many games, even in the Epworth League, is worth what they're asking for him."

Cedric Durst, the outfielder Huggins liked in St. Paul when scouting Koenig and Collins in 1925, was now a Yankee. Before New York could swing a deal with the Saints, the Browns had purchased him. After a trade that sent pitcher "Sad Sam" Jones to St. Louis, Durst became a Yankee. "I'm glad to be here now, with the Yankees," he said. "It seems like a hard assignment to horn in on an outfield of Ruth, Meusel, Combs, and Pascual, but you can't blame a man for trying."

From St. Paul came right-handed pitcher George Pipgras. In a trade with the White Sox, the Yanks obtained two players for Aaron Ward in second baseman Ray Morehart and catcher Johnny Grabowski. "He's a good batter," Huggins said about Morehart. He also received praise from veteran star infielder Rabbit Maranville of the Braves for his fielding: "I like the way that guy gets in front of the ball. A grounder has to bore a tunnel to get by him. Not bad on the way he covers second base on force outs and double plays."

Former Phillies manager Art Fletcher took Fred Merkle's place on the coaching staff, and would serve as Huggins's right-hand man and third base coach.

In Fort Myers, Ty Cobb was wearing an Athletics uniform and became friends with the town's most prestigious resident. "Fort Myers was once a dead city, but now alive due to the Athletics," said Thomas Edison. One day, the great inventor grabbed a bat and stepped in to hit against the newest member of the Philadelphia outfield. Cobb lobbed one over the plate. Edison swung and drilled a line drive back at Cobb. "I can hardly be charged with an error on that," Cobb laughed after ducking and falling on his back. "If you're that spry when you're eighty, Ty, you ought to be playing ball," replied Edison.

"I want to take this opportunity to express my appreciation to every baseball fan in the country," said Cobb. "Without them, there would not be a game."

"Who's going to win the American League, Ty?" asked a sportswriter.

"Well, the A's ought to finish second, but Detroit will win it, now that the Tigers are freed of the drag of their old manager, who never knew the hit-and-run game, and how to direct the club," Cobb said in a sarcastic manner, then paused to catch his breath. "That's what they say in Detroit; it kind of hurts. Did I do so bad managing the Tigers?"

Connie Mack signed two other seasoned veterans to his 1927 squad. Eddie Collins, who once starred for the Mackmen before being sold to the White Sox, was now the starting second baseman for the A's, and outfielder Zach Wheat, after spending his entire brilliant major league career with the

12. Babe Ruth, the Legend—1927

Dodgers, was now an Athletic. "While I was in the National League, I didn't get the opportunity to see Ty Cobb, but knew what a great player he was," said Wheat. "Since we have been together, I have been amazed by his baseball instincts. He knows how to make great plays and he can put them through."

The Athletics came to St. Petersburg on March 17 to play the Braves at Waterfront Park in a rare exhibition season double-header before a large crowd of 2,500. In the fourth inning, Collins was at bat with Cobb, 2 for 4 in the game, on deck. Frank Wilson, the umpire who had called Lazzeri a busher the year before, was behind the plate, and that meant trouble. The arbitrator had feuded with Cobb during his American League umpiring days; however, all seemed okay in this game until Wilson suddenly wheeled around to inform the on-deck batter that he was out of the game. Cobb dropped his bat and headed to the Athletics dugout to get his sweater and mitt as A's coach Kid Gleason charged from the coach's box to argue. The umpire warned Gleason that the game would be forfeited if Cobb did not leave. The A's coach replied by daring him. "This game is a forfeit to the Braves, nine to nothing!" shouted the umpire.

Why did the umpire toss Cobb? According to Boston catcher Frank Gibson, Cobb and Collins carried on a conversion when Collins was at bat, and Cobb commented that there was an awful odor in the neighborhood.

With Cobb ineligible to play in the nightcap, three-quarters of the crowd departed. Many asked for a refund but were denied. When Wilson took his position for the second game, he was booed and hissed. Without warning, he sprinted toward the stands, grabbed a fan by the shirt, and shook a fist before returning to his position.

Cobb was informed the next day that he was currently banned from playing in any games that Wilson was umpiring. Three times during the game, the crowd chanted, "We want Cobb!" When the two teams met again, a foul ball smashed the windshield of Cobb's six-thousand-dollar car. The day turned out to be costly for Cobb when informed by Landis that he was fined $100 for the comment that had led to his game ejection.

The Yankees were predicted to finish behind Philadelphia in 1927. According to sportswriter James Harrison, the Yankees were improved over the previous season with stronger catching and a more experienced infield; however, he was concerned about the age of the Yanks pitching staff. "They will need more strength at short and second," commented Cobb. "They were fortunate with a new combination there last season. Still the Yanks are good, darn good, but I think Connie has a better team."

Huggins disagreed. "If our club develops a few more pitchers, we ought to have little to worry about."

Most were picking the Athletics with the addition of Cobb, the pitching of Grove, and with the younger players, like Al Simmons, being a year older and wiser. But there were questions as to whether Cobb, Collins, and Wheat, all forty and past their primes, were just names. Some claimed that Mack was sacrificing speed and defense for more batting; others said that Mack overestimated baseball reputations as the way to win ballgames. A Yankee said the addition of Cobb would hurt more than help. "Cobb will have those A's 'nuts' by the time the season is half over. He 'nutted' up the Tigers and he'll do the same thing with the A's, mark my words."

The addition of Speaker to an already strong hitting attack made the Senators a threat to recapture the pennant. "With good pitching and breaks this team would run away with the pennant."

With a new manager, Detroit was expected to be better. "Cobb mishandled the pitchers, and they never recovered." Former Tigers third baseman and American League umpire George Morriarity was the team's new pilot.

"No use in kidding ourselves. The Indians outfield is not as strong without Speaker," said an Indians official. Without centerfielder and manager Tris Speaker, the Indians were expected to struggle. "If it wasn't for the loss of Speaker I would say the Indians rank as an even bet with the A's."

Ray Schalk, the new manager of the White Sox, believed his team's infield was the best in the American League. He also had a good pitching staff that ranked third in the league in 1926, but Huggins didn't see them as a contender. "The White Sox haven't enough besides pitching to take them to the top."

"The Browns are not going to win every day, but they're going to hustle every day. I'll guarantee a fighting team if nothing else," said St. Louis manager Dan Howley, one of five new managers in the American League.

"You tell the public what you think of the team; it will be more interesting," is how Red Sox manager Bill Carrigan answered the question about how Boston would be in 1927. He knew he had an uphill battle in order to return the franchise to the days when he had managed them to the 1915 and 1916 World Championships.

A sea of fans gathered outside of Yankee Stadium on opening day. As with the 1926 World Series, trolley cars, the subway, and taxicabs delivered fans by the hundreds. By three o'clock, all the unreserved seats were filled and there were no empty seats by game time. New York versus the Philadelphia Athletics to start the season was a World Series–like feeling. A major league record crowd of 72,000 packed Yankee Stadium. Fans stood in rows behind the back rows and packed the runways. "We had to be careful about overloading runways to comply with fire and police rules or we would have sold more

12. Babe Ruth, the Legend—1927

tickets to persons willing to stand," said a Yankees official. "It looks like a capacity crowd," the New York players said as they stepped onto the field.

The two teams lined up and marched to the centerfield flagpole. Once they were there, the band played the National Anthem as the American flag was hoisted along with a "1926 American League Champions" banner.

Waite Hoyt, a sixteen-game winner in 1926, footed the pitcher's mound. He knew he had a tough battle ahead. Connie Mack had stacked his lineup with six lefties, and his starting pitcher would be Lefty Grove.

Eddie Collins hit Hoyt's first offering on the ground. Koenig made the play and retired the leadoff batter. After the next batter also grounded to Koenig, Cobb received a "glorious hand" as he made his first plate appearance as a member of the A's. The veteran grounded to Gehrig for the final out of the inning.

After a walk and a sacrifice to begin the Yankees' first, Cochrane held onto Ruth's tip for strike three, and Gehrig swung and missed for a strikeout. Grove struck out Meusel and Lazzeri to begin the second inning. In awe over the pitcher's speed, longtime baseball writer Joe Villa wrote, "No lefthander this writer has seen in the last forty years has equaled Grove's speedsters. The phenomenal Rube Wadell, known for his smoke, would have looked slow in comparison."

Hoyt was unable to match Grove's speed, but kept the opponent off the board with a variety of pitches and by using his head. He threw a changeup, curveball, and fastball, and never used the same pitch in succession.

"It took four innings for New York to size up the speed of Lefty Grove's fastball." Before New York batted in the fifth, Huggins ordered his batters to stop swinging and just try to meet the ball with quick, snappy cuts. The Yankees produced four runs in the next two innings for a 4–0 lead. In the bottom of the seventh, Koenig whistled an RBI triple. Then in a surprising move, Ben Pascal batted for Ruth and came through with a hit to score another run. Gehrig followed by bringing the crowd to its feet with a long drive to right-center. Cobb, sprinting towards the fence, caught up with the ball to end the inning. "Although Cobb is in his fortieth year, he hadn't slowed down a bit."

"Black spots before the eyes from looking at Grove's speedsters?" a writer asked Huggins about Ruth after the Yankees' 8–3 win.

"Nothing of the sort," Huggins shot back. "Ruth complained of feeling ill on the bench during the game and I let him rest, since the game seemed then precisely near in the bag."

A healthy Babe Ruth returned to the lineup the following day and pounded out two hits in a 10–4 win over the A's, although Koenig was the hitting star of the day by going five for five. Meusel took the honors a day later with three hits and four RBI in New York's nine-run, fourteen-hit attack. However, the New York hurlers struggled to hold the lead, including Cy Moore, who allowed four runs in 4.2 innings in his major league debut. The game ended in a tie when called on account of darkness. Ruth hit his first home run of 1927 during game four of the season in a 6–3 win over the A's.

Boston came to Yankee Stadium with a familiar face. After a fine 1926 season at St. Paul, the Red Sox paid $50,000 for shortstop Pee Wee Wanninger, who had already committed four errors through the first four games of the season. Feeling he was a disappointment, the Red Sox attempted to ship him back to St. Paul, but the shortstop, believing he belonged in the majors, balked. A deal was made that sent him to the Reds. Following a dismal season, Wanninger agreed to return to St. Paul. He would never appear in another major league game.

The Yankees were 6–0 following three wins in a row against Boston. They finally lost two in a row before rebounding to score thirteen in a seven-run win over the A's, with Combs, Meusel, and Lazzeri collecting three hits apiece, and Gehrig smacking his third home run of the season. The day's pitching heroics went to Cy Moore, who allowed just one hit and a walk in 4⅔ innings to earn his first big league win. "Unless I am dead wrong, Moore is another Cy Young," said the Yankees manager. "He is built for hard work, he had a low fastball that's a wonder, and as soon as he masters control, he ought to win many games for us this year."

In Philadelphia, a middle-aged man had introduced himself to Ruth as Johnny Sylvester's uncle. "I thought you would like to know, Mr. Ruth, that Johnny is making a remarkable recovery. He certainly would like to thank you and I want to thank you on behalf of the family."

"That's fine," said Ruth. "I'm certainly glad to hear it. You tell Johnny I was asking for him and telling him to keep up the good work." After the two men shook hands, and Johnny's uncle walked away, Ruth asked, "Now who in the hell is Johnny Sylvester?"

Tris Speaker received a warm welcome from Yankees fans when he made his first appearance at Yankee Stadium in a Senators uniform. The Yankees squandered a 4–0 lead and lost.

When May began, the Yankees and Athletics were 9–5 and tied for first place. The Yankees were batting .369, with Gehrig quietly hitting .447; Koenig, Collins, and Meusel were all above .400. Ruth, batting just .273, began the month by belting two home runs, his fifth and sixth of the season, in a 7–3 win over Philadelphia in front of a home crowd of 70,000. Gehrig also hit his fifth. Little did anyone realize that Ruth and Gehrig were about to engage in baseball's first great home run race.

13

Lindy! Lindy! Lindy!—1927

"He's coming to see me pitch? I think I'll ask him for an autographed airplane."—Waite Hoyt

It had finally stopped raining by 4:15 at New York's Curtis Field on the morning of May 20, 1927. And there was more good news about the weather: the forecast called for clear skies in the Northeast.

Charles Lindbergh, deciding to head to the airfield after being unable to sleep in his hotel room, ordered the *Spirit of St. Louis* to be taken to the runway. Three hours later, the plane's gas tanks were topped off with 451 gallons to increase its total weight to 5,050 pounds. Lindbergh approached the plane, climbed into the cockpit, then jumped out to take one final walk around the *Spirit*. He stared down the path of the runway to note his marked spot to abort the takeoff in case his airplane was still on the ground. He then looked at the homes, the telephone wires, and an ambulance beyond the runway.

"I'll be in Paris tomorrow," Lindbergh told B.F. Mahoney, the twenty-six year-old president of Ryan Airlines.

"I'll see you in Paris," said Richard Byrd as he shook the pilot's hand.

"What will you do when you reach Paris?" someone asked.

"I'll probably go to sleep," answered Lindbergh.

Lindbergh opened the door to the *Spirit* and looked inside. "It's like getting into a death chamber," he said, "and if I get out in Paris it will be like a pardon from the Governor."

As Lindbergh began to ride the *Spirit* down the runway, the spectators tossed their hats in the air as they cheered. The plane began to gradually gain speed, then hit a bump and staggered into the air before dropping to the muddy runway. The plane lifted again, this time a bit higher, but fell to the mud once again.

By this time Lindbergh had passed the abort marker, but had no intention to stop. Meanwhile, the frightened spectators began to panic: "He can't make it!" "He's going too slow!" "For God's sakes, why doesn't he pick up speed?"

The *Spirit* leapt into the air again, this time about ten feet above the ground, slowly gained height, and cleared the telephone wires and trees by only twenty feet. "He's off!"

"I didn't think he'd make it," said Byrd. "He's got nerve."

"Do you think he'll make it to Paris?" someone asked.

"I certainly do," replied Byrd. "The chances in his favor are three to one. He has the gas, the weather outlook is good, and of course, he has the courage and ability."

A few minutes later, another airplane took off from the field. When that plane returned, the pilot reported that Lindbergh was going fast and every cylinder of the engine was hitting perfectly. "He must have been moving better than one hundred miles per hour."

Nine days before Lindbergh's departure, Ruth belted two home runs at St. Louis to total eight for the season. His second home run, off hard-throwing Ernie Nevers, landed in the centerfield bleachers; the second home run ever to reach those bleachers at Sportsman's Park (the other being Ruth's 1926 World Series homer). "Yes, that's a good park to hit in," Ruth said of Sportsman's Park. "So is Detroit, and so is Cleveland. Comiskey Park is even better since they extended the grandstand, and Shibe Park is good too. They are all good except the [Yankee] Stadium. But the best of all was the Polo Grounds. Boy, how I use to sock 'em there. I cried when they took me out of the Polo Grounds."

The Yankees swept the four-game series in St. Louis, and increased their winning streak to six when they swept their rain-shortened series at Detroit. "I have a better club than I had in 1926," announced Huggins. "My pitchers are pitching as well as they did a year ago, and in the case of Hoyt, much better. Gehrig, Lazzeri, and Koenig are much improved as a result of experience, my outfield hasn't a single fault, and my catching has been strengthened by the addition of Grabowski."

The Yankees made it seven straight with a 4–3 win at Cleveland. Huggins called on Moore when Shocker proved ineffective in the first two innings, and the thirty-year-old rookie allowed just four hits in seven-plus innings. In the top of the ninth, with the game tied, 3–3, the Yankees had runners on the corners with one out and Moore due up. Knowing Moore was a weak hitter, Huggins signaled for a squeeze play, and the pitcher came through with his first major league hit by popping a bunt out of the first baseman's reach to score the go-ahead run.

MOORE: "You want to know my impression of what?"

FRANK GRAHAM (*New York Sun* sportswriter): "The American League hitters?"

MOORE: "I haven't pitched against American League hitting much. That game was the most pitching I've done since I joined the Yankees. I'll have to pitch against all of them before I can have an impression."
GRAHAM: "You throw a sinker, don't you?"
MOORE: "Sure. Not all the time, though. Just once in a while. Besides, I've got a curve, though some fellows will tell you I haven't. Don't pay any attention to them. I've got a slow ball and a curve ball."
GRAHAM: "Is the sinker tough on the arm?"
MOORE: "No, because it's a natural delivery."

On May 20, Gehrig stepped into the batter's box at the moment that Lindbergh was flying over Nova Scotia. The Yankees first baseman, off to a fantastic start, was hitting .429 with nine homers through thirty games. George Uhle, known to be a Yankees nemesis, cooled him off for the time being by striking him out on curve balls. The next time Gehrig came to the plate, Uhle resorted to fastballs to record another strikeout. The Indians won, 2–1, in just forty-seven minutes to snap the Yanks' win streak at seven.

When night fell, Lindbergh had flown over the last area of land and was now over the open Atlantic. His progress would be unknown for the next several hours. That night at Yankee Stadium, ring announcer Joe Humphries asked the crowd of 50,000 boxing fans to stand and observe one minute of silence and prayer for Lindbergh's success.

There was good news the next morning: Lindbergh had been seen by an independent vessel off the coast of Ireland. People jammed the streets and crowded the newsstands for the latest updates. The *New York Times* was flooded by ten thousand phone calls from excited citizens wanting to know the aviator's progress.

The sun was bright that afternoon in Cleveland as the Indians took the field. There was a band on hand and a turnout of fifteen thousand ready to celebrate the anticipated good news. In the first inning came an announcement that Lindbergh was approaching Paris. "The Yankees celebrated by knocking Emil Levsen out of the box and scoring three runs." Three singles and Ruth's double did the damage. Another double by Ruth resulted in another run and a 4–0 lead, but Cleveland fought back to cut the lead to one after six innings.

In the bottom of the seventh came the news over the wire: Lindbergh had done it! Word spread through the stands like wildfire, and the game came to a halt. As the band broke into the National Anthem, the crowd stood and removed their hats.

"Sock one on the nose!" a fan yelled to Indians catcher Luke Sewell during his at bat. Sewell responded by tagging one to score a run to tie the game, 4–4. In the twelfth inning, Moore threw ball four on a 3–2 pitch with two outs and the bases loaded to force in the winning run.

"We underestimated the Yankees," admitted Connie Mack. "Miller Huggins has a better team than last year." The Athletics were 21–17, in third place, and four games behind New York (25–13). "Our boys are trying hard to win, but they are not pulling together. The weather conditions have hampered our pitchers, and some of the regulars are weak at bat. The season is still competitively young, however, and soon the team will show its real strength."

The Yankees traveled to Philadelphia for a five-game series, including a Memorial Day double-header. Before 40,000 in the morning game, New York tagged Grove for eight runs on fifteen hits, but lost 9–8. In front of another 40,000 in the afternoon contest, Ruth turned the jeers to cheers when he hammered one over the centerfield wall for a 6–5 Yankees win. Moore starred once again by allowing no runs in four innings for his fifth win. The next day, the Yanks scored twenty-eight runs to win both ends of a double-header from the Athletics. Gehrig collected four hits, including his twelfth home run. Ruth homered in both games to give him sixteen through the end of May. In 1921, he had hit his sixteenth on June 3. When asked if he was going to break his home run record, or equal it, he replied, "I dunno. But I'll be in there swinging."

New York began June with another win in Philadelphia to put them seven games ahead and 9–3 in the season series against the team that was favored to win the pennant.

At Yankee Stadium the home team trailed the White Sox by five as the game headed into the bottom of the ninth. Combs and Ruth singled to begin the inning. Gehrig followed by lining a double off the screen in right field to score one. Cedric Durst, subbing for Meusel, made his third hit of the game to score Ruth and Gehrig to cut the lead to two. "Push em-up, Tony!" the crowd yelled as Lazzeri came to the plate, and he responded by knocking one over the fence to tie the game. A tremendous ovation followed as he rounded the bases. The Yanks eventually won the game in eleven innings on a hit by Morehart.

A day later, the Yanks were down to Chicago, but once again rallied for another win. In the seventh Morehart remained hot by knocking a three-run inside-the-park home run. Ruth followed with a triple, and then to everyone's surprise, he stole home. The Yanks won 8–3 for their third straight win over Chicago.

Against Cleveland, Ruth powered a tremendous home run to row twelve in right centerfield. As he rounded the bases, Indians catcher Luke Sewell picked up Ruth's bat and looked it over, "even sniffed it as if it was pretend or filled with iron. He conceded it was real, just longer and heavier than everyone else's." Later in the game, Ruth hit another round tripper, and after belting another one the following day he had twenty-one in sixty-three games.

"Lindy's coming! Lindy's coming!" It echoed through New York City on June 16, a day declared as Lindbergh Day. Schools and business were closed. The city was decorated with flags and signs to honor the American hero.

Following his visit to Washington, D.C., where he received the Flying Cross—a symbol of appreciation—from the president, Lindbergh arrived in New York on Mayor Walker's yacht at 12:40. An estimated four million people lined the streets, or peeked from their windows, to get a glimpse of Lindbergh as he traveled in an open car. Men waved their hats and children waved to the hero as his car passed by. When the procession reached Wall Street a ticker-tape parade began. The shredded paper was so thick that Lindbergh could hardly be seen.

The parade stopped when it reached the mayor's two huge grandstands at City Hall. Lindbergh joined the mayor and other government officials on the grandstands, and was introduced by Mayor Walker. "New York City is yours," the mayor told Lindbergh. "I don't give it to you; you won it." The mayor proceeded to pin the Medal of Valor of the city to Lindbergh's lapel.

"I never expected anything like this," Lindbergh told the crowd. "I simply cannot find the words to describe my feelings. All I can say is the welcome is wonderful, wonderful."

"Lindy's coming!" Lindbergh's parade was heading to Yankee Stadium for the Yankees-Browns game. "I feel a homer coming," Ruth told his teammates. "My left ear itched. That's a sure sign." But to Ruth's disappointment, there was no sign of the pilot when the game was to begin at 3:30. The game was delayed before finally starting without Lindbergh at 3:55.

In the bottom of the first, Ruth got hold of a pitch by Tom Zachery and delivered it to the seats in left centerfield. "I had been saving that home run for Lindbergh, and then he doesn't show," Ruth said with sadness.

"Gee, Dad. That's a peach," a boy said to his father. "Did you see that?"

"Yes son, I saw it," the dad replied. "But keep watching. Lindy will be here any minute."

Gehrig followed with a home run to almost the exact spot as Ruth's. "It's very sad that the great exhibition of the Bust-em Twins should have gone for naught," wrote Harrison.

When the game ended with an 8–1 Yankees win, there was still no sign of Lindbergh. As the crowd began to depart a sudden cheer was heard from the left-field entrance, along with chants of "Lindy! Lindy! Lindy!" The procession had finally arrived with Lindbergh in the back of an open car, smiling

Hoping to put on an impressive performance on Lindbergh Day, both members of the heart of Murderers' Row delivered. Unfortunately, Lindbergh did not arrive in time to witness the Ruth and Gehrig round-trippers. The two sluggers would engage in a home run race throughout the summer to capture the attention of the entire nation (National Baseball Hall of Fame, Cooperstown, New York).

and waving. When the car stopped at the empty box that was reserved for Lindbergh, the hero shook hands with Colonel Ruppert, and the two spoke for a few minutes before Lindbergh departed. "It's too bad you couldn't have been here earlier," the Colonel told him. When Lindbergh arrived, Ruth was in the shower. The two would have to meet on some other day.

Lindbergh was rushed from Yankee Stadium to downtown for a meeting at the Hotel Brevort on Fifth Avenue and Eighth Street, where he received a diploma, a medal, and a check for $25,000 in honor of the Orteig Prize.

Ruth now had seven more home runs than Gehrig. The Yankees' first baseman decreased the gap when he blasted two in an 8–4 win over the Browns. He hit another one the next day in Boston. Ruth smacked a pair the next day to give him twenty-four on the season. His second, a tremendous blast that was, once again, said to be the farthest ever at Fenway Park, cleared the confines of the ballpark and rolled through a vacant lot before stopping at a garage door "where six men and two boys fell on it." Two days later, Gehrig did what Ruth had never done—hit three home runs at Fenway Park in one game, to give him twenty-one for the season.

"I never had to force Gehrig's development as a first baseman," said Huggins. "Almost all he knows about the bag he learned the best way—by experience. When he learns how to make a certain play, he doesn't forget it. He's a pretty darn good first baseman right now, and as he gets better all the time I guess I won't have to worry about him for a while."

After sweeping the Browns and Red Sox in succession, the Yankees were riding a nine-game winning streak. Their record was 44–17, and they were ten games ahead of the next best team. Their hitting attack was outstanding, the fielding was better than the season before with the improvement of Koenig and Lazzeri, and the pitching was doing well.

"I never had his likes before," Huggins said after Cy Moore hurled 5.2 innings of shutout ball to earn saves in both games of a double-header. "Moore is the best rescue man I have had since I've been a manager. He is in a class by himself."

Another pitcher off to a good start was Dutch Ruether, now 6–1 with an ERA below 3.00 after beating the Red Sox. "It tickled me to pitch that victory over the Red Sox," Ruether said in the train's dining car as he feasted on a club sandwich. "Maybe I do not deserve much credit with Gehrig helping me so much with three home runs, but I had a personal satisfaction in the affair at that. It was hot today at Fenway Park." Ruether claimed he had lost twelve pounds from pitching on a humid and muggy day. "But you get the weight back after you take a few drinks of water after the game." The thirty-three-year-old Ruether was pitching on experience and whatever else he had to offer. He had not thrown a curve in three seasons. "I just mix 'em up—fast ones and slow ones."

Ruether said he appreciated working for Huggins, and loved the fact that he was not a manager who called every pitch. "He relies on a fellow's experience of being able to pitch without being told. I'd wish he'd give me more work. Today was the first I had pitched in over two weeks. June 8 was the last time I started." But he accepted the fact that there were younger hurlers on the staff who deserved to take their turns in the rotation. "I have no kick coming."

The second-place Athletics were back at Yankee Stadium for a six-game series, beginning with back-to-back double-headers. Trailing New York by eight games, they had to make their move. Before fifty-five thousand, the A's swept the first twin bill. In the first game, with the bases loaded, two outs in the ninth, Gehrig was at the plate. This time the star first baseman swung and missed a curve on a full count.

Philadelphia won the first of two the following day. Huggins called on his rescue man to start the second game, and Moore came through by allowing just five hits in a 7–3 Yanks win. Ruether increased his record to 7–1 with a win the next day, and the Yanks won the last game 9–8 to earn a split in the six-game series. The A's had arrived behind by eight, and left trailing by the same number with six fewer games on the schedule.

Following the embarrassment of whiffing with the bases loaded in the one-run loss, Gehrig clobbered four home runs in the next five games to go one up on Ruth. The Babe hit one against Boston to pull even at twenty-five, but Gehrig poked one more before the end of the series.

The four-game series sweep of the Red Sox increased the Yanks' winning streak to seven and upped their season record to 51–20. Next on the schedule was a four-game home-and-home series with the red-hot Washington Senators, who were fresh off sweeping the A's to take second place. They were on an eight-game winning streak, but 10 ½ behind the Yankees. Thinking back to when the Yanks had nearly surrendered a big lead in 1926, Washington had hopes of a repeat in 1927. They figured if they could sweep the series, or even take three of four, it could start the Yankees on a downward spiral.

Thirty thousand fans crammed into Washington's Griffith Stadium on July 3. Hod Lisenbee, a rookie with a 3–0 season record against New York, was Washington's starting pitcher. Before the crowd had settled into their seats, Ruth hit one that landed in a concrete sun parlor beyond the centerfield wall. Washington slugger Goose Goslin matched Ruth's clout in the same inning to give the Senators a 2–1 lead. In the bottom of the fifth, Tris Speaker, leading the Nats with a .343 batting average, singled, Goslin walked, and Joe Judge hit one down the right field line. A peanut vendor on the field saw the ball coming, made a gallant effort to dodge the hit, but was struck by the ball. Both runners scored on the play; however, the umpires called the vendor for interference and ordered the second runner back to third base. The arbitrators then called time to shoo all the on-field vendors into the stands. As play was about to resume, an intoxicated fan opened the centerfield gate and found a seat in the outfield grass. When an umpire waved him off the field, he waved back. Ruth said something, and the fan responded by turning, pawing the dirt, and shouting, "hee-haw." The police led the drunk off the field, and the game finally resumed.

The next batter singled to score two runs, giving Washington a 6–3 lead. New York fought back, with Lazzeri hitting one that barely stayed inside the foul line before landing in the leftfield seats to cut the lead to 6–5. Washington held on to win, and gained a game on New York.

The two teams mingled as they traveled on the same train to resume the series at New York. Huggins chatted with Washington coach Al Schacht about the pennant race. "Well, all I hope is you drop twenty straight and then start on a losing streak," Schacht told Huggins. Members from both teams laughed, except for Huggins, who failed to find humor in Schacht's wisecrack.

The biggest crowd in baseball history, 72,641, packed Yankee Stadium. Hungry for revenge from the day before, the Yankees crushed their nearest competitor by scoring eight runs in four innings off starting pitcher Sloppy Thurston, and added four more after Harris sent in Walter Johnson for a 12–1 win. Gehrig smacked one off Johnson to put him one ahead of Ruth. In the nightcap, Gehrig tagged starting pitcher General Crowder for a grand slam in the first inning to infuriate the Washington manager. Believing that Crowder lacked good judgment, he made a waiver deal with the Browns to bring Tom Zachery back to Washington in exchange for Crowder. "There are few flingers who can win without thinking, and I don't believe that Crowder is one of them," said Harris. He would have second thoughts when Crowder won twenty for the Browns in 1928. New York won the nightcap, 21–1. Ruth, although with no homers on the day, knocked out five hits.

Bump Hadley was a very nervous young man. Being assigned to start against the Yankees the day after they had murdered Washington's pitching for thirty-three runs did not sit well with the rookie. He looked for sympathy among the other Washington pitchers, but found none:

> THURSTON: "The Yanks could pound anything and would on the slightest provocation. They treated me badly."
> MARBERRY: "Boy, there are worse things than facing the Yankees, but tell me what it is."
> BURKE: "I'm just a young fellow myself, Bump. I used to think I was a pitcher, but the Yankees knocked that notion out of my head."

JOHNSON: "It strikes me that the Yankees show no more respect for my years and service than a young fellow who is just breaking in."

Hadley did find support when his teammates gave him a 5–0 lead before he took the hill in the bottom of the first, but when he gave way to two hits and two walks to four of the first five batters he faced, he was replaced. Slowly, the Yankees pecked away until they tied the game when Gehrig tripled and scored on Lazzeri's sacrifice fly in the seventh inning. In the bottom of the ninth, Lazzeri sent one into the leftfield seats for another Yankees victory.

14

Baseball's Greatest Team—1927

"Miller Huggins has the strongest team seen in the majors for the last thirty-five years. The Yankees are playing better than Frank Chance's Cubs, who established the record at 116 victories in a single year."

—Detroit sportswriter

Was there a way to slow down the 1927 Yankees? Perhaps the answer was injuries. The slack fell to team trainer Doc Woods when the casualties began to mount in midseason. Shocker, Pennock, Hoyt, Dugan, Koenig, and Gehrig were all hurting. "It isn't broke," Woods said in regard to Shocker's ankle injury. "We had it X-rayed to prove it. Pennock hasn't any broken ribs, either. He has nothing more than a few muscle bruises. Hoyt's arm is still weak, but he ought to be able to strengthen it by pitching a little batting practice each day. All three will be back soon, and winning."

"It sounds funny, but I can feel a sore arm coming on and I want Doctor Knight [an osteopath in Rochester] to look at it," said Dutch Ruether. "I'm sure it's nothing serious, but I don't want to take any chances."

Koenig was out with a leg injury, and Dugan had missed a few games when his lame knee began to throb. When Koenig went down, Lazzeri shifted to shortstop and Morehart filled in at second base. "I was hoping to have a good year at second base," Lazzeri said regretfully. "When I was a kid I played everywhere, as any kid does. One day I wanted to pitch, the next day catch. Finally, I settled down in the infield but not at one position. When I broke into professional baseball and got with the Salt Lake City club, I played all around the infield the first year, spending most of my time at first base. Then I moved to shortstop in 1925. Last year Hug put me at second base and I've gotten that I'd rather play there than anywhere else."

At Navin Field, Gehrig hit one past the centerfield flagpole at the deepest part of the park. With a sore ankle, Gehrig limped into third base for a triple.

"With any speed he would have made four bases on the drive." In the second game, Ruth hit one deep to center, but not as far as Gehrig's drive. He was able to round the bases for his twenty-seventh home run.

The Yankees scored eighteen runs in their first two games at Detroit, but settled for a split. They scored nineteen a day later in a 19–7 win for a sum of seventy-seven runs in their last six games. In the nineteen-run attack, Ruth went 5-for-6 to lift his season average to .373. Two of his five hits were homers to give him the league lead with twenty-nine through seventy-nine games, and put him four ahead of his 1921 pace. Gehrig had twenty-eight in the same number of games, and was batting .400. The next day, Gehrig hit another one by the Navin Field flagpole. Sore leg or not, he would have circled the bases, but the stadium's ground rule limited the hit to a double.

Moore went two for three against the Tigers to become four hundred dollars richer. His three hits for the season won bets with Ruth and Pennock, both certain that he was too weak a hitter to reach that number. "I was a bum hitter in the Sally League," Moore said with a laugh as he gingered four yellow-backed one-hundred dollar bills. "But, boy, I'm a good hitter up here."

Shocker showed no signs of an ankle injury when he shut out the Indians, Ruth hit his thirtieth home run, and the Yankees closed their series in Cleveland by coming back from a six-run deficit to win by one. They had scored three in the ninth off their nemesis, George Uhle. They then swept the Browns in St. Louis to make it 11–0 versus the Browns in 1927. Gehrig hit two out in the series to take the lead over Ruth with thirty-one. At Chicago, Ruth hit the first upper-deck home run at Comiskey Park to tie the home run race.

Before 83,000 at Yankee Stadium on the evening of July 21, Jack Dempsey kayoed Jack Sharkey, a top-ranked contender, to earn another fight against the man who had defeated him the year before to take his heavyweight title. The fight with Sharkey was a playoff for the right to face Gene Tunney.

"I was fouled," Sharkey said in regard to Dempsey's low punches prior to the knockout blow. He had been in command by connecting on several punches through the first six rounds that gave Dempsey a bloody nose and mouth and a cut above and below his right eye. Dempsey figured the only way he could win was to get close enough to his opponent to land a single power punch. With his head pushed against Sharkey's chest, he threw the low blows that Sharkey believed were too low. When Sharkey turned to complain to the referee, Dempsey threw a left hook that sent Sharkey to the canvas to end the fight. "I didn't foul him," said Jack Dempsey. "I hit him with hard rights to the beltline, and as his guard dropped, brought a left in the jaw that finished the job."

The Senators went 13–6 on their trip out west, yet lost a half game to

14. Baseball's Greatest Team—1927

New York. "How are we going to catch a team that rarely loses?" asked a frustrated Bucky Harris. "We had a winning streak of ten and another of seven, yet we just about held our own." The Yankees were 65–26 and thirteen games ahead of the second-place Senators. "We are out so far, not because other teams have slipped since last year, but because we have improved," reasoned Huggins. "Most of the other teams, barring the Indians, have improved, but we have improved to a greater extent.

"Lazzeri is a better player this year, and so is Koenig. The big guy on first base is better. Ruth is just as good ... pardon me, very good this year. Meusel is playing the best baseball of his life. Combs is the best centerfielder in the league. My catchers are doing great, and hitting, too. The pitching is balanced and Moore has been a great help."

SPORTSWRITER: "I see John McGraw said the Orioles were the best team the game ever saw."
HUGGINS: "Yes."
SPORTSWRITER: "Do you think the Orioles could have beaten your Yankees?"
HUGGINS: "I don't know."
SPORTSWRITER: "Did you ever play against the Orioles?"
HUGGINS: "Are you trying to kid me? Say, I didn't break into the majors until 1903."

"I don't think the Yankees could touch the old Red Sox," snorted Bill Carrigan when asked to compare his Red Sox from the previous decade to the

The 1927 New York Yankees (National Baseball Hall of Fame, Cooperstown, New York).

1927 Yankees. "The Yankees are great slash and cut guys, but I don't think they'd be slashing and cutting against Shore, Ruth, Leonard, and Mays. A defense such as I had in those days would stop the Yankees."

The Yankees celebrated their return home by sweeping the Browns to make it fifteen straight over St. Louis in 1927. They scored forty runs in the four-game sweep with Ruth hitting three homers to Gehrig's two to take a 34–33 lead. Before the end of July, Gehrig socked two more to retake the lead. It was known that the Yankees were going to take the pennant. The question was, who would win this home run race? The sportswriters were surprised to learn that Gehrig was uninterested. "Not once this season have I come up to the plate with the determination of getting a circuit smash," Gehrig told them. "A single in a pinch means more than a home run. I follow nobody's style. I have no advice to give on home run hitting."

Gehrig began August with two home runs against Detroit to put him three up on the Babe. Ruth hit one before the Tigers left town: Gehrig 37, Ruth 35.

"This is the most disappointing season of my career," said Connie Mack as his A's prepared to host the Yankees. "I thought I had finally gotten a pennant winner—after so many years of experimenting." Mack's Athletics were a disappointing 55–50, leading to questions about whether Mack was overvaluing Cobb and the other veterans. "Cobb, Collins, and Wheat have done everything I've expected of them, despite that injuries have happened to them. I didn't expect them to go the entire route of 154 games," said Mack. "Lack of pitching is what killed the chances of the Athletics. When the season opened, I thought we had the most balanced pitching staff in the league. I figured my three righties—Gray, Rommel, and Ehmke—would turn in approximately fifty victories. With the season over half over, they have turned in one-third that number. If it wasn't for my southpaws—Grove, Walberg, and Pate—I don't know where we would be." When asked about the Yankees, Mack replied, "A club with great batting that is getting the best pitching in the American League."

In a one-game series at Philadelphia, Walberg was on the verge of becoming the first pitcher to shut out the Yankees in 1927 when, in the top of the ninth, Gehrig hit home run number thirty-eight. The A's won, 8–1, with Cobb collecting three hits to lift his season average to .329. "When Connie Mack tells me he does not need me, I will hang up the old uniform." On August 25 in St. Louis, Cobb went 5-for-5 to lift his season average to .354.

Cobb's red-hot bat appeared to rub off on the A's. Beginning with their 8–1 win over New York, the A's won seventeen of twenty-one to move back into second place. The right-handed pitching that Mack had written off combined for 14 of those 17 wins.

14. Baseball's Greatest Team—1927

When the Yanks traveled to Washington, Ruth was in a 0–11 slump. He broke out of it with three hits, including his thirty-sixth home run into the left-centerfield stands, off Tom Zachery. At Chicago, Ruth connected with a Tommy Thomas pitch and drove it over right field upper deck to become the first player to hit a home run over the Comiskey Park outfield roof. In the top of the eleventh of a 2–2 game, Ruth hit a curveball over the leftfield fence to tie Gerhig for the home run lead.

"The Cubs pitching will smother the New York hitters," said a baseball expert. The Cubs looked like the team that would face the Yankees in the 1927 World Series. Led by the power hitting of Hack Wilson and the pitching of Charlie Root, the Cubs were five games ahead of the Pirates and 7½ up on the Cardinals until they slumped at the end of August to allow the Pirates to catch up, and when Pittsburgh beat Chicago 4–3 on September 1, the Pirates were in first place.

Like the Cubs, the Yankees were suddenly in a slump. Following a loss in the final game of the series at Chicago, they dropped three straight in Cleveland. "A slump?" asked an amused Mark Roth, the traveling secretary of the Yankees. "Back in 1908, when I was a baseball writer covering the Yanks, they started west for the second time with a lead of five games and everybody was picking them to win the pennant, including managers of other teams. They played twenty-two games, tied one, and lost the rest. Now that's a slump." Roth's story was grossly exaggerated, but his point was the Yankees were in no slump, or if they were they quickly broke it by winning eight in a row.

The Yankees scored thirty-two runs in a three-game sweep at St. Louis to make it 18-0 against the Browns for the season. Ruth hit two home runs to Gehrig's one in the series to take the lead by one.

Against Boston, Ruth hit another one to take the lead by two. The Yanks won, again, to finish August at 89–37 and with a seventeen-game lead. With the outcome of the American League pennant race known, all eyes were on the home run race. With two outs in the first inning at Philadelphia, Ruth tagged Walberg for a home run over the right field wall. Gehrig followed by hitting one out of sight. The ball cleared the street behind the right field wall and landed on a rooftop. One inning later, Gehrig hit another one: Ruth 44, Gehrig 43.

On Labor Day, in Boston, Gehrig homered to right to once again tie Ruth for the lead. The Red Sox went on to win the game, 12–11, in eighteen innings with Hoyt taking the loss. "You know what's the most distressing feeling in the World?" asked Hoyt. Several Yankees looked at him as they waited for the answer. "It comes when you're in there pitching a tight game, and meaning to pitch inside to a hitter who murders the ball on outside pitches, and you see the ball start for the outside when it leaves your hand."

Gehrig homered again at Boston to tie Ruth. Ruth came up the following inning and blasted one. When the ball landed far beyond the centerfield barrier, it was called the longest home run ever hit at Fenway Park. In the nightcap, Ruth did it again to take the lead by two: Ruth 47, Gehrig 45.

"While it is not likely he will go as high as fifty-nine, which he reached in 1921, he is generally favored by all ball players as the winner in the struggle with Gehrig." The next day, Ruth hit two to take a 49–45 lead. Twenty-one games remained for Ruth to equal or break his home run record.

The Browns were in danger of being swept in the twenty-two-game season series with the Yankees when they arrived in New York. They had four chances left to win one game to avoid the embarrassment. In the first game, Hoyt hurled a three-hit shutout for his twentieth win of the season. Ruth drove in four runs in a 9–3 win in the second game of the series. Moore, in another rare starting assignment, pitched a seven-hit, 1–0 shutout in the third game. The Browns did manage to salvage the final game of the season series to avoid the sweep. "Taking pity, we let them win the twenty-second game," according to Ruth, who hit his fiftieth home run.

Ruth homered twice in a double-header win over the Indians to go up by seven on Gehrig. The double win clinched the pennant for the Yankees, but there were no celebrations. It had been known for weeks that the Yankees would do it.

"What are my plans for the World Series? I haven't any," said Huggins. "Not right now. In the first place, I do not know which club we will meet, though I guess it will be the Pirates. Until I know, I am unlikely to make any plans. The series is two weeks off and so much might happen before then."

Ruth hit number fifty-three a few days later, although the hitting star of the day was, of all people, Cy Moore. After he singled for his first career hit at Yankee Stadium, he came up later in the game and homered! He also pitched his eighteenth win of the season.

Ruth hit his fifty-fourth against the White Sox to equal his 1920 total. When he went to right field after the inning, a boy came out of the stands with the home run ball and a pen. Ruth gladly signed it for him.

Detroit pitcher Sam Gibson goose-egged Murderers' Row for eight innings, but in the ninth Ruth homered, his fifty-fifth. One day later, the Yankees were down by a run in the bottom of the ninth with Koenig on first and Ruth at the plate. Ruth belted one that crashed into row six of the right field bleachers with so much power that it chipped a seat. He carried his bat as he

14. Baseball's Greatest Team—1927

rounded the bases, something Ruth often did after hitting a walk-off homer, when a boy in knickerbockers met him at third base. He patted his idol with one hand while he grabbed Ruth's bat with the other. Not wanting to part with his bat, Ruth held on and dragged the boy across home plate "like the tail of a comet."

"Ladies and gentlemen of the radio audience: We are in Chicago," announced Graham McNamee.

"The most impressive spectacle that any of us have ever seen," added Phil Carlin, "a crowd of 140,000 to 150,000."

At Soldier Field in Chicago, on the evening of September 22, 1927, Dempsey and Tunney were about to square off in a ten-round rematch for the heavyweight crown. Dempsey was declared the underdog for the first time since he had won the title from Jess Willard in 1919.

Shortly after the two fighters entered the ring, referee Dave Barry called them to the center of the ring to explain the rules: "Now I want to get one point clear. In the event of a knockdown, the man scoring the knockdown will go to the furthest neutral corner. Is that clear?" The two boxers nodded.

Tunney took charge from the beginning. He connected with several punches, and had Dempsey on the ropes and staggering. The challenger was bleeding. He was flatfooted, tired, and having trouble breathing, but wasn't about to surrender.

The two men exchanged light blows to begin the seventh round, and then Dempsey began to score. He delivered a hard right and left to the champ's face that backed him to the ropes, and then followed with several punches to send the bewildered boxer to the canvas. "Dempsey has Tunney down!" screamed McNamee.

Tunney was down and in danger of being counted out. However, the referee had not begun to count. Dempsey had failed to retreat to a neutral corner, per Dave Barry's pre-fight instructions. "Go to a neutral corner!" shouted Barry, and by the time Dempsey responded, Tunney had received five extra seconds. The champ appeared to come to his senses when Barry's count was at 3 or 4, but he remained on the canvas after looking across the ring and seeing his manager signaling for him to stay down until the count was higher. Tunney was on his feet on the count of nine, which was really fourteen with the extra five seconds.

The champ began to backpedal around the ring in an attempt to stay away from the challenger for the rest of the round. "Come on and fight," Dempsey told him. After the bell, Tunney went back to his corner, where he received a heated lecture from his trainer. In the eighth round, Tunney took charge again, and even knocked the challenger to one knee. When Dempsey dropped, Barry mysteriously began his count without reminding the champ of the rules.

Dempsey got up after one second, but had nothing left. Tunney won the decision in ten rounds to retain the title. "I realized the time had come to hang up my gloves and leave the ring," Dempsey said years later. "I was thirty-two years old, but I felt a hell of a lot older."

Connie Mack brought his Athletics to town for their last game against the Yankees in 1927, minus Ty Cobb. A few days before, the great outfielder shook hands with Mack and his teammates, waved to the fans, and said farewell. He finished the season with a .357 batting average. He decided to call it a season and said he was unsure about 1928. The writers speculated that he was going to retire.

Gehrig finally hit one for his first home run in three weeks. He would hit one more to finish the season with forty-seven homers. In that same game, Ruth sent one over the fence against Lefty Grove for a grand slam. He was now two away from tying his record, and three away from sixty with three games remaining.

Washington arrived at Yankee Stadium for the final series of the season. There were two outs and nobody on base when Ruth came to the plate for his first at bat of the series against Yankee killer Hod Lisenbee, winner in seven of his eight decisions against the Yanks in 1927. With two strikes, Lisenbee threw a changeup, low and outside. Ruth swung, and the ball sailed to the bleachers in right center field for home run number fifty-eight.

Ruth came to the plate in the bottom of the second with the Yanks in the midst of a seven-run rally, and the slugger connected again. This time the ball headed towards the leftfield bleachers, looking like the one that might tie the record. The ball hit the fence and rolled towards the infield. Ruth rounded second and made it to third for his eighth triple of the season.

In the bottom of the fifth, Ruth was at bat with the bases loaded. On the mound was young Paul Hopkins, pitching in just his second major league game. With a full count, Hopkins threw one that Ruth later described as "a fastball right through the middle with a three and two count." It was tailor made for the Babe. He sent the pitch halfway up the right field bleachers for a grand slam. Home run number fifty-nine! "Hopkins should be grateful. Less than twenty-four hours ago he was unknown. Now he is celebrated as the man who pitched the ball that Babe belted to tie the record."

"What did you say his name was?" asked Ruth. "Hopkins, eh? Very good."

After the game, Ruth was approached in the clubhouse by "a tall, good-looking chap, his black hair shower-pasted." "Autograph this for me, will you, Babe?" asked the tall lad. "Who was that?" asked Ruth after the visitor had departed. "That was the guy you hit your first home run off of today—Hod Lisenbee."

Lefthander Tom Zachery pitched the second game of the series for Washington. He was booed by 10,000 fans for walking Ruth in the first inning on four pitches. Ruth singled in his next two at bats, and then he came up in the bottom of the eighth in a 2–2 game, and with Koenig on third base. Pitching very carefully, Zachery tossed ball one before getting a strike over. He made his next offering. Ruth swung, and the ball headed toward the right field bleachers.

Could this be it? Was it far enough? Would it stay fair?

Right-fielder Sam Rice drifted back until he ran out of room. The ball landed in the crowd, and had stayed fair by twenty yards. Home run! Sixty! A new record! Ten thousand fans, sounding three times that number, went wild as Ruth circled the bases with a big smile and doffed his cap to the fans.

The 1927 Yankees set an American League record with 110 wins and finished nineteen games ahead of the second-place Athletics. They set a new record for runs scored (975) and home runs (158), and led the American League in almost every offensive category. Their pitching staff led the league in team ERA. Waite Hoyt led the league in wins (22). Cy Moore won 19 games, led the league in saves (13), and posted the league's lowest earned run average (2.28).

It was off to Pittsburgh to meet the Pirates in the World Series. After checking into their hotel, the Yankees headed to Forbes Field for their practice session a day before the start of the World Series. A Pirates fan spotted Ruth climbing into a taxi and yelled, "You'll not hit any home runs off of our pitchers."

"Come out to the ballpark, and the Babe will show you a sample of what he is going to do in the series," Yankees bat boy Eddie Bennett told the fan.

The Pirates had finished their practice session and headed to the seats to watch the Yankees. "Gee! They're big guys!" Pirates centerfielder Lloyd Waner told his brother Paul, the Pittsburgh starting right-fielder, in reference to seeing Ruth and Gehrig for the first time in his life. Ruth stepped into the batting cage, and his first hit cleared the fence in centerfield by a lot. "Holy smoke!" said a Pirates pitcher. "Does he do that often?" His next drive found a resting place in the right-field grandstand. He hit another one deep to centerfield before yielding to Gehrig.

As the Pirates watched in awe, Gehrig sent one over the fence in right field that barely missed landing in the upper tier. His next hit, although not as powerful as the first, landed in the stands.

The Yankees won Game One, mostly due to Pittsburgh misplays. "If you made mistakes they beat you," recalled Lloyd Waner. "In the first game there was a double play ball that went through our second baseman's legs and they scored a bunch of runs and beat us, 5–4."

Lloyd Waner was referring to the third inning, with the game tied 1-1, when Pirates second baseman Larry Granthan booted Keonig's grounder with one out. There was no missed double play chance, but the error would prove costly. Ruth followed with his second single of the game, Gehrig and Meusel both walked to force in a run, and another run scored on Lazzeri's fielder's choice. The third run of the inning came home on another Pirates error to give New York a 4–1 lead.

Hoyt gave up two singles with one out in the bottom of the eighth of a two-run game. Huggins, taking no chances, called on Moore, who got out of the jam but allowed an RBI single to cut the Yankees' lead to 5–4. Moore, however, retired the Pirates in order in the ninth to nail down the win.

"When will Hug learn that Pipgras will never make it as a pitcher?" a sportswriter asked. Huggins had a hunch about his starting pitcher for Game Two. Pipgras had won ten games, including his last four decisions, since the manager had inserted him into the starting rotation when his pitching staff was decimated with injuries.

The Pirates scored first, but quickly fell behind when New York put three on the board in the third inning. Combs and Koenig singled, and Combs scored when Lloyd Waner bobbled Koenig's hit for an error. Gehrig followed Ruth's long fly out with a double to score Koenig, and after Meusel reached base on an infield hit, Lazzeri hit a fly ball deep enough to score Gehrig for a 3–1 lead. In the top of the eighth, New York added three more on singles by Meusel and Lazzeri, followed by two walks and a hit batsman. Koenig came through with his third hit of the day to make it a 6–1 lead. Piprgras went on to pitch the complete-game win to give the Yankees a 2–0 lead in the series. The series would now head to New York. "I don't think we'll come back here," predicted Huggins. "Not that I dislike this town. But it looks as though we should end this series in New York."

Huggins started nineteen-game winner Herb Pennock in Game Three before over 60,000 at Yankee Stadium. The Yankees hurler was given an early two-run lead when Murderers' Row scored twice in their first at bat. Combs singled and Koenig beat out an infield hit for his fifth hit of the series. After Ruth struck out, Gehrig blasted a two-run triple to the base of the left-centerfield wall.

The Pirates were unable to solve Pennock. The Yanks' lefty sent the opposition down in order for seven innings. In the bottom of the seventh, the Yankees' bats came to life. A hit, a bunt and two fielder's choices scored one.

14. Baseball's Greatest Team—1927

Combs singled to make it 4–0 and Koenig followed with another hit—a double—to score another one, and to force the Pirates to make a pitching change. Left-hander Mike Cvengros got the call to pitch to Babe Ruth.

Ruth dug his cleats into the batter's box and took a few practice swings. When he saw a pitch to his liking, he swung and powered the baseball into the right field bleachers. "Torn scorecards floated down from the upper deck of the vast stadium as the illustrious one stepped on first, turned his head to assure himself that the ball had found a safe haven, then on to second, third, and home, and ahead of him danced Professor Combs and Marcus K."

Pennock retired the first batter in the eighth inning, but the next batter singled to break up the no-hitter bid, and the hope of a shutout vanished when the next batter hit an RBI doubled. The Pirates would get another hit but no more runs in the Yankees' 8–1 win.

Ruth did it again in Game Four. With a runner on base in the fifth inning, he sent a towering drive to deep right-centerfield. "Paul Waner in right field and Lloyd Waner in center each took a few steps in the direction of the ball's skyward path. Then the two Waners stopped dead...."

On the verge of being swept in four games, the Pirates fought back to tie the score against Cy Moore. In the bottom of the ninth, with the game still tied 3–3, Combs walked on four pitches. Koenig legged out a bunt down the third base line for his ninth hit in eighteen at bats in the series, and Pirates pitcher Johnny Miljus uncorked a wild pitch to advance the runners. Ruth received an intentional pass to load the bases with nobody out. Then the Pirates' hurler settled down and struck out Gehrig.

"Let's try a squeeze play, Hug," suggested Pat Collins as Meusel walked to the plate.

"Let's sacrifice," another player recommended.

"Take a chance, Hug," said another player in favor of bunting.

Huggins didn't reply. The manager and his player watched Meusel go down swinging for the second out of the inning.

Tony Lazzeri strolled up to home plate with the bases still loaded, two outs, and one run needed to win the World Series. As the batter swung and missed for strike one, Huggins finally spoke: "Listen, we don't have to take a chance at all. That fellow is bearing down too hard. It isn't in the cards for him to get away with it. If Tony doesn't hit one, he'll wild pitch as sure as fate."

Miljus's next pitch sailed by the catcher and bounced to the backstop. Combs sprinted down the third base line and crossed home with the winning run to make the Yankees World Champions.

"You called it, Hug!" howled Pat Collins. "You called it!"

"Nice work, gang," Huggins said in the victorious New York clubhouse. "You put it over. I knew you could!" And then he ducked away from the noise and confusion, and the newspapermen who pounded at his office door. It was the players' triumph and he wanted them to have the credit. For that was Huggins's way.

15

Break Up the Yankees—1928

> "Throw the Yankees out of the league and give the other teams a chance!"—A disgruntled Philadelphia Athletics fan

Babe Ruth discovered that he would share the spotlight from now on. When he arrived in St. Petersburg for spring training in 1928, he was accompanied by the 1927 American League MVP, Lou Gehrig. The two sluggers were greeted by several newspapermen, and were presented with large bouquets of beautiful flowers by a host of pretty women who posed for photos with the two home run stars. They were then taken to the Princess Martha Hotel where Ruth, said to be looking very fit at 224 pounds, changed into knickers and a white sweater, ate breakfast, and headed to the Jungle Club to shoot thirty-six holes. Gehrig, who detested golf, took a pass. "I ain't going to demean myself by chasing after golf balls," he said. "When I want to converse with nature, I'll take an automobile."

"Sixty-one or bust," was buzzing around Lake Crescent Park. "Why don't you change up and hit into leftfield?" a writer asked Ruth. The question went unanswered. "Would you rather hit .400 than sixty-one homers?"

"I would say not!" snapped Ruth. "The fans would rather see me hit a home run to right than three doubles to left. Anyway, sixty-one home runs would be about right for this year. Yes sir, that wouldn't be a bad idea at all."

Gone from the Yankees were Ray Morehart, Dutch Ruether, and Urban Shocker. Morehart was sent to St. Paul. Ruether, finishing 13–6 after an 8–1 start in '27, was now pitching for San Francisco of the Pacific Coast League. Shocker declined New York's offer and announced his winter job of radio sales was now a full-time career. "He says he's quit and I'm going to take his word," said Huggins. "In cases like this we put a player's name on the voluntary retired list."

Huggins and the Yankees may or may not have been aware that Shocker was ill. A winner of forty-nine games since returning to the Yanks in 1925,

Shocker didn't appear in the 1927 World Series, perhaps because he was ailing. On December 20, 1927, he was placed under the care of a physician for a heart condition.

With Ruether and Shocker gone, Huggins would rely on two rookie hurlers in Hank Johnson and Al Shealy, plus George Pipgras. Thirty-eight-year-old Stan Coveleski was another newcomer to the pitching staff. After a twenty-win 1925 season with Washington, injuries caused his career to decline. Shortly after pitching the opening-day win for the Senators in 1927, he was released, and Huggins claimed him. "I hurt my arm during the training trip last season, and it was never right," said Coveleski. He worked out with the Yankees but appeared in no games when accompanying the team on a road trip. One day in St. Louis, he knocked on the manager's door at Buckingham Hotel. "I come to say goodbye, Hug. I know my arm isn't going to be any good this year. I'm going home to Shamokin [Pennsylvania]. If it feels better in the spring, can I have a trial with you in St. Petersburg?"

"You can have a trial next spring, or any spring," replied Huggins. "You've been on the square with me, and I won't forget it."

Other newcomers were rookies Bill Dickey, Leo Durocher, Sammy Byrd, and veteran third baseman Gene Robertson. Word was that the 5'7", 150-pound Robertson would take over as the starting third baseman, but Huggins made it clear that job would remain with Joe Dugan. "Sure Robertson is a good ballplayer," the manager said, "but Dugan is going to start for us, and he's going to stay in there as long as he delivers the goods."

Bill Dickey was considered the prize rookie in camp. He was a solid left-handed hitting catcher with an excellent throwing arm. He was 6'1", weighed 180, and spoke with a slow and broad Ozark drawl. While growing up in Kensett, Arkansas, he dreamed of being a locomotive engineer, perhaps influenced by his father's career of working on the railroad. He was a pitcher throughout high school and his first year at Little Rock College. He saw less competition for his team's catching position for his 1925 semi-pro team, so he decided to become a catcher. In 1926, he played at Muskogee, Oklahoma, and Little Rock of the Southern Association. Feeling he needed more seasoning, Little Rock sent him to Jackson, Mississippi, of the Class D Cotton States league. Yankees scout Johnny Nee believed Dickey was good enough to make the jump from Class D to the major leagues.

Miller Huggins was high on rookie infielder Leo Durocher. "He's as fine a young shortstop as I ever saw in a Southern training camp," the manager said to the host of reporters as they watched Durocher spare a slow grounder while charging ahead and making an off-balance throw to Gehrig. As he watched the completion of the play, Huggins's eyes softened as he smiled like a proud father watching his son. "Never lose that self-assurance that you are the best," Huggins would tell Durocher. "And you'll be here when those guys with strong backs and weak minds are gone, because little guys like us can win games. We can beat 'em up here," he'd say while taping his head.

The brash and daring Durocher failed to use his head when disobeying a team rule, an oversight that landed him in hot water. Huggins had warned his team about staying away from certain social events in St. Petersburg, especially one in particular at another hotel. Durocher had received an invitation to that hotel party from a wealthy female friend. The rookie infielder accepted, and happened to have a tuxedo to wear for the occasion. There was a challenge of making it through the hotel lobby without being seen. He knew his manager would disapprove, and if his teammates saw him in a tuxedo, he'd be down to his underwear before he reached the door. He knew of a service entrance that Babe Ruth used to avoid the fans. Durocher used that entrance, walked through an alley, turned the corner, and—"Oh God!" Sitting on a bench before him were Huggins, Fletcher, and O'Leary. "One thing I will say for myself—I brought their conversation to a sudden halt," Durocher would later say. "Lovely evening, gentlemen," Durocher said, and then he made a bow. He dove into a waiting limousine he had ordered and told the driver to step on it. The next morning, he found a note on his locker that instructed him to see the manager.

HUGGINS: "Son, did you come down here to wear evening clothes?"
DUROCHER: "No sir, Mr. Huggins, I came down here to play baseball. But Mister Huggins, this was a very fine affair and I had an invitation and, of course, it was a back-tie affair, and I had to wear evening clothes and—"
HUGGINS: "And you had them, didn't you? You packed them into that fancy trunk of yours, didn't you? Let me give you a tip. You put them back into that trunk and don't let me ever see you with those things on again. Do you understand?"
DUROCHER: "Yes sir, Mister Huggins."

The writers were nearly unanimous in picking the Yankees to win a third consecutive pennant. "Overconfidence, lack of pitching, and the unseen uprising of a strong rival" were mentioned by the *New York Times* as reasons how the Yankees could be overthrown. "It's not easy to win three pennants in succession," said Bucky Harris. "Our team captured the American League flag in 1924 and 1925, but couldn't get in front in 1926. Perhaps the Yankees will experience the same difficulty this year following two championships. At least, I hope so." The Washington manager questioned the Yankees' pitching, claiming that "Hoyt and Pennock are a year older and Shocker's retirement puts question marks up for their hurling."

Huggins restated that other pitchers would pick up the slack for the departed Ruether and Shocker. "Even if they don't, I doubt there will be a difference of nineteen games between the Yankees of last year and this year."

The Athletics, viewed as the biggest threat to the Yankees, would have Ty Cobb for another season, and they signed Tris Speaker when Clark Griffith elected to pass on the veteran for 1928. "Cobb was a great help last season," said Mack. "He will be very useful this year, and with Speaker in the outfield, we will be very strong in that department."

"I really wanted to retire," said Cobb, now showing a little gray along the temples, but looking fit for age forty-one. "I'm going to play one more year. Then I am through."

"I am unable to run back and pull down those long line drives like I used to," said Speaker. He also mentioned that he was going to back up another ten feet in centerfield. There was a time when Speaker played extremely shallow at his position—so shallow, in fact, that he was close to the second base bag. "I was often criticized in those days for playing too close to the second base bag, but in those days, when scientific baseball was in vogue, it was mighty handy. Now with free swingers and the lively ball one can't play deep enough."

The Yankees endured a rough spring, but the manager remained confident. "Everything is fine and we have enjoyed a great training season. And we will beat the hell out of those Buffalo Bisons this afternoon."

Not quite. They lost to the Bisons, and they lost Lazzeri. The slugging second baseman strained his side while swinging at a wide pitch. He was sent back to New York for examination, where it was announced that he sustained a torn muscle and would be unavailable for the start of the season. Durocher would play in his place.

Another loss to Buffalo made it six straight defeats for the Yankees to drop their exhibition season record to 1–9. Gehrig attributed the slow start to the Florida sun. "When you try to bat you have to squint your eyes like this [gives example]. After we get up north where the glare isn't so bad, we'll start hitting."

As the Yanks continued their exhibition season through the South, they began to hit, just as Gehrig had predicted. However, they continued to lose through "one of the most disastrous spring training campaigns," scoring just six wins in twenty games, and finished 3–10 against major league teams. They dropped their last exhibition game at Brooklyn, 7–2, and they headed to Philadelphia to begin the season. "They're playing possum," warned a National League scout. "They will suddenly come to life and have the last laugh on everyone."

Twenty-five thousand fans braved the frigid elements at Shibe Park. They came prepared with blankets, layers of clothing, and turned-up coat collars. The women in attendance wore their best sable coats. The temperature was thirty-seven at 8:00 a.m. By game time it had warmed up to forty-five. Richard Vidmer of the *New York Times* believed that the game needed to be postponed.

Before taking the field for pregame warmups, Miller Huggins gathered his troops and gave them a pep talk: "You are starting another season, and I want to see you start it well. Most of the fellows on this club have been in baseball long enough to know what it's all about, and know that a good start is worth having. You should win the pennant again, but not as easily as you did last year, not because you are not strong as you were last year but because the law of averages doesn't give you two seasons in a row like that."

Philadelphia outfielder Al Simmons was ready with a headset plastered to his ear, plus a scorecard and pencil in hand as he lay in his hospital bed. He

Opening day, 1928. Left to right: Lou Gehrig, Tris Speaker, Ty Cobb, Babe Ruth (National Baseball Hall of Fame, Cooperstown, New York).

looked pale but showed no effects of a tonsil bobbing. Like Lazzeri, he would miss the start of the season. While tuned into the game's broadcast, he smiled when hearing his roommate during a pregame interview. "I wonder if Al Simmons is listening down at the hospital," said Ty Cobb. "I hope he is, and I want to let him know his old buddies at Shibe Park miss him out here today."

"We're going to knock the A's off again," Ruth told the radio announcer.

"Best wait until the game is over, Babe," Simmons said.

"Whiff him!" shouted Simmons as Ruth stepped in for his first at bat of the season. He then heard the crack of the bat, then a pause.... "Max [Bishop, second baseman of the A's] gathered it up and threw to Joe Hauser [first baseman]."

New York scored two runs in the second when Grove walked Meusel, Durocher, and Collins. With two outs, the bases loaded, Pennock singled to score two. In the next inning, Ruth walked, Gehrig and Meusel singled to score one. Durocher followed by clearing the bases with a double that made Simmons groan. The spirits of the A's ill outfielder turned when his teammates rallied to cut the score to 5–3. "Here we go, and on to first place," he said. The Yankees scored two more in the seventh inning on RBIs by Gehrig and Meusel, and they added one more in the next inning for an impressive 8–3 win. "They're all right," said a relieved Miller Huggins with a smile. "I knew they would be." He added, "This game shows me that there isn't anything wrong with this ball club. The men composing it are the same who won the pennant and World championship last year. We are just as good as they were a year ago."

In the season's second game, with the temperature reaching the sixties, Gehrig smacked his first home run of the season. The ball cleared the right centerfield wall, then sailed over Twentieth Street and into a second story opened window. "If some old Philadelphia furniture hadn't interrupted its flight it probably would have gone onto 120th street." Later in the inning, Meusel and Dugan singled, and Durocher hit a triple off the leftfield wall to score both runners. Combs hit a long line drive over Speaker. As the Yankees centerfielder rounded the bases, the veteran outfielder looked all of his forty years as he chased the ball. Combs beat the throw to the plate for an inside-the-park homer to cap a five-run second inning. Later, Meusel hit a two run blast over the right field wall for a 7–0 lead. The A's rallied and cut the lead to 8–7 before Hoyt was called to the rescue to save the game.

For the first time in ten years, Boston was excited about their Red Sox. "Boston extends you hearty greetings on your season and the sincere wish that your efforts will be rewarded in a most successful season," the mayor of Boston said in a telegram he sent to Bill Carrigan following their opening day win at

15. Break Up the Yankees—1928

Washington. The Red Sox would get off to a surprisingly good start before reality set in, and Boston would finish last for the sixth time during the 1920s.

At Boston, the Yanks built an early 7–0 lead en route to their third consecutive win. Gehrig hit his second home run and Pipgras allowed just five hits. New York won the next game, 10–7, with Durocher making his second consecutive two-hit game. But the biggest news of the game was Ruth's first home run of the season.

Light-hitting Leo Duroher was tabbed a "hitless wonder" during spring training. Ruth said he tried to help the rookie became a better hitter when suggesting he would hit .400 by becoming a switch hitter. By doing that he could bat "two-hundred right-handed and two-hundred left." All kidding aside, Huggins announced that he intended on making Durocher a switch batter, but the way he was going he decided to let him continue to bat just right-handed since he was now 6-for-16 through the season's first four games.

The Yankee Stadium upper deck now extended completely down the third baseline with 12,000 additional seats expanding its capacity to 70,000. Fifty-five thousand came to Yankee Stadium to watch the home opener against the Athletics, including Johnny Sylvester.

Johnny Sylvester was invited to the Yankees' home opener in 1927, however, his mother, fearful of his temporary illness and the chilly weather, announced that Johnny would be unable to attend, but would be "pulling for" Ruth to homer. Contacted by a writer from the *New York Times* following the game, Johnny told him, "He did fine," in reference to Ruth's 1927 opening day performance.

Now, 1½ years after the two had met for the first time, Johnny and Babe were together again. The two posed for the photographers. One of the photos from that day would be framed and placed on the wall in the Sylvester residence.

As "The Star-Spangled Banner" was played, the World Series Championship banner was hoisted along with the American flag. Then the attention turned to the Yankees players while they received their 1927 World Champions diamond rings.

Lefty Grove and George Pipgras were locked in a pitcher's duel for four innings. In the top of the fifth, Bishop and Cobb singled, and Speaker followed with a grounder through the middle. Durocher made a dive for the ball, but missed. As the ball rolled into shallow centerfield, Durocher got up, took a few steps toward the outfield, and accidentally brushed Cobb as he rounded second base. Bishop easily scored, but Cobb, delayed temporarily when bumping into the New York second baseman, was thrown out at third base by Combs, much to the delight of the hometown crowd, to end the inning. As

Durocher headed back to the Yankees dugout on the third base side, he encountered Cobb along the way. "You get in my way again, you fresh busher, and I will step on your face," Cobb warned him.

Durocher, amazed to be on the same field as Ty Cobb, made no reply. When Ruth returned to the dugout after the inning, he asked what Cobb had said. When the rookie told him, Ruth replied, "Well, kid, the next time he comes to bat, call him a penny-pincher." The green rookie was clueless to the meaning of penny-pincher, but judging by the laughter among his teammates, he had a feeling it was uncomplimentary. He was also unaware of how much Cobb resented that name, and how it made him fighting mad.

The next time Cobb came to the plate Durocher shouted the insult and the A's outfielder began to shout and point while pacing toward the second baseman. The home plate umpire intervened by holding Cobb as he instructed him to return to the batter's box.

In the bottom of the seventh, Durocher tripled and eventually came around to score to tie the game. In the ninth, Cobb tripled and scored on Speaker's fly out to give the A's a 2–1 lead, which held up for a win. Following the final out, Durocher saw Cobb sprinting toward the New York dugout. He immediately hurried to the safety of the Yankees' clubhouse. Ruth put an arm around Cobb and said, "Now what are you going to do? You don't want to hit the kid, do you?" Cobb, deciding that Ruth was right, let it go.

Lazzeri was back in the lineup the next day and Durocher went to the bench. The Yanks lost 10–0, with Rube Walberg hurling the shutout for the A's. The season before, it had taken over one hundred games before New York was shut out by Lefty Grove. In 1928, it took just eight games.

"I am not conceding the pennant to the Yankees this year any more than I did a year ago when I was the last manager in the league to proclaim my club out of the race," said Bucky Harris. "I felt no matter how far the Yankees were ahead, we always had a chance."

Harris selected Hod Lisenbee (7–2 versus the Yanks in 1927) to pitch the first game of the series. The pitcher who had served Ruth's fifty-eighth home run in 1927 gave way to two by Ruth in a 4–0 Yankees win. New York won 12–4 in the second game of the series with every Yankees starter driving in a run.

Ruth began the month of May by blasting a 430-foot home run to centerfield at Washington. "It was a Ruthian shot of the first order." Only one other time had a ball been hit to that spot—by Ruth, during the previous season.

"Hey, cousin, are you going to pitch today?" Ruth asked Tommy Thomas of the White Sox, who was 0–7 lifetime versus the Yankees. The pitcher nodded to assure Ruth that he would be starting. "Well, you can't stop a guy from trying," said Ruth. Thomas tried but gave way to six earned runs before departing after the third inning. Ruth, going four for four, homered again. Dugan went three for three and hit a grand slam in a 10–4 win to make Pennock 5–0 on the season. Thirty thousand came out for the next game and saw Pipgras strike out eight in a 7–0 win. Fifty-five thousand were on hand for the third game of the series, which New York won, 4–2. Coveleski got the start and earned his first win in two years. And New York won again the following day with Gehrig smacking his third homer of the season. Shealy, striking out seven in his major league debut the week before, became 3–0 with a win in the series' fourth game.

The Indians, now under the direction of rookie manager Roger Peckinpaugh, responded to their new boss by winning 12 of their first 16 games. After George Uhle hurled a four-hit shutout to snap New York's ten-game winning streak, the Tribe led 2–0 the next game until Ruth batted against Hudlin, a curveball specialist, who accidentally hung one that Ruth swatted halfway up the leftfield bleachers for a three-run homer. Pipgras did the rest for his fifth straight win of the season.

The Yankees kept their winning ways alive when Gehrig hit a grand slam against Cleveland. Bob Meusel, leading the Yanks with a .376 average, doubled in the winning run with his third hit of the day, and Shealy got another win. The next day, the rookie hurler went the last four innings to earn the win. "A game young man," Huggins said about Shealy, and added that he made up for less ability with guts and smarts. "You can tell by looking at him."

Shealy was filling in as the Yankees rescue man for the injured Wilcy Moore (out with a sore arm). "I don't know what to do with all of this spare time," said Moore. "I haven't laid off this long since I broke my wrist in 1926." Three years before, he fixed an arm injury by pitching until the soreness was gone. He felt he could do the same now, but claimed he needed warmer weather.

Two more wins followed to up the Yankees' record to 20–5. In win number twenty, Koenig and Lazzeri handled six chances apiece without committing an error and turned two double plays to leave Tigers manager George Moriarty feeling frustrated. "How do you beat a team that scores seven runs a day and cuts off seven runs on the other side?"

With Jude Landis in the crowd, the Yankees went on to complete the sweep over Detroit. Ruth tripled and blasted two home runs to give him eleven for the season and five in his last seven games. Koenig, who hit an inside-the-park home run, extended his hitting streak to eleven, Gehrig made three hits, and Grabowski, accepting any playing time he could get, went 3 for 3 to prove no matter who Huggins used, the Yankees won.

Durocher returned to the starting lineup in Boston when Koenig suffered a lumbago attack. Huggins instructed him to bat left-handed for the first time against right-handed pitchers. He went 1 for 8 while batting from the left side in a double-header. Batting lefty the next day, Durocher went 3-for-6 to boost his season average to .378.

New York traveled to Philadelphia for a six-game series. Forty-five thousand fans packed Shibe Park (a ballpark with a capacity of thirty-three thousand) for a Memorial Day double-header. The aisles were full and there were fans were atop the scoreboard. "So thick were the fans in leftfield, the stands looked like they were triple decked."

With the score 6–5 in the top of the ninth, Durocher, batting left-handed, singled, Ruth was hit by a pitch, Gehrig hit into a fielder's choice, and Meusel walked to load the bases. Lazzeri followed with a triple, his third hit of the game, to clear the bases for a 9–5 lead.

In the bottom of the ninth, Moore, back from his injury, allowed a single and a walk, and then uncorked a wild pitch. He proceeded to strike out a batter, but when he threw two balls to the next batter, he noticed Hoyt trotting from the bullpen to the pitcher's mound. Moore was shocked. Wasn't he the Yankees' closer? He refused to yield. Huggins responded by being adamant and persistent until the pitcher reluctantly obeyed.

Philadelphia did score two but fell two runs shy. The Yanks won again, 9–7. The Athletics took the nightcap, 5–2, on three RBI by Speaker and two by Cochrane. It was Pipgras's first loss of the season.

"I'm tired," Huggins said as he sat at a table at the Root Garden restaurant in the Adelphia Hotel. "Two tough games like that take a lot out of me. We had some good pitching out there from Pennock and Hoyt. That Pennock is a smart one. He didn't pitch an overhand curve all afternoon. Pitching sidearm had made it easier for him because he's had a sore arm for more than a week."

Huggins paused to place his order for a fruit cocktail, a boiled mutton chop, a baked potato, a salad, Camembert cheese, and coffee.

"What pleased me today was Gehrig's home run. We looked like a weak hitting club in that first game until the seventh inning ... then Combs singles, Ruth walks, and Gehrig hits the ball into the leftfield stands, winning the ball game ... that's good hitting ... one smack and the other fellow is licked ... that's the kind of ball club this is ... never can tell when one on the team is going to get one smack and win the game."

Before another more than capacity crowd at Shibe Park, the Yankees took both ends of a double-header, with Gerhig socking his eighth homer; a three-run blast to leftfield to break a 1–1 tie. In the nightcap, they evened the score with Walberg for shutting them out the month before. When the A's left-

15. Break Up the Yankees—1928

hander departed in the third inning, he was trailing 7–0. Ruth homered in the first and Dugan hit two out in a 4-for-4 day to lift his average to .344. Later in the game, Ruth hit another one, his sixteenth of the season, in a 9–2 win.

In the fifth game of the series, Coveleski pitched against Quinn for "about eighty years of spit balling." Coveleski pitched the win for his fourth straight win. New York beat Lefty Grove for the second time in the series to take five of the six games. "It looks like they have knocked the armchair out from under me again," Mack said.

"Break up the Yankees," cried fans from other cities around the American League, claiming the Yankees to be too good. "Get other American League clubs to go out and buy high-class players like we have done," responded Ed Barrow. "We couldn't win pennants until we spent money in the open market for championship material. We had to take chances and, it must be remembered, that we did not get a single player from a rival club for nothing."

New York was now 31–7 and eight games ahead of the second-place A's. "The Athletics are so far behind that it will cost them ten cents to send the champions a postcard." The Yankees' team batting average was .315. They had scored forty more runs than the next best team. Seven of their eight starters were batting over .300: Ruth was hitting .366, Durocher .356, Gehrig .348, Meusel .325, Dugan .347, Lazzeri .333, and Koenig .330. Pipgras was 8–1, Pennock 7–1, and Hoyt 4–1. "I'd rather wait until we make a swing around the west before I commit myself," Huggins replied when asked about winning the pennant. "A road trip is the best test for a team. I'll know more about my pitchers then."

The swing through the west began with five consecutive wins to increase the Yanks' season record to 39–8. Gehrig slugged three home runs, Ruth hit two, and Pipgras won his tenth game. "I'll be right when the warm weather comes around," Pipgras quipped to a writer.

The Yankees obtained George Pipgras from Frazee's Red Sox in January of 1923 in exchange for a backup catcher, who lasted for one full season in Boston. Four weeks later, the Yankees received Herb Pennock in another trade with Boston. "The rape of the Red Sox now was complete!" In July of that year, Harry Frazee sold the Red Sox.

Pipgras was assigned as the Yankees' batting practice pitcher in 1923 and 1924 to work on his control. "I found the way to acquire control is to pitch in games. Pitching batting practice never helped my control." During the 1925 spring training session at St. Petersburg, he developed a sore arm. To cure the injury, he wrapped scalding hot towels around his lame arm. The treatment worked, but the blistering heat had permanently scarred his right shoulder.

The Yankees farmed Pipgras to Atlanta in 1925 and to St. Paul in 1926.

He began the 1927 season on the Yankees roster, but rarely played. "Pipgras needs a lot of work," Huggins told the sportswriters. On June 29, Huggins gave him his first starting assignment, and Pipgras responded by allowing just three hits in a win over the Red Sox. With a spot in the rotation for the rest of the season, he won ten games and pitched a win in the 1927 World Series.

A Sunday crowd of over forty thousand packed Comiskey Park to see Babe Ruth, Lou Gehrig, and the awesome Yankees attack. They saw Ruth smash a drive to right centerfield that "traveled at unbelievable speed." A fan in the bleachers reached out but couldn't hold the hot smash, which fell back onto the field. "One of the hardest hit balls of his career," declared Harrison. In the top of the ninth, Ruth hit one into the upper deck in leftfield. Later in the series, Ruth hit another home run, his twenty-third. That same day, Gehrig hit two homers and two triples. He also pounded one to right field which, like Ruth's smash, a fan in the bleachers was unable to hold. The ball fell onto the field, only this time the umpires called it a double. "Your correspondent was certain that the ball had gone into the stand," wrote Harrison.

The St. Louis Browns were two games above five hundred and their fans were behind them. St. Louis owner Phil Ball promised a housecleaning during the 1927 season, and he did not lie. Just five players remained from the previous season. Gone were all-time Browns greats George Sisler and Ken Williams.

A Browns record home crowd of thirty thousand appeared for the last game of the series after the Browns doubled their 1927 total wins against New York by taking two of the first three games. The large turnout showed progress for the Browns. They had fewer than three thousand on opening day, and fewer than three hundred for another home game. Ruth and Gerhig entertained the fans by homering, and Hoyt won his ninth game. New York was now 43–12 and 8½ up on the second-place Athletics.

A Wednesday crowd of thirty-five thousand watched the Yankees take a 5–2 lead in a five-run third inning. Pat Collins got things going with a home run, Gehrig scored two with an RBI hit and Pascual scored one with a hit, and another run scored when Cobb slipped in the outfield. The A's, however, rallied for a 10–5 win. Cobb redeemed himself with a double in a four-run ninth inning, one of three hits for him on the day to lift his batting average to .326.

In the nightcap, Grabowski whacked a three-run homer in the seventh to break a 1–1 tie, and one inning later he nailed a two-run double in a 9–3 win. Pipgras allowed just four hits and struck out eight in winning his twelfth of the season.

Hank Johnson was built like a prize fighter: with broad shoulders, big hands, a thick neck, and muscular arms. He stood at 5'11" and weighed 175. He was from Bradenton, Florida, where his older brother, Gilbert, a former

15. Break Up the Yankees—1928

hurler at the University of Florida, tutored him. He wanted to be an outfielder until his brother taught him how to throw a curve. "But I played some outfield in Milwaukee last year and hit .333." Against the Athletics, he matched Grove for five innings in a scoreless duel. Lazzeri finally broke the ice with his sixth home run of the year. New York added another one in the sixth, and in the seventh, Koenig lashed a two-run double for a 4–0 lead. Johnson sent the A's down in order in the ninth to complete his shutout.

Following two losses to Boston, Pipgras hurled a three-hit shutout to increase his record to 13–2. He allowed just three hits and retired seventeen in a row at one point. New York, 46–15, headed to Philadelphia for a three game series. During batting practice, Ruth hit one over the right field wall.

BENGOUGH: "Quite a smack, Babe."
RUTH: "It's all timing."
BENGOUGH: "Timing my eye. I can time 'em but I can't hit them over the infield."
COMBS: "This is a pretty good park to hit in."
GEHRIG: "It is for me."
RUTH: "The Giants' park was the best one to hit in."
COLLINS: "What park?"
RUTH: "The Polo Grounds. I'd make one hundred homers if I played there. And our club would make two hundred."
COMBS: "We had that many last season."
COLLINS: "What are we making this year?"
RUTH: "We must be. I got twenty-eight. Lou has got sixteen. How many do you have, Bob?"
MEUSEL: "Four."
Lazzeri drills one over the wall.
RUTH: "Look at Tony hit one."
  Ruth turns to the A's dugout.
RUTH: "Hey! How are you going to beat the Yankees?!"
  Grabowski hits one over the leftfield wall.
PASCUAL: "That's about twenty home runs we made today."
GAZELLA: "Yeh! But they don't count until after 3:30."
RUTH: "Well, let's get a few after 3:30."

There were no New York homers after 3:30, although the Yankees did beat Lefty Grove and the A's, 7–4. Once again, Huggins matched Johnson with Grove, and the Yankees rookie allowed just five hits and struck out six for his fourth win before eighteen thousand unhappy fans who booed the hometown team.

The Yankees won again the next day to make it nine wins in ten games against the A's in 1928 and increase their league to twelve games. Ruth hit home runs number twenty-nine and thirty to remain ahead of his 1927 pace.

His second homer sailed high over the right field wall, flew across Twentieth Street and landed atop a tin roof. "It was an authentic wallop."

The newly built grandstand in leftfield was used for the first time when the A's came to Yankee Stadium for a double-header before sixty thousand fans. Huggins sent Johnson to the mound. This time the A's were ready and made three runs in the first inning. In the bottom of the third, Combs walked and Koenig doubled to left center. Ruth followed with a two-run single and Gehrig gave New York a 4–3 lead when he hit one into the right centerfield bleachers, his seventeenth in 1928. In the sixth, with the Yanks ahead 6–5, Koenig singled, Ruth walked, and Gehrig hit one that landed on the track in centerfield. Koenig easily scored, although the A's had a play on Ruth. Cochrane was in position for the relay throw, but Ruth shoved him out of the way. The ball rolled all the way to the backstop to allow Gehrig to round the bases and score. The Athletics screamed in protest about Ruth, but to deaf ears. New York won 12–6, and Koenig made four hits in the game to lift his average to .410 since returning to the lineup following his brief illness.

In the nightcap, Lazzeri went 3-for-4 with two home runs in another Yankees win. Lazerri, with seven hits on the day, increased his batting average to .362. New York was now 52–16 and 13½ ahead of Philadelphia. "It's all over but the shouting, and there isn't any shouting to be done."

16

Collapse—1928

> "Flowers bloom and their fragrance fills the air, rivers still run downhill and winter follows fall. But alas! No longer are the Yanks in a class by themselves."
> —Richard Vidmer of the *New York Times*

The Yankees received a scare at Washington. After Ruth doubled in the top of the eighth, Gehrig followed with a long fly out. Ruth tagged on the play, made a hard slide into third base, and immediately clutched his shoulder. "I thought for sure he was hurt badly on that play," Huggins said after the game, "but it's just a bit bruised." It turned out to be more than just that. Ruth's back was also sore from swinging too hard. Nonetheless, Ruth ignored the pain and continued to play.

Koenig continued to hit by going 4-for-6 to lift his season average to .357. Gehrig also made four hits to boost his average to .368, and Lazzeri singled in the winning run in a Yankees 7–6 win at Washington to make their record 53–17. They were still 13 games ahead of Philadelphia with the season approaching its halfway point.

A lieutenant of the Watertown Police Department was riding with the town's chief of police when he pointed to a house in their village at Forty-five Quincy Street. "Babe Ruth's wife lives over there," he said.

"We always thought that 'Mrs. Kinder' had been divorced from Babe Ruth, and that was the general feeling around the neighborhood," said A.W. Sweet, who lived with his wife and two daughters in the house directly across from the Kinders. "Everyone said the same thing and that was pretty much taken for granted." The neighbors said that the Kinders were secluded. They described Helen as quiet, quite attractive, and "a young matron with no social aspirations." "Only the mother and father of the doctor would visit them, and not very often," said Sweet. Sometimes the doctor's brother, who lived within a block of the Kinders, would stop by, but never the Babe. The Sweets heard rumors of Ruth visiting often, but they claimed to have never seen him. "They frequently went out at night by themselves, and always came home very late."

The Kinders attracted attention by owning a large new sedan of an expensive make in a neighborhood where luxury automobiles never appeared. The neighbors were more baffled when Helen took taxis instead of the family's sedan. She often taxied to a shop at Watertown Square to buy magazines. She enjoyed reading, but dreaded reading about people burning to death. "That would be a terrible way to die," she would say. According to the shopkeeper, Helen would spend 50 cents when most spent 15 to 20 cents per sale.

The neighbors said the Kinders owned a Doberman pinscher police dog (different from the bull terrier that Ruth had given his daughter in 1925) that was valued at $400, but also said the dog wasn't there for very long. "I remember that dog," said Ruth Olson, who was closest to Helen among the neighbors. "Walter [her brother] would walk him." Olson said there were no photos of Ruth hanging in the Kinders' home, but she knew that Helen was Ruth's wife when she saw a newspaper photo of Helen and Dorothy with Ruth. "I was the only person in the neighborhood who knew Helen was not Doctor Kinder's wife." Feeling that it was nobody's business, she never said a word.

Dorothy was known by the neighbors as "Dorothy Kinder." They described her as a sweet-faced little girl with sparkling eyes and a ready smile. They also recalled the only time she was around was during the summers and holidays. Following the summer when the Kinders relocated to Watertown, Dorothy was sent to boarding school at the Academy of the Assumption in Wellesley Hills, Massachusetts. Helen assured her that the time would go by quickly, and that she would visit, but she never did. Babe also never came, leaving his daughter feeling the way he had felt during his years at St. Mary's—like an unloved child.

Dorothy was unaware of the circumstances of her birth, and wouldn't know until 1980, when the person she had known as her "aunt" spoke on her deathbed. While visiting California in 1920, Ruth had an affair with a young lady named Juanita Jennings. Before leaving he told her to call him whenever she was in New York. A few months later, she called to tell him that she was pregnant with his child. Ruth agreed to pay and arrange for everything. Jennings came to New York, gave birth to Dorothy, and Ruth handled the rest, even made it so the birth was completely confidential. Newspaper writers tried but nobody ever found a single record, which led to the assumtion that Dorothy was adopted.

Ruth had hired a heavyset black woman in her early thirties named Fanny Bailey to take care of his baby. Bailey once told Dorothy she was so small at birth, she could hold her in the palm of her hand. Bailey also said when she

16. Collapse—1928

took her for a walk she would cover the baby carriage with a veil so nobody saw a scrawny and frail-looking baby, perhaps the reason why the Ruths kept Dorothy hidden for over a year after her birth.

Dorothy would later recall her happiest times of her childhood were with Fanny Bailey. She cherished the memories of sitting in a high chair before a wood-burning stove and singing along with her. She also enjoyed helping her prepare the family meals by washing the vegetables.

When the first semester ended at her new school, Dorothy was excited to go home to Watertown to be with Fanny Bailey. She was bitterly disappointed to learn that she was no longer employed by Helen.

Claire Hodgson was frustrated. "No woman likes to hide her love, but this woman had no choice." She loved Babe Ruth. He loved her. Her home was his, yet there were no photos of the two of them together, or of Ruth, for fear someone might become suspicious. She never pressured him, but when they did speak about the future it always came down to, "I'm a Catholic, I'm married, and I have a kid. We can't get divorced," and Claire had no choice but to settle for friendship with the man she loved.

On July 5, Urban Shocker officially retired from baseball. "He didn't have much besides his spitter in the last few years, but he was smarter than everyone else and that much harder to beat," said Browns manager Dan Howley. Shocker revealed his health issues. "I've had a bum heart for some time," he told the *New York Journal-American*. "You've seen me sitting up late in my Pullman berth. I couldn't lie down. Choked when I did." When asked if he was aware of the pitcher's heart condition, Huggins replied, "Oh, sure."

Shocker felt healthy enough to rejoin the Yankees in May, and even hurled for two innings in one game before deciding he needed more time to recover. He went to his home in St. Louis, and then opted for a different environment to regain his health. "I'm going to Denver to fight this thing," he said. Shocker was also going there for another reason. Against his doctor's orders, he was going to hurl in a semi-pro tournament. "Nothing mattered if you put a baseball into his hands," said his wife, who had pleaded with her husband not to pitch in the tournament. "His love for the game was more powerful than twenty physicians." Although extremely weak, he pitched one game, was shelled, and went directly from the game to a hospital bed, suffering from pneumonia.

The Yankees were on the field taking batting practice before meeting the Browns.

RUTH: "Swell bunting, Stanley [Coveleski]."
KOENIG: "Who bunts on this team?"
RUTH: "I can bunt."

GRABOWSKI: "I remember one day in Chicago when you bunted. I was catching for the White Sox that day."
BENGOUGH: "You mean the time Hug signaled for a bunt and Babe hit?"
GRABOWSKI: "Yeh."
RUTH: "I nearly knocked [Earl] Sheely [first baseman of the White Sox] down with that one."
BENGOUGH: "Did Hug rave, though?"
RUTH: "Hello, Cuzz. You going to pitch?"
HAL WILTSE [Browns pitcher]: "Yep."
PASCUAL: "Yah! Ol' cousin Wiltse!"
RUTH: "I'm a son of a gun if he ain't my cousin. Every time he pitches I get a home run; sometimes two."

Ruth didn't homer, but Meusel hit his sixth of the season in another Yankees win.

At Yankee Stadium the Yankees won the next one in classic Ruthian fashion. They were trailing, 8–6, with two outs and nobody on base in the bottom of the ninth, when Ruth came to the plate with first base unoccupied. Nonetheless, the White Sox elected to pitch to him. Ruth got one down the middle of the plate to his liking. He swung and "whack!" a deep fly ball to right field that left little doubt in anybody's mind that Ruth had just won the game. The crowd stormed the field and mobbed Ruth as he rounded the bases. Ruth, knowing he had to touch home plate to officially let his run count, knocked over customers in an attempt to barge his way to the plate. After touching home, he shoved his way to the dugout and into the hallway leading to the clubhouse.

A very special visitor was in attendance the next day. Mrs. Mary (Mamie) Moberly of Baltimore, Babe's one and only sibling, called "a charming little lady," was making her first appearance at Yankee Stadium. Wanting to do something special for his sister, Ruth asked his teammates what he should do. "Give her a wristwatch," someone suggested.

"Great!" Ruth said.

"Give her a homer," was another suggestion.

"Give her two homers," someone else said.

"Now you're talking, kid," said Ruth.

The watch was beautifully jeweled, fashioned to look like a baseball, and with Ruth's signature therein. Ruth presented to her as she sat in a first row field box by the visitors' dugout. True to his word, Ruth drove two into the seats to give him five in as many days. Through eighty-eight games he had thirty-eight home runs to stay ahead of his 1927 pace.

Pipgras hurled a four-hit shutout the next day for his seventeenth win with Ruth hitting another home run. In the last game of the series, the Yankees

16. Collapse—1928

were ahead 3–0 and looked promising for an eighth consecutive win until the White Sox rallied against Johnson and Moore to take a 6–4 win. New York, now 66–24, were 10½ ahead and about to hit the road for twenty-one games. All seemed fine, although some believed there was cause for concern. The pitching staff was beginning to show signs of fatigue. Hoyt said he was feeling pain in his right shoulder. "It started three weeks ago and spread through the arm and into the hand, so that one day last week the first two fingers were quite numb. The pain is not severe but it is persistent." Ruth's shoulder was still hurting, and so was Lazzeri's, to the point where he stayed out of the lineup. Dugan's back was bothering him, Pennock and Pipgras were tired, Johnson was walking too many batters, Shealy needed more time to develop, and Moore, so brilliant in 1927, was ineffective this season. "If you ask me, I think Moore is thinking too much about his arm," said Huggins. "If he can forget about it, I think you will see a great improvement in him."

"Once upon a time there was a Yankee pitcher who lasted the full nine innings." At Detroit the Yankees' pitchers gave up twenty-six runs in three losses. In Cleveland, the staff yielded two dozen in a 24–6 loss. It took the New York batters twelve runs to salvage the last game of the series, 12–9.

The Yankees, with a season record of 70–31 when July ended, were now feeling the pressure. Their league lead was now down to 5½ games. The Athletics were red-hot, and climbed back into contention by going 25–6 since being swept by the Yankees on July 1 to fall 13½ games behind.

Mack made changes to add fire to his lineup. Both Speaker and Cobb went to the bench; Speaker was not hitting and Cobb wasn't covering ground. In their place Mack inserted Mule Haas and Bing Miller. At first base the manager made an interesting move by assigning the position to a pitcher, Ossie Orwoll.

The A's closed out July by outscoring the Browns 34–11 in their four-game sweep in St. Louis, and Browns manager Dan Howley offered no excuses. "I gave them the best I had in the way of pitching, and they beat the tar out of it." The Athletics began August by winning two games to trim the Yankees' lead to a too-close-for-comfort 4½ games. The Yanks won their first game of the new month in St. Louis with Ruth hitting his forty-second home run. Meusel also hit one, and Johnson went 5-for-5 while hurling the victory, a sign that he might play a key role in New York's drive to the pennant. Ruth went hitless the next day as New York lost in fifteen innings, and a day later they were shut out by Sam Gray and the Browns, 8–0, to extend their scoreless streak to twenty-one consecutive innings. Nobody on the struggling Yankees was struggling more than Koenig. Just one for 16 at the plate, he had made two errors in the shutout loss at St. Louis. He also made two miscues at

Chicago to cost the Yankees another game, and allowed the A's to reduce the lead to 3½ games.

The Yankees' problems were mounting: Lazzeri was injured, Dugan appeared to be wilting in the summer heat, Robertson wasn't hitting as he had earlier in the season, Moore was still ineffective, and the left side of the infield was in disarray. Hoyt was still hurting, Shealy was proving unreliable, Coveleski had a dead arm, and Pipgras had lost fourteen pounds during the season. To aid the worn-out pitching staff, Huggins relied on his connections with the St. Paul Saints and acquired left-hander Fred Heimach. Formerly with the A's and Red Sox, he had won thirty-four games in less than two seasons for the Saints.

The Yankees traveled to Albany for an exhibition game that drew twelve thousand. Following the game, they caught a 1:45 a.m. train for Boston. As the team slept during the trip, Combs dreamed about a 6–1 New York victory over the Red Sox. The next morning he told Heimach about his dream.

"Boy, is he fast," a surprised Huggins said in the dugout after watching his new hurler work the first inning. The newcomer got off to a slow start by allowing two walks and a hit for one run. After that, he retired the next fifteen in a row. He allowed just three more hits, no more walks, and struck out eight in a Yankees 7–1 win.

Perhaps inspired by Heimach's performance, Pipgras struck out six and won his nineteenth game. Gehrig got three of the team's six hits in the 5–2 win, including his twentieth home run, "a walloping blow" over the right field wall to score three runs. The Yankees first baseman did it again the following day by drilling one to left center that hit the top of the wall, then bounced up and through two steel poles that supported a sign, for a three-run homer and another 5–2 Yankees win.

The Yankees returned home to begin a fourteen-game home stand while still holding a 4½ game lead. Against the Red Sox, Pennock hurled a three-hit shutout in an 8–0 win for New York's fifth win in a row. Koenig seemed to find his stroke again by going 4-for-4 with a pair of doubles. "The burden is on the A's," insisted Huggins. "We went bad for a while, but we finally came back with a five-game winning streak." When asked about Philadelphia, Huggins answered, "They have showed that they are a great club. They may do it, and if they do they will deserve the pennant. At the present, they are playing the best ball in the major leagues."

Four weeks away was a four-game series at Yankee Stadium between the two American League frontrunners. The series would begin with a doubleheader on Sunday, September 9. The series would also be the season's final series between the two teams.

16. Collapse—1928

New York lost two in a row to Chicago, but lost no ground to the Athletics. Pipgras lasted just two innings in one of the defeats. Ruth pounded a homer in each game to give him forty-five for the season. One of the blasts, said to be the farthest ever hit at Yankee Stadium, almost left the confines of the stadium. "The clients applauded furiously." The Yanks managed to bounced back to take the last game of the series.

Against Cleveland, the Yanks built a 7–0 lead. Through six innings, Pipgras allowed just two base runners. In the seventh he walked two, gave up two hits, and hit a batter. Huggins called on Moore, but the struggling relief specialist was touched for an RBI double. An infield out scored another run to cut the lead to 7–5. In the eighth, Moore's troubles continued with a leadoff hit that persuaded Huggins to call on Hoyt, who got out of the inning and pitched through the ninth to give Pipgras his twentieth win.

Hoyt pitched his sixteenth win of the season three days later. Pennock was next in the rotation, but there was a problem: the left-hander was injured. "He may be out for a few days or several weeks," Huggins said while shaking his head pessimistically. When asked about the extent of the injury, Huggins replied, "The most I can say is we aren't satisfied with his condition."

"Isn't this a swell break?" Pennock asked sarcastically as he ruefully looked at his pitching arm baking under a heat lamp. "A fine time for the old soup bone to turn sour just when I ought to be giving the boys a hand to keep us in front, but I think the other pitchers can carry the team without me."

"When did your arm go lame?" asked a reporter.

"I don't know exactly when it happened or why. I guess it's just one of those things. It came so suddenly. That's why I think it is neuritis."

Another setback followed a week later when Lazzeri's shoulder injury worsened. "I don't expect Lazzeri to play regularly for the rest of the season," Huggins announced. He mentioned that he could hardly throw. "I think he tore a muscle in his shoulder. It is not serious, but might be if he keeps playing. Rest is the only cure. He will be in uniform everyday and available to pinch-hit."

Huggins had a replacement for Lazzeri in the smooth-fielding Durocher, but what about for Pennock? With no suitable substitute on his staff, the manager looked elsewhere and found someone in Washington left-hander Tom Zachery, the man best known for serving up Ruth's sixtieth home run the season before. "He's a smart, clever southpaw who has plenty of experience and is in excellent condition right now," said Huggins. "I expect him to deliver for the Yanks."

"You'll be working today, Zach," Huggins told his new pitcher upon his arrival, and came through. His sharp curve, his cunning slow ball, and his craftiness in mixing his pitches "left the Detroit batters swinging in empty air." With the game tied 3–3 in the bottom of the eighth, Gehrig surprised the Tigers with a bunt for a hit, Ruth singled, and Meusel hit a fly ball to score Gehrig to make Zachery's Yankees debut a success in a 4–3 win.

The Yankees beat Detroit in the next game for a series sweep to finish their home stand at 9–6. Their league lead, now at four full games, was one less than when the home stand had begun.

At Washington, former Yankee "Sad Sam" Jones beat Waite Hoyt and his former mates, 3–1. For Hoyt it was just the fourth loss of the season. Ruth, still ahead of his home run record pace, hit number forty-seven. The surging A's won again to make it 45 wins in their last 57 games, and knocked another game off the Yankees' lead.

Inside Washington's Wardmen Park Hotel, James Harrison heard a knock at his door. Babe Ruth entered. He looked unhappy as he walked directly to the window and peeked at the pool below. "Going to jump?" Harrison asked.

"Nah," said Ruth. Ruth slumped into a chair and stretched his long legs. "I was figuring. If we win 18 of our last 28 games, we ought to win," he told the *New York Times* sportswriter.

"But what about your home run record?" Harrison asked. The record was secondary for Ruth. What he most desired was another pennant, and the opportunity to play in his ninth World Series.

Lazzeri was sent to see a specialist in Philadelphia to have his shoulder examined. While he was at the doctor's office, a phone call came through. It was A's third baseman Jimmie Dykes calling with a message for Lazzeri. When the doctor told the Yankees' second baseman that Dykes requested he "pull Lazzeri's arm out of its socket to make sure he would be out until October," that made Lazzeri angry. "All they need are Johnson, Hoyt, and Pipgras to sweep the series next week."

September began with a Yankees win over the Senators, 8–3. Meusel led the way by going 4 for 4 and Pipgras won his twenty-second. At Philadelphia, the Athletics won again, 14–2, over Boston to finish a successful 16–6 home stand. The game was the last of the season at Shibe Park until, hopefully, the World Series. In the win, Lefty Grove won his thirteenth consecutive game for his twenty-first win of the season. "There are two things Grove is doing this year," according to a Philadelphia sportswriter. "He is not trying to fan every batter, and he's giving fewer bases on balls. His control is better and he has learned many things about opposing batsmen." Last season at the approximate number of innings he had pitched this season, he had walked 61 and struck out 137. This season he had walked 49 and struck out 127. Recently against Cleveland, he fanned 5 in a row on 17 pitches. "Nobody told me a thing," said Grove, attributing his baseball success to nobody but himself. "I studied the batters like I did in the International League." Grove's current season record was 21–6. Five of the six losses were to the Yankees.

Before fifteen thousand at Washington, the Yankees made just four hits in a 2–0 loss. Coupled with another Athletics victory, New York's lead was now down to two games.

Gray skies held the crowd to 30,000 on Labor Day at Yankee Stadium. Gehrig homered to help the Yankees built an 8–0 lead after three innings. But the Red Sox rallied for five against Heimach in the fourth, and after the bullpen failed, Hoyt was once again called upon, and he threw $3\frac{1}{3}$ innings to preserve the win. However, the Yanks dropped the nightcap, 4–3. Fortunately for the Yankees, the A's dropped a pair in Washington.

The hottest ticket in sports was one for the Yankees-Athletics doubleheader, now just six days away. Five thousand customers waited through a rainstorm at the Yankees 42nd Street office for tickets. Then came an announcement that all reserved seats had been sold, and fans who were unable to get a ticket would have to wait until game day, when forty thousand grandstand seats and 20,000 bleacher tickets would go on sale. That consolation was unsatisfactory. With a potential riot about to erupt, a call was made to the 42nd Street police reserves, who rushed to the scene to quell the disturbance. For the rest of the afternoon, police remained on duty to turn away any prospective customers, or those who weren't. One customer approached the scene and casually walked toward the Yankees office until a policeman rudely grabbed him and yanked him back into the street. "Where do you think you're going?" the officer asked.

"Upstairs," replied the young man, who then continued on his way.

"Who do you think you are?" the policeman asked as he headed him off.

"Leo Durocher, the second baseman."

"Oh, yeah? Since when has Tony Lazzeri been benched?"

Inside the Yankees office, Yankees scout Paul Krichell spoke to reporters about the Athletics. "I am hoping that the A's play Hauser and Hale, because our boys have the Indian sign on those birds."

"Yes, and we have it on some other A's too," Durocher said as he walked into the meeting. "I'm getting my vocabulary spruced up so I can say things to the A's as soon as they come out of the clubhouse."

"They're liable to be groggy," Krichell said about the fact that they would play three consecutive double-headers before returning to Yankee Stadium.

On September 5, the Yankees split two with Washington to remain two games ahead of Philadelphia. Two days later, they would play another doubleheader for their twenty-third twin bill of the season. "Not since 1886, when the double-header habit was introduced into baseball, have I heard of so many double-up games," said Huggins.

The Yankees scored just one run in their next twin bill and dropped both games to Washington. At Boston, the Athletics won their double-header to finally pull even with the Yankees. In the first game, Lefty Grove won his fourteenth in a row, 1–0. He allowed just four hits and struck out eleven.

On September 8, one day before the Yankees-Athletics showdown, 25,000 fans at Fenway Park cheered for the Athletics, the sentimental favorite among most sports fans throughout the country. The writers would later admit they too were for Connie Mack and Ty Cobb to finish on top.

Down by two runs in the bottom of the eighth of the first game, Mack sent Orsoll in to pitch. In the top of the tenth, Orwoll singled to put the lead runner on third base. Max Bishop followed with a hit to send the go-ahead run across the plate. Orsoll then retired the Red Sox in order for the win.

The final score of the A's first-game win was posted on the Yankee Stadium scoreboard. For the first time in three seasons, the Yankees were not in the league lead in the month of September. Heading into the bottom of the seventh, the Yankees were trailing, 3–2, to the Senators. Attempting to fire up his team, Huggins grabbed a bat, stepped up to the bat rack, and began to pound away, making resounding thumps that were heard in all four corners of the stadium.

Combs began the

Rookie infielder Leo Durocher was brash, daring, couldn't keep his mouth shut, and sometimes needed Ruth to bail him out of trouble (National Baseball Hall of Fame, Cooperstown, New York).

16. Collapse—1928

inning with a bunt and beat the third baseman's throw to first base for a hit. After Koenig reached base on an error, Gehrig (switched to third in the batting order) smashed one on the ground that the second baseman was unable to handle. Combs rounded third and continued home to tie the game, 3–3.

The slumping Babe Ruth, who had not homered since August 30, came to the plate. He was now behind his 1927 pace, but as he had said, winning the pennant was more important.

Ruth clouted one to deep right field that cleared the barrier and fell into the bleachers for his forty-eighth home run. Hats and scorecards littered the field as Ruth rounded the bases. As he touched home plate, he tipped his cap to the fans. New York now led 6–3. Johnson hurled the last two innings without giving up a hit. The manager's message had been heard. "Bring on the A's!" the confident Yankees shouted in their clubhouse.

At Boston, the A's won the nightcap, 7–4, to end the day one-half game ahead of the Yankees. As Mack led his team away after winning the second contest, the Boston crowd stood and cheered.

Before the sun set in the Bronx that evening, three gentlemen arrived at Yankee Stadium with soapboxes, sandwiches, and bottles of soda pop. At 1:30 a.m., there were 60 to 70 people lined up. The count was up to 20,000 when the sun rose the next morning.

17

Completing the Dynasty—1928

> "I want to take this occasion to thank every member of the team for the fight they have put up in the interest of the New York fans and their club owner, Colonel Ruppert."
> —Miller Huggins

The fans came by automobile, special trains, foot, and even bicycles. A man rode his bike from Reading, Pennsylvania, to Yankee Stadium. "I got a reserve ticket, but I can't find a place to park this bike," the young man told Yankees club secretary Charlie McManus. "There is one problem I can't solve," said McManus.

The gates opened at 9:00 a.m.—two hours before scheduled. By noon, sixty thousand spectators were inside the stadium, while fans on the outside furiously attempted to get tickets. Some came with rain checks, but there were no tickets remaining.

Ruppert had built Yankee Stadium, even added to the capacity before this season, so every fan who wanted to see Babe Ruth and the Yankees would be admitted. Today's crowd was far beyond what he could have ever imagined.

There were repeated announcements at Grand Central Station and surrounding stations that the double-header was sold out. Every inch of the Yankee Stadium seating area was taken. Fans packed the aisles, flooded the runways, and stood 4 to 5 deep behind the back rows. An estimated 5,000 additional fans crowded the rooftops of buildings that overlooked the field. When the total figures were tallied, it was estimated the record crowd was 85,265: 81,622 paid and 3,643 used passes. Receipts totaled $115,000.

"Get me a morning paper. I want to see who is going to pitch the games today," said Urban Shocker when awakening in his hospital bed at 6:00 a.m.

"But you can't read. Your condition is not such to permit it," replied his nurse.

"Oh, yes, I can read. I must see who pitched yesterday, and who will be

17. Completing the Dynasty—1928

A record crowd of 85,265 invaded every space of Yankee Stadium to see the Yankee and Athletics double-header on September 9, 1928 (National Baseball Hall of Fame, Cooperstown, New York).

hurling today," insisted Shocker. "I'll be better today," he said thirty minutes later. "I'll be able to enjoy the two victories of the Yanks today." But forty minutes later, Urban Shocker was "conscious to the last and unaware of the pending tragedy." He was thirty eight years-old when he died.

"He played the game to the last," said Mrs. Shocker, who was reported to be deeply grieved. "If the Yankees had not lost the lead in the American League, he would still be alive. He began to sink when his 'beloved Yankees,' as he called them, dropped two games and Philadelphia won two games [two days before]. His condition grew worse on Saturday [the day before] when the Athletics went into the lead."

Shocker had recovered from pneumonia, but his illness had weakened his heart and wore him out. He had never lost hope of recovery, and in fact was so confident that he had instructed his eighteen-year-old son to shorten his visit to Denver and return home to St. Louis.

Unaware of Shocker's passing, the Yankees took the field. At 2:05, George Pipgras threw the first pitch of the game. He started by striking out A's leadoff man Max Bishop. Mule Haas followed with a fly ball, which Meusel dropped after making a long run. Haas rounded first, slipped, and Koenig, after taking Meusel's throw, walked over to apply the tag. Cochrane ended the inning by grounding out to Gehrig.

In the Yankees first, Combs singled against A's starter Jack Quinn. He advanced to second on Koenig's ground out, and to third on Gehrig's long fly. Ruth struck out on a 2–2 pitch, much to the delight of the Philadelphia fans. They cheered louder when Ruth whiffed on three pitches in the bottom of the fourth.

There was still no score through five innings. In the top of the sixth, Yankees third baseman Gene Robertson made a spectacular diving catch on a sacrifice attempt. Haas then attempted to steal, but was thrown out to end the inning.

In the bottom of the sixth, the Yankees' bats came to life. "They broke out with the thunder that made them feared from Boston to St. Louis and earned them the title of the Ball Busters from the Bronx." Combs and Keonig singled to start the inning, and Gehrig doubled to score Combs. Ruth was purposely passed to load the bases for Meusel, who tagged a long drive to center. Haas made a long ran before making the catch for a long out, but the drive was deep enough to allow Koenig to tag and score the game's second run. Lazzeri, healthy enough to return to the lineup, followed with a hit to score Gehrig for a 3–0 lead.

In the bottom of the eighth, with a runner on base, Gehrig drove a deep drive that fell into right-centerfield. A run scored as Gehrig rounded second and stopped at third. When he looked into the outfield and noticed A's second baseman Max Bishop drop Haas's relay throw, Gehrig responded by taking off for home and slid in ahead of the throw to score for another run. Ruth followed with a long fly to right field that thumped the top of the wall for a double. After taking third on a sacrifice by Meusel, he scored when Lazzeri made his third hit of the game. Pipgras took care of the A's the rest of the way, finishing with seven strikeouts to win his twenty-third game.

Huggins went with Heimach in the nightcap. Mack selected left-hander Rube Walberg.

Combs led off the bottom of the first with a three-bagger, and scored on Koenig's groundout to Bishop. After that, Walberg would retire the next sixteen in a row. The Philadelphia bats were quiet until the sixth, when Cochrane beat out a grounder to Dugan, and Simmons followed by driving one into the right field seats to give his team their first lead of the day.

In the bottom of the seventh, with Philadelphia ahead 3–1, Gehrig walked, Ruth hit into a fielder's choice, and Meusel finally got a hit off of Walberg. Following Lazzeri's out, Huggins sent Pascal to hit for Dugan, and he came through with a single to score a run and send Gehrig to third. Huggins made another move by sending Gazella to bat for Bengough. On the first pitch, Pascal stole second. The A's then purposely walked Gazella to load the bases. Huggins sent up a third consecutive pinch hitter, Pat Collins, who walked to force home the tying run.

Koenig singled to start the Yanks' eighth inning, and Gehrig doubled. Ruth was purposely passed to load the bases for Meusel. With a full count, Meusel swung, and when he connected there was little doubt where the ball was heading. The crowd jumped to its feet and let out a roar that was deafening. Hats were thrown onto the field, including Panamas, felts, old straw hats, and caps. Scorecards and newspapers, torn to flakes, floated down from the upper decks. When Meusel crossed home plate, Ruth greeted him with a big bear hug. The Yankees celebrated in their dugout, while across the field Mack looked straight ahead as he rubbed his chin.

Hoyt, who entered the game in the top of the eighth, retired the Athletics in order for his nineteenth win of the season and complete the double-header sweep. When the day had begun, the Yankees were a half game behind the A's. Now they were back in first place with a 1½-game lead.

Following the double-header, as the two teams headed down the same tunnel to get to their clubhouses, Cocahran and Lazzeri began to jabber. Without warning, the A's catcher jumped the New York second baseman. Ruth grabbed his teammate and pulled him into the Yankees' dressing room.

"We broke their hearts today," Ruth said in his booming voice in the happy Yankees clubhouse. Meusel, last to enter the clubhouse, was greeted with a handshake by O'Leary and Ruth and a pat on the back by Heimach. Bengough leaped onto the outfielder's back. Fletcher forcefully removed the backup catcher. "I hit a curve ball, about the fastest he could throw," Meusel told the press, but would not comment further on his grand slam.

Huggins, taking the win calmly, said to Mark Roth, "We ought to play them every day."

"The same old A's," Hoyt and some of the Yankees began to sing. The pitcher opened the door and hollered the song, his voice echoed and carried around the corner to the A's dressing room. The defeated Athletics heard the tune as they dressed in silence. Not a single member of the team would speak to the press.

The Yankees party was disrupted, and the mood of the postgame celebration turned to sorrow when they were informed about the passing of Urban Shocker. Details about their reaction went unrecorded.

The ticket line for the third game of the series extended for two blocks, but ticket demand was minimal in comparison to the double-header. Fifty thousand were in attendance, including around 1,000 fans from Philadelphia, substantially fewer than September 9. Connie Mack was going with Lefty Grove. Huggins countered with the man he always pitched against the A's ace, Hank Johnson.

The Athletics built a 3–0 lead after four innings, which appeared safe by the way Grove was going. The fiery left-hander struck out three in the first two innings. He whiffed Ruth in the bottom of the fourth, much to the enjoyment of the Athletics fans in attendance, who hooted the slugger as he headed back to the New York dugout.

The Yankees finally broke through for one in the seventh to cut the lead to 3–1. The A's threatened in the eighth with two singles to put runner on first and second with only one out. Thinking he could catch the Yankees off guard, Mack called for a double steal, but Pat Collins upset the strategy by throwing Simmons out at third base. Bing Miller followed with a pop fly into right field that looked like it might drop for a hit and score the base runner on second base until Babe Ruth, charging at full speed, reached out and made the catch to end the inning.

In the bottom of the eighth, Combs walked on a full count, and Koenig hit a hard line that third baseman Jimmie Dykes knocked down. With no play at first base, Dykes threw anyway. His hurried, low throw skipped by the first baseman to allow Combs to move up to third base.

Grove now had runners on first and third with nobody out and with Gehrig and Ruth due up. Perhaps thinking too much about dealing with the heart of Murderers' Row lineup, he uncorked a wild pitch to allow Combs scored to reduce the deficit to 3–2. Grove followed with another wild one. Gehrig ducked, but the ball hit his bat and fell to leftfield for a hit. Koenig scored to tie the game.

Babe Ruth tried to bunt, but fouled for strike one. With a count of one ball and one strike, Huggins signaled to Art Fletcher in the coach's box, who relayed the signal to Ruth to swing away. The next pitch was a fast ball. Ruth swung, and a loud crack echoed throughout the park. The ball headed to right field, and fell into the bleachers for Ruth's forty-ninth home run of the season. As the crowd went wild, several hats landed on the field as Ruth trotted the bases with a wide grin, looking at the ground. He was still smiling after he entered the dugout.

Down by three in the top of the ninth, Mack sent in Cobb to pinch-hit for Dykes. After being fooled by Johnson on a changeup for strike one, he lifted a pop fly down the third base line. Koenig ran over to make the catch in what was Cobb's final plate appearance of his career.

Mack sent up Eddie Collins to pinch-hit, and he popped up to almost the same spot that Cobb had for the second out. With two outs, Mack sent up another pinch hitter in Walt French, much to the disappointment of the New York fans, who had hollered for Tris Speaker. A fly out to Meusel and the game was over. New York won, 6–3, to increase their first-place lead to 2½ games.

"I'm just lucky against the Macks," said Johnson with a big smile after winning his fifth game in sixth tries against the Athletics.

"What a jinx these Yankees are to me," moaned Lefty Grove, now 1–6 versus New York in 1928. "Why must they upset me when I can beat the other teams so easily?"

"That kid has nerve," Huggins said about his winning pitcher. "Nothing bothers him. He's the same with men on base and with the bases empty. He has enormous faith in himself, which is a great thing in his favor."

17. Completing the Dynasty—1928

Before thirty-five thousand for the final game of the series, Philadelphia owned a 3–2 lead in the bottom of the eighth. There was one out with the tying run in scoring position and Gehrig at the plate, but the Yankees slugger struck out. When he swung and missed for strike three, the crowd let out a groan.

Once again, the A's opted to intentionally pass Ruth to pitch to Meusel, but this time they did not pitch to him. A's pitcher Howard Ehmke threw one inside that struck the batter. Taking exception, Meusel headed to the mound with his fists clinched and his right arm cocked. Ehmke walked off the mound in the direction of the batter. Home plate umpire Bill Dineen got between the two angry ballplayers and instructed Meusel to take his base.

Bases loaded, and up came Lazzeri. On his next pitch, Ehmke twisted his knee and was forced to retire for the game. "It was the worst blow I ever got when I was forced to quit against the champions, for I don't remember pitching a better game," said Ehmke. "There were only four men between me and the victory. The first up was Lazzeri and I wanted to show him up for the crowd because of all the trouble we had."

Orwoll came on and pitched three straight balls to walk in the tying run. Huggins then sent Gazella to bat for Robertson, but the pinch batter flew out to end the inning.

Hoyt retired the first two batters in the top of the ninth, and then had two strikes on Bishop when the A's second sacker swung and drove one deep to right field. Ruth never even turned to look. The home run gave the A's a 4–3 lead.

Combs struck out to end the game. The A's had managed to salvage a win at Yankee Stadium to cut the Yanks' lead to 1½ games. Fifteen games remained on the Yankees' schedule, all on the road. Before the Yankees and Athletics headed west, Cobb made an announcement that 1928 would be his final season. "Guess it's time to get out of the game and play with my kids before they grow up and leave me," he said. "And there's that trip to Europe I promised Mrs. Cobb this year."

Something Cobb desired was to finish his great career with a World Series Championship. He had appeared in three consecutive World Series (1907–1909) during his career, but had never played on a World Series champion. He also mentioned that he wanted the Athletics to win for their manager, whom he considered "the squarest man in baseball."

St. Louis was the first stop for the Yankees. The morning before the first game, they paid their last respects to their former teammate. Nearly one thousand persons attended Urban Shocker's funeral at the All Saints Church. Robertson, Hoyt, Gazella, and Gehrig served as pallbearers.

"I feel safer here," said Dugan as he stepped off the train in Chicago. "We are through with St. Louis. I figured that to be the hardest stop of the trip. Winning three of four games there didn't look so rough but the Browns are a good club."

Koenig hardly played in the series at St. Louis due to a game ejection and a heel injury. Durocher took his place in the lineup and went 3 for 6 with three RBI in the last game of the series while batting in Koenig's second spot in the Yankees' batting order. "I will miss Koenig if he can't play," said Huggins. "Mark always hit well at Comiskey Park. Durocher will be able to take care of the fielding all right, but if he hits as well as he did in the last game in St. Louis we may be safe. I always like to watch Durocher at short for that's where he belongs. What a ballplayer he is for his size; what a crest of gameness. He's going to be even better in a few years."

Was this a message for Koenig? He was back in the lineup for the first game at Chicago, and socked two hits to boost his season average to .315, but the Yanks lost in twelve innings. Hoyt, pitching for the third consecutive day, and for the fifth time in the last eight days, took the loss.

Hoping to produce more runs, or perhaps to help Ruth break out of a batting slump, Huggins switched Ruth and Gehrig back to their original places in the batting order. During the game Ruth joined the injured when he pulled a ligament in his leg while running from first to third and retired for the day. The Yankees managed to win 5–2 behind the pitching of Zachery, who helped his cause by belting a two-run homer.

Ruth was back in the lineup the next day, but went 0 for 3 to drop his batting average to .075 on the current road trip. The Yankees lost to Tommy Thomas and the White Sox. "Even a blind pig will find an acorn if he keeps rooting long enough." Thomas had finally posted a career win over the Yankees.

Was two consecutive days off enough rest for Hoyt? Huggins must have thought so. He started Hoyt in the first game at Cleveland, and Hoyt came through by tossing a four-hit shutout for his twentieth win of the season. A loss the next day went harmless since the Athletics also lost to remain two behind. The last game of the series resulted in a Yankees 10–1 rout. The Yankees now traveled to Detroit to finish out the season with a two-game lead and needing three wins to clinch the pennant.

At Detroit, Ruth homered in the first inning to help New York rally for a 4–1 lead. Hoyt, making another start, allowed two more runs, but held the lead for a 4–3 win. Ruth also homered in the second game of the doubleheader, his fifty-second of the season. The Yankees rallied to make it 6–0, but at a cost. Earle Combs broke his arm during the game, and would be lost for the season.

17. Completing the Dynasty—1928

The Tigers roared back against Heimach and Shealy to cut the lead to three. With the sun now beginning to set, the seventh inning was declared as the last inning. In the bottom of the seventh, the Tigers threatened by putting two on base.

Two Tigers on base, two outs, and Tigers slugging outfielder Fatty Fothergill, a dangerous hitter with three hits on the day, including a two-run triple, at the plate. As the batter got ready, "Time!" was called by Durocher from his position at second base. "There's a man hitting out of turn," he told umpire Bill Dineen as he paced toward home plate. The umpire examined his lineup card. "Fothergill is the right man batting," he said. "Fothergill?" questioned Durocher as he squinted. "Oh, from where I am standing it looked like two men up there."

Fothergill was sensitive to the slightest criticism about his weight, but to hear this from a rookie who had been riding him all season was enough to make him curse and make the veins in his neck stick out. So enraged was Fothergill, he lost focus and left his bat on his shoulder as three strikes whizzed by to end the game. After strike three, he dropped his bat and took off for Durocher. The loud-mouthed rookie ran for the dugout, but Fothergill got there before he did. Durocher then turned to the outfield, but Fothergill, moving well for his size, cut off his path. Durocher continued to run for his life until Ruth, once again, came to his rescue. As Ruth explained to Fothergill why a fresh busher wasn't worth his time, Durocher ducked into the safety of the jubilant New York clubhouse. "That's the way I want you to play, son," Huggins said with a smile as he patted the rookie on the back.

A win the next day clinched the 1928 American League pennant. New York put four on the board in the first when hits by Meusel and Robertson made it 4–0. A Ruth home run, his fifty-third, made it 8–1 in the fourth inning. Pipgras pitched a complete game for his twenty-fourth win and the Yankees' 100th win of the season. "Whee, what a relief that it's over at last!" said Huggins. "Over and in—safe by a whisker. I don't mind telling you fellows of the press that there were times during this part of the season that I thought we were sunk, with so many accidents and all. Don't congratulate me. Congratulate the team–a fine bunch of athletes who kept trying every minute in the face of devastating handicaps."

The Yankees' pennant-clinching victory was posted on the Comiskey Park scoreboard. At that moment, Connie Mack wiped his furrowed brow, Eddie Collins took a few steps in the coach's box with his head down, and Ty Cobb sat quietly at the end of the dugout. "It's all over!" yelled a Chicago player. "Wait until 1929, Connie," yelled another player.

There was one more New York injury on the last day of the season when a hard grounder suddenly skipped and caught Gehrig off guard. Blood covered his face and uniform and also ran from his ears. A woman in a box seat screamed at the sight, and then fainted. Later that evening, Gehrig said his jaw ached, and since he was unable to chew, he passed on dinner. It happened in the seventh inning, the same inning he hit his final home run of the season to finish with twenty-seven. Ruth also homered, his fifty-fourth.

"It's going to take more than a slap on the kisser to keep me out," said Gehrig, "I want to earn my share in the playoffs, and I got a feeling it will be the winner's profit. We're going to show up those Cards, even though we are cripples."

Gehrig, only twenty-five years old, had another great season by batting over .370 for the second consecutive season. He also made over two hundred hits and led the league in doubles and RBI for the second year in a row. His home run total fell by twenty, since opposing pitchers were now working carefully against him.

Due to a rash of injuries and an overworked New York pitching staff, the Yankees were viewed as the underdog in the 1928 World Series. "Pipgras and Hoyt have pitched 11 of 13 games from September 15th to the 28th," mentioned an Athletics player who, like his teammates, was pulling for the Cardinals. "The Yankees have been in a hitting slump since their second trip in the West," added the Philadelphia player. "Where are they going to finish if they don't get a hitting attack going for their wobbly pitchers? In one stretch of games we noticed that Ruth made just 1 hit in 16 at bats. If the Babe is silenced for the series, it will be worse than the Pittsburgh series last season."

Lazzeri was still ailing, but would play. Combs and Pennock would be out. Durst and Pascal would platoon in Combs's place and take his place at the top of the order. Zachery was slated to start in place of Pennock.

In spite of the injuries, the Yanks were confident, especially Leo Durocher, who was picking the Yankees to win in a breeze. "I hate to be kept waiting in getting my base hits," he said while on the field during the Yankees' practice session at Yankee Stadium a day before the first game of the series. "If I can't get into the World Series myself I'm going to tell the other boys how to hit homers. Babe, come over here and let me give you a lesson."

Ruth responded by heaving his mitt at Durocher, who ducked in time to avoid it from hitting him on the head. "Can you beat that kid?" said Ruth. "'The All-American Out.' That's what [Harry] Heilmann [of the Tigers] was calling him in Detroit. When little Leo can hit the ball that far, watch out for the rest of them."

Although Hornsby was long gone, the Cardinals were virtually the same

17. Completing the Dynasty—1928

team from two seasons ago when they beat the Yankees in seven games. Bill McKechnie came over from Pittsburgh to manage, and Frankie Frisch, now playing second base, proved valuable in helping the Cards win six more games than in 1927. Jim Bottomley was still the team's cleanup hitter, and they still had the same tough pitching staff which beat the Yanks in 1926, including Pete Alexander. Now forty-one, and not chalking up the whiffs like he once had, his experience and pinpoint control helped him record sixteen wins in 1928.

Hoyt looked anything but tired in Game One. He faced just one over the minimum through the first four innings. The only Cardinal to reach base was when Hoyt missed on a full count. Bill Sherdel, a loser in both of his decisions in the 1926 World Series, gave up a run in the first inning when Ruth and Gehrig his back-to-back doubles. In the fourth, Ruth doubled before Meusel sent one high into the right field seats for a 3–0 Yankees lead. In the fifth, the Cards finally got a hit, and in the seventh Bottomley tagged Hoyt for a solo homer. The Yanks got it back in the eighth when Ruth followed Koenig's hit with his third hit of the game, and Gehrig singled to score Koenig. The Yanks won, 4–1, with Hoyt allowing just three hits while striking out six.

Over sixty thousand fans applauded Alexander as he stepped onto the mound at Yankee Stadium for the first time since he saved Game Seven of the 1926 World Series. But for Alexander, it didn't start off well when Durst lined a hit to right and Ruth walked.

Up came Lou Gehrig, who went 1 for 8 against Alexander in 1926. Thinking of what had worked two years before, Alexander pitched Gehrig in the same manner, only this time Gehrig sent the first pitch into the right field bleachers to give the Yanks a 3–0 lead. "I pitched him a screwball," Alexander told the sportswriters after the game. "Lou could not hit the screwball in 1926, but he hit the hell out of it today."

Meusel looked at strike three for the second out of the inning. Up came Tony Lazzeri for the much anticipated at bat after the result from the seventh game of the 1926 World Series. The pitcher won the battle, again, by inducing Lazerri to tap one back to the mound for the third out of the inning.

Pipgras issued a walk and two hits to score a run and put runners on the corners in the top of the second. Huggins, noticing a flaw in the pitcher's mechanics, called time and made a trip to the mound to tell Pipgras to stop throwing sidearm and go with his usual overhand delivery. The next batter grounded to Lazzeri, and the second baseman, still playing with a lame throwing arm, threw high to first base to allow a run to score. Pipgras induced the next batter to bounce into a double play—Koenig to Lazzeri to Gehrig. Another run scored during the twin killing to tie the game 3–3.

The Cardinals put a runner on base in the fourth and fifth innings, but were unable to score. "He's pitching better than he was in that other inning," Huggins told his team in the dugout in reference to Pipgras. "He is still using too much sidearm but he's getting higher before letting go of the ball." Pipgras was in complete command after the top of the fourth. He retired ten Cardinals in a row before yielding a hit and a walk and finished the day with eight strikeouts.

The Yankees retook the lead in the bottom of the second by manufacturing a run on a walk, a sacrifice, and Durst's second hit of the game. In the third, the Yankees sent Alexander to the showers with a four-run rally to take an 8–3 lead. "My fortunes lay in the fact that I couldn't hit the corners," said Alexander, who offered no alibis. "Bum control and too many Yankee base hits—that explains the game."

The Yankees added one more run in a 9–3 win to take a 2–0 lead. The series would now head to St. Louis for games three and four, and five if necessary. "We couldn't beat anybody with the kind of pitching we got," said a disappointed Bill McKechnie on the train ride to St. Louis, "and we can't seem to hit. We are in a slump. I have to say this for the Yankees; they beat the best we got."

"How can I write my piece when I'm sitting on a bridge game?" Ruth asked while on the train heading to St. Louis in reference to his writing job for one of the newspapers during the World Series. But unlike the other players who were hired to write for various newspapers, Ruth had support. He clapped twice and his ghostwriter appeared.

Unlike Ruth, Hoyt did his own writing. "But the train moves so fast that I can't hit the keys. Clear out those old creaky typewriters and give me a pencil. I'll do my story longhand."

Jesse Haines beat the Yankees twice in 1926 while posting a 1.08 ERA. He began Game Three by retiring the Yankees in order in the top of the first. In the bottom of the first, two infield hits after one out started a threat for St. Louis. Bottomley lined one to center. Durst attempted a shoe-string catch, but missed. Two runners scored to give St. Louis their first lead of the series.

Gehrig led off the top of the second with a blast into the right field pavilion to put the Yanks on the board. Two innings later, he lined one to center field. St. Louis outfielder Taylor Douthit whiffed on a shoestring catch try, and Gehrig rounded the bases for his second home run to give New York a 3–2 lead. "He should have caught it," McKechnie would later say about the play. "He catches a dozen balls like that every season."

In the top of the sixth, with Ruth on second and Gehrig on first in a tie game, 3–3, Meusel grounded to the third baseman, who threw to second to

17. Completing the Dynasty—1928

force Gehrig. The relay throw to first was not in time, but on the throw, Ruth, being overly aggressive on the base paths as usual, rounded third and came barreling toward home plate. "A guy would be safer in the World War," an opposing player once said about colliding with Ruth on the base paths. Bottomly threw to Cardinals catcher Jimmie Wilson. Ruth crashed into the catcher with enough force to knock him on his back and jar the ball from his mitt. Wilson recovered and threw to second in an attempt to get Meusel, but his throw sailed into the outfield to allow the runner to reach third. Lazzeri followed with a walk, and then the two base runners executed a double steal with Meusel scoring to give the Yanks a 6–3 lead.

"We played terrible, terrible," said the St. Louis manager after watching his team make three errors and leave eight on base in a 7–3 loss. "They beat us twice in New York but they did not beat us today. We beat ourselves."

Wilson sat in front of his locker with his head down and looking too tired to take off his uniform. "Where did Ruth hurt you?" a writer asked him. "He didn't hurt me," Wilson replied. "I'm all right. He did not hurt me." He then shook his head. A reporter asked him another question, which he did not answer.

"He's all right. The Babe didn't hurt him," said McKechnie about his catcher as he leaned over and gave him a playful tap to the jaw. "See. He's a tough guy," he said with a smile.

In the top of the seventh in Game Four, Ruth came to the plate with his team trailing 2–1. He was 1 for 3 on the day with his one hit being his first home run of the series. This time, Bill Sherdel quickly got two strikes past him. Ruth, disagreeing with the umpire's call for strike two, turned to protest. Wilson, the St. Louis catcher, quickly whipped the ball back to Sherdel, who quickly chucked one down the middle for strike three. Ruth, busy protesting, never saw the pitch. The crowd, thinking this was strike three, roared.

"You can't do this," Ruth shouted to the pitcher.

"The hell I can't. I just did," replied Sherdel, believing he had struck Ruth out on a quick pitch: a legal pitch in the National League, but not in the American League. The rule allowed a pitcher to pitch whenever a batter was in the batter's box. Before the World Series, the two leagues agreed to disallow it, and home plate umpire Pfirman of the National League declared, "Ruth isn't out. Sherdel will have to pitch all over to him."

"But it's legal!" pleaded McKechnie. "It is a perfectly legal pitch according to the National League rules."

The other umpires backed the decision. Ruth, laughing at the Cardinals as they were overruled in their protest, stepped back in the batter's box, and as he got ready for the next pitch, he struck a conversation with the pitcher.

RUTH: "The National League is a hell of a league."
SHERDEL: "It sure it."
RUTH: "Put one right here and I'll knock it out of the park for you."

Sherdel threw a curve ball, and Ruth backed his promise by drilling it over the right field roof and onto Grand Boulevard for his second home run of the game. Gehrig followed by sending the ball atop the roof over the right field pavilion for his fourth home run of the series to equal Ruth's 1926 home run record. It was also his ninth RBI to tie Meusel's 1923 World Series RBI record.

Meusel followed with a single, and McKechinie, with his team down by a run and facing a World Series sweep, sent Alexander to the mound. The first batter he faced was Lazzeri, and finally, the Yankees second baseman got a hit off of his archrival with the help of a St. Louis outfielder who had lost the ball in the sun. Meusel scampered to third on the hit. Dugan followed with a ground ball to Frisch, who threw too late to get Meusel at home. Earle Combs, making his only World Series plate appearance, hit a line drive to right field to score Lazzeri for the fourth run of the inning and a 5–2 lead.

Durst led off the Yankees eighth with a round-tripper, and then Ruth did it again by homering to right field for his third of the game.

The World Series ended with Ruth's long gallop and stab in foul territory to make the catch for the final out of the World Series. The Yankees were World Champions once again.

The return trip to New York City was a wild celebration. "We were as crazy as a bunch of wild Indians," Ruth would recall. "When you win two straight World Series without a loss it calls for something special." Led by Ruth, the Yankees stormed through each train car. Ruth punched a hole through every straw hat he could lay his hands on, an old favorite prank of his. He also took pleasure in tearing shirts off the backs of his teammates. Realizing they had not seen Ruppert during their celebration, Ruth and the others sought to find him. They knocked on the door of his drawing room. "Go away," the Colonel answered. "I've already turned in and want to get some sleep."

"This is no night for sleeping," Ruth yelled.

Ruppert once again told him to go away, but Ruth just laughed. Ruth then signaled to Gehrig, and the two sluggers put their shoulders through the door. Ruth reached inside to unlatch the lock, opened the door, and tumbled into the room with Gehrig, Collins, and a few other teammates. Noticing the colonel was wearing an expensive lavender silk nightshirt, Ruth said he was going to rip it off. "Don't do it, Mr. Ruth," warned Ruppert. "This is custom-made silk."

"Aw, I only want a piece of it," said Ruth.

"Mr. Ruth, you are suspended."

Riiiip!

Huggins, never a drinker due to his health issues, stayed away from the party while quietly celebrating in private, but wasn't spared from their shenanigans. "Did anyone see my false teeth?" he asked the following morning as he searched the train.

18
Tragedy—1929

> "This thing has licked me. I don't care if I ever play baseball again. I'm through. The only thing I want is to get away from it all and go somewhere alone."
>
> —Babe Ruth

On January 11, 1929, A.W. Sweet was taking a late Friday evening stroll through his neighborhood in Watertown when he noticed a glow in the Kinders' home, which he discounted as an electrical lamp. When he entered his house at Forty-six Quincy Street, he went directly to a window to observe the house across from his. "The dentist and his wife aren't usually home at this hour," he said to his wife. "Mrs. Kinder has been confined to her home the last two or three days with a bad cold," his wife replied.

Sweet became startled when he noticed that the glow had expanded. "That's not an electric light," he said. "That's a fire." He quickly exited his home, charged across the street, and hammered on the front door. As he frantically pounded away, he heard the sound of crackling flames from within. Receiving no reply, he sprinted down the road, where he encountered two women who had seen the fire from behind the house while driving along Waverly Avenue. They had pulled over, stepped out of their vehicle, and searched for an alarm box. "Are you going to turn on an alarm?" one of the ladies asked. "I don't know where there is an alarm box," replied Sweet, "but I'll go down this street, and you go down Waverly Avenue and look for one."

When Sweet was finally able to locate an alarm box, he pulled the switch. By the time the fire apparatus had arrived, shortly after 10:00, the house was a mass of flames. "Mrs. Kinder is in the house," Sweet told Watertown Police Sergeant John J. Igoe. Fireman John Kelly, another fireman, and a patrolman broke down the front door and entered the burning structure. They crawled their way through "choking smoke" and remained on their hands and knees while climbing the steps to the second floor. When they passed through the doorway of the master bedroom, Kelly came across Helen's unconscious body, ten feet from her burning bed. The three men carried her from her burning home and to the next door residence at 35 Quincy Street. A doctor was summoned. The report was that Helen's face was blistered on one side but not badly burned. Another report claimed she was "severely burned about the body." Two men from the Box 52 Association, a fire prevention organization which responded to all blazes within the community, arrived before the doctor. Knowledgeable of medical procedures, they tried "artificial respiration," but were unable to revive her. When the two doctors arrived, they examined the patient and pronounced her dead. Helen was thirty-one years old.

A neighbor was aware that Doctor Kinder went to Boston that evening to watch boxing at the Boston Garden. A page was made at the arena. When Kinder reached a telephone, Reverend John W. Down of Watertown told him, "Your house is on fire."

"My wife is there," replied Kinder. "I asked her to come to the fight but she said she did not care to do so."

Back in Watertown, shortly after the last flames were extinguished, the phone rang in the destroyed front hallway of the Kinders' residence. Unsure what to do, Watertown Fire Chief John O'Hearn let it ring several times before deciding to pick up the receiver.

> CALLER: "Who is this?"
> O'HEARN: "The fire chief."
> CALLER: "What are you doing there?"
> O'HEARN: "There's been a fire in the house."
> CALLER: "What number?"
> O'HEARN: "I don't know—It's the last house on the street."
> CALLER: "That's my house—What's wrong?"
> O'HEARN: "There's been a fire here."
> CALLER: "Anybody hurt?"
> O'HEARN: "Yes, a woman was burned."
> CALLER: "I'll be right out."

Doctor Kinder was in a state of collapse when he arrived to the scene. He asked a few questions, and then vanished.

Two hours later, William Kinder, Jr., the doctor's brother and neighbor, phoned the Watertown Police Station to ask for pins, rings, and other jewelry belonging to his "sister-in-law" to be turned over to him. He also asked for letters, pictures, and papers. His requests were denied. The police had a box in their possession that Sergeant John Igoe had taken from the wreckage containing letters addressed to Mrs. Babe Ruth and Mrs. Helen Ruth.

The story of the fire with a photo of Helen Kinder appeared on the front

Helen and Dorothy did not spend much time together after Mrs. Ruth and Dr. Kinder began living together in Watertown, Massachusetts, in May of 1927 (National Baseball Hall of Fame, Cooperstown, New York).

page of Boston's Saturday morning newspapers. The neighbors confirmed that the woman in the photos was the one they knew as Mrs. Kinder; however, other sources recognized her not to be the dentist's wife, but Mrs. Babe Ruth. That same morning, Lieutenant Riley of the Watertown Police Department paid a visit to William Kinder, Jr.'s Watertown home. When he arrived, he encountered Kinder Jr. and his wife talking to someone he immediately recognized as the caretaker for Babe Ruth's daughter. Riley, a friend of Ruth's, knew Fanny Bailey from his few visits to Home Plate Farm. After asking questions, Riley departed but stationed a watchman to stakeout the residence.

The Watertown police wanted answers. They interviewed the doctor's father, who told them that Helen and his son had married in Montreal in August of 1927. He added that he had met her a long time ago following her legal separation.

Babe Ruth went an entire day without knowing of the events in Watertown. On Saturday evening, around twenty-four hours after the tragedy, he and Claire were at Joe Dugan's home when he was informed by a phone call from Art Crowley, a good friend of his in Boston (other sources say a messenger delivered the news to him). He wept upon receiving the news and quickly made arrangements to immediately depart for Boston. Before midnight, he sent a telegram to Crowley asking him to meet him at the Boston train station the next morning.

"Arthur, isn't this a tough break to get?" Ruth asked his friend when they met the next morning in at 7:00 in Boston. Ruth inquired about his daughter. When told that she was in the School of Assumptions Sisters at Wellesley, he talked about visiting her. Crowley advised against it for fear it would frighten the child. He took Ruth to the Brunswick Hotel, the same hotel where the Yankees had stayed when they were in town to play the Red Sox. After checking into suite number 574, they called for room service, but Ruth was in no mood to eat. At 8:45 the two men headed to the St. Cecilia Church in Boston's Back Bay to attend 9 a.m. mass. During the service, Ruth let out a loud "half-sob" that alarmed those who were seated around him.

While Ruth attended the service a Watertown police officer reported that Fanny Bailey had returned to Kinder Jr.'s home. He told Riley that he saw her leave by taxi and followed the cab until it reached Bailey's home. The lieutenant instructed a member of his staff to fetch her and bring her into police headquarters for questioning.

When asked whether Mrs. Kinder was in fact Mrs. Ruth, Bailey denied the connection. Riley then informed her that he knew Ruth, visited Home Plate Farm, and knew her as Ruths' maid. She then gave in, admitted that she had accompanied Mrs. Ruth to the Watertown home, but left for another job after Dorothy was sent to Wellesley to live, since she did not care to stay and do just the housecleaning.

Following the service, Crowley took Ruth back to their hotel, where they were greeted by two other close friends of Ruth's: John Feeney, an attorney, and Thomas McNaney. They went to Ruth's suite, where they filled him in on the happenings at Watertown. They also helped him prepare a statement for the press.

The news had reached the Woodford family. Shortly before Sunday afternoon, two of Helen's sisters, Nora and Catherine, traveled from their South Boston home to see the undertaker to confirm the identity of their sister. Afterwards, they went to the Brunswick Hotel to talk to Ruth. After waiting for over an hour in the lobby, they were escorted to Ruth's suite.

The police picked up Kinder Jr. and took him to the station for questioning. "Oh, Babe Ruth, he's a buddy of the doctors," he said. He confirmed his dad's story that Helen and her brother were married in Montreal, but failed to recall the exact date. He also was unable to remember Helen's maiden name. "Mrs. Kinder had married when very young, and Dorothy was from her previous marriage," he added. When told by the police that he was seen speaking with Mrs. Bailey, he confessed to everything he knew.

Atop the investigators' interview list was Doctor Kinder. However, the doctor's whereabouts were unknown. The police made it clear that there was no evidence of criminal activity, but desired to speak with him.

"His story is a damnable lie," Thomas Woodford said upon hearing Kinder's claim of having married his sister in Montreal. "Ruth and my sister were making plans to live together again." His sister had a different story, claiming that Ruth wanted to marry another woman and Helen agreed to a quiet divorce in Reno, but with a condition that her husband pay her $100,000. She said Ruth had disagreed and Christy Walsh had tried to negotiate with the two parties but failed. "It isn't true," Ruth said when asked, and wouldn't further comment.

Thomas Woodford had more to say. He believed that foul play was involved, "and the police do not have all the facts behind the death of my sister. What is there to prove that the house wasn't fired? What is there to prove that she wasn't murdered?" He also mentioned that she may have been drugged in order to prevent her from escaping the blaze. "Helen told me she knew a doctor who would give her opium tablets," added another brother.

"I am sure Mrs. Ruth did not take drugs or sleeping pills," said Ruth Olson, the neighbor who was closest to Helen. "She spoke to me about attending wild parties long ago, but there was nothing to indicate that she lived that kind of life while living with Doctor Kinder."

The Medical Examiner, Doctor George West, made it clear that his findings showed no foul play. "There is nothing about the body that is inconsistent with death in a burning building." He noted that the cause of death was suffocation and incineration. "So far as we can judge, the woman was overcome by smoke but was sufficiently aroused to stagger to her feet and then fell to the floor." A state inspector's examination of the premises determined the cause to be overloaded wires in the sun parlor added by Kinder after purchasing the home. "The wiring of the house gave indications that amateurs tinkered with them. Also, there many extension cords running everywhere. From indications of sort where the flames were the longest, it is very likely that the wires were overloaded."

Doctor Kinder voluntarily visited the Watertown police headquarters with his attorney. He appeared calm and collected as he answered questions for two hours while expressing great sorrow at Helen's passing, and confirmed that her severe cold was why she was unable to accompany him to the fights that evening. Kinder said that he had taken Mrs. Ruth into his house as a friend because she was estranged from her husband and had no other place to go. "She never told anyone that she was his wife, although she may have to avoid embarrassment." He also said that Ruth never visited, but believed that he knew his wife was living there, and that he would make trips to New York City with Helene and Dorothy so they could spend time with Ruth.

"What I'm going to say I can say in very few words," Ruth told twenty news reporters inside his hotel suite. He paused, took a deep breath, and read the words from a sheet of hotel stationery. "I have not lived with my wife for three years. In that period, I have only seen her a few times. I have done everything to comply with her wishes." He paused again as tears tumbled down his cheeks. He tried to continue, but his sobs chocked his words. His massive chest rose as he took another deep breath. His eyes twitched as he reached into his pocket for a handkerchief. "Her death comes as a great shock to me. Please leave my wife alone. Please let her stay dead. That's all I'm going to say."

Ruth crumpled the piece of stationery and tossed it into the fireplace. "Let me alone, boys," he told the newsmen. A few reporters shook his big hand as they headed to the door. When the last reporter left the suite, Ruth shut the door and turned the key to lock it.

One day later, Ruth sat in the living room of the Woodford residence in South Boston. He was alone with Helen's sister, Joanne McCarthy, as he was informed of the Woodford family's plans for Dorothy. She told him that a petition would be filed after the burial, and that her family had hired a Major Judson Harrington of the Harrington & Harrington law firm.

Ruth listened. When she finished, he angrily rose and shouted, "Never!" as he pointed. "I'll stand for almost anything but that. You can never have Dorothy—that much I'll tell you right now."

"We're going to make every effort to have Dorothy with us," a member of the Woodford family told the press. "In our opinion, Ruth is not suitable to bring up, be a custodian of Dorothy or administer of her estate." When asked for his side of the story, Ruth said nothing, except he wanted peace until after the burial.

A second autopsy was conducted by a medical examiner who was believed to have more sophisticated equipment. His findings confirmed the original examination, and verified that foul play was uninvolved. "There has been no evidence that a crime was committed," said Massachusetts State detective Edward O'Neil. He announced the case closed unless new evidence came about.

Helen's body was then taken to the Woodford South Boston residence with a police escort. Two hundred persons were present when the hearse arrived at the home. When the casket was brought inside the home, Joanna and another sister were so overcome, they collapsed. The coffin was placed inside the living room. The lid was removed, and the first well-wishers were admitted to pay their last respects.

"There's the Babe," someone said among the crowd of approximately five thousand camped outside the Woodford residence. Ruth was accompanied by Arthur Crowley, Michael H. Crowley (Boston police superintendent and Arthur's father), Feeney, and McNaney. He removed his hat after the party stepped out of their automobile and walked to the front door. Ruth said no words when his party was greeted by the residents of the home.

The kitchen clock struck midnight as Ruth stepped inside the house. "Over here, Babe," said Joanne McCarthy. Ruth nodded, and then walked to the living room.

Flowers were everywhere in the parlor, including floral tributes from Miller Huggins, Colonel Ruppert, Herb Pennock, Lou Gehrig, and other members of the Yankees. Gehrig also sent a letter to express his condolences:

> Dear George, my heart-felt sympathy in your great loss. May the Almighty grant you and Dorothy sufficient strength to bear up during your bereavement. Your sincere friend, Lou Gehrig. Key West, Florida, where happiness reigns on a fishing trip which I wish you shared.

A huge basket of roses and lilies from Ruth filled the room. He had also sent a blanket with an inscription: "Forever rest in peace."

Ruth slowly approached the bench beside the casket. He knelt down, reached the rail with his left hand, and made the sign of the cross. He looked at the woman he was married to for fourteen years with a glassy stare for five minutes; he was described as appearing as though he were looking through her. Or perhaps he pictured their life together: from the first time they met followed by their brief romance leading to marriage as teenagers when a proud Babe Ruth wanted his friends to meet her to know that she was his wife. "I'm proud of you, Babe," she said when he had reached stardom. "And I'm proud of you," he replied. She always came to the ballpark to see him pitch, and was always immaculately dressed and groomed. "These were happy times," Ruth would tell his friends. But then came the tough times, beginning with the difficulty of dealing with Ruth's achieving fame and fortune, and his mishandling of their finances. Their quarrels over his refusal to allow her to handle the family financial affairs, to his lack of time spent with Helen and Dorothy, to the other women: Juanita Jennings, Delores Dixon, and Claire Hodgson. The turbulent year of 1925: his illness, the bellyache, time away from the game, his worst season, and their separation. Helen's difficulties: her nervous condition, her breakdowns, and trying her best to cope as a single mom. And finally, the tragedy that took her life.

As Ruth looked at his wife for the last time, his chest and broad shoulders caved in when he vented his feelings. "Oh-oh-oh-Helen-oh-oh." His load sobs echoed through the three-story home as his tears fell onto Helen's silken death clothes.

Ruth tried to rise but was too weak. The Crowleys stepped forward to help. "Oh-oh, wait," pleaded Ruth. "Come on, Babe," Feeney said as he stepped forward.

The four men escorted Ruth from the living room. When they reached the front door, they encountered the Woodford family. "I've made all the arrangements," Feeney told them in reference to the funeral the next day.

19

Remarried—1929

"We're not going on a honeymoon. We're going to work and win another pennant."–Mrs. Babe Ruth

Dorothy Ruth sat alone in a "drab, gray waiting room" at the Foundling Hospital feeling unloved and without a purpose in life. She had not heard from her mother for too long, or perhaps not since her last visit to Watertown. She had not seen her father for an even longer period. One night she lay awake thinking that her parents had died, and nobody wanted to tell her.

The child was frightened from the first day she had arrived at her boarding school. Dorothy was alone and without friends since she was too timid to mingle with the other children. The other students went home to their families on the weekends while Dorothy remained in school. She tried to be strong with hope that her parents would visit in the near future, but they never did. During the night she kept her dorm awake by crying so hard that a nun was assigned to sleep in her room. "When that didn't work, they simply told me to shut up."

On a cold morning in January, two nuns woke Dorothy and instructed her to get dressed and pack her belongings. She had no idea why, but did as she was told. "Trust in God: everything will be all right," they told her during their train trip to New York City. After they arrived, she was placed in the Foundling Hospital. Following a sleepless night in a huge room with dark shadows, she was taken to see Sister Xavier, the mother supervisor of the hospital, who told her she was going to live with a Miss Dooley, an employee of the hospital, until her father came for her. (According to another source, that had been arranged by Ruth's lawyer.)

Dorothy moved into Miss Dooley's three-story brownstone building in Brooklyn, but under a different name. Her temporary guardian told her that her name was Marie Harrington. The child protested, but had no choice. The name was marked on her clothes, her books, and even her gym suit.

19. Remarried—1929

During her stay in Brooklyn, Miss Dooley had told her that her mom had gone to heaven and left her $50,000 which was placed into a trust. On January 29, Helen's will was revealed. "I give and bequeath unto my husband, George Herman Ruth, the sum of five (5.00) dollars and it is my will that this provision be in lieu and bar of every right and interest in and to my estate." It was unsurprising and understood why Ruth would feel "slighted," but it was unknown why Helen also left her mother and seven siblings five dollars apiece. "Shocked" is what the Woodfords told the reporters, but refused to comment, although they did mention they would not contest the will. "Mrs. Ruth's family is delighted that Dorothy is fully provided for," their family attorney said in a statement. "They raise no questions about the money left for them."

Helen's will referred to Dorothy as her "beloved ward," which once again raised questions about the child's birth records. When asked about Dorothy's history, Helen's attorney, James J. Conlin, refused to reply.

The door opened in the waiting room of the Foundling Hospital, and to Dorothy's amazement, her dad appeared. Thrilled to finally see a parent, she ran to him and jumped into his arms. But her joy quickly turned to anger when she saw another woman. "Claire is going to be your new mother," Ruth told her.

"Where's my real mother?" Dorothy demanded. When her question went unanswered, she asked again, and then ran for the door when her dad remained silent. Ruth reached down and grabbed Dorothy before she made it to the doorway, and lifted her back into his arms. "She's not my mother, and she never will be my mother!" Dorothy screamed.

Claire handed her a gift she had brought. Dorothy responded by tearing the gift to shreds. As the child continued to rave, her dad informed her that he and Claire were going to marry and she would be living with them. Dorothy was bitterly disappointed, but at least she had a parent back in her life.

Helen's passing opened the door for Ruth and Claire to marry. His engagement appeared to be agreeable to the Woodfords to allow him to have custody of his daughter, since a battle never followed. It may have also helped that Ruth had taken care of all of Helen's funeral costs. "You've done very nicely toward us," Helen's mother had told Ruth as they traveled in the same car en route to the funeral. When hearing this, one of Helen's sisters nodded in agreement. "I want to do right by you," Ruth replied. At the funeral, Ruth stood beside Mrs. Woodford and one of Helen's sisters at the edge of the grave with his head bowed. He wept with the others when the Our Father was recited as the coffin was lowered into the grave.

"If I'm getting married, it's news to me," Ruth told reporters when asked before the Yankees played the Dodgers in an exhibition game at Ebbets Field.

"But everybody knows more about my life than I do." He added, "No, I'm not getting married. But maybe you know something I don't."

The next day, Babe and Claire arrived at the New York city clerk's office shortly after the closing hour. "I want a license," Ruth said.

"A marriage license?" asked the city clerk, who dealt with many kinds of licenses.

"That's it," said Ruth.

"When?" reporters kept inquiring when hearing the news about his marriage application. "Some time this week," Ruth told them.

The writers were not content with his answer. They snooped around Claire's apartment building, questioned the doorman and elevator operator, but received no answers. They were also denied access and their request to ring Claire's apartment doorbell was refused. Later that day, they saw the couple dressed in dinner clothes as they left their building with two other women and three men.

"When?" they asked.

"Sometime this week," Ruth answered before climbing into a waiting limousine.

On April 17, the day the Yankees were scheduled to begin the 1929 season, the wedding party arrived at 5:45 a.m. by limousine at the church where Claire worshipped, the Roman Catholic Church of St. Gregory the Great on West Nineteenth Street. "Hello, Babe," someone said among the 250 admirers who stood outside the church doors. "Hello, fellows," Ruth replied as he walked up the church steps. The groom was dressed in a double-breasted serge suit with a matted brown tie, a white shirt, and tan shoes. The bride, "looking pretty and charming, and a trifle sleepy," wore a violet Georgette dress trimmed with crystal beads, grey silk stockings, black suede slippers with steel buckles, and a purple turban. The church altar was decorated with three vases of lilies and carnations.

Ruth appeared nervous by twisting and squirming during the ceremony while Mrs. Ruth looked very much as ease as they stood before Doctor William F. Hughes, the pastor of St. Gregory, who officiated the wedding.

Ruth's "I do" boomed through the church. When the ceremony concluded, a photographer's camera let off a loud and bright flash that caused everybody to flinch. Ruth appeared to be annoyed as he put a protective arm around his wife, but soon showed a broad smile as his guests came forward to shake his hand.

REPORTER: "Where are you going for your honeymoon?"
RUTH: "To the ballpark, I guess."
REPORTER: "Why was the marriage planned so early?"
RUTH: "That's hard to answer."
REPORTER: "Did you stay up all night?"

Babe and Claire on opening day at Yankee Stadium in 1929. Claire told Babe that it may not a good idea to blow her kisses every time he hit a homer (National Baseball Hall of Fame, Cooperstown, New York).

RUTH: "No, I got a good night's rest. I got up at 4:30."
REPORTER: "Will there be a party?"
RUTH: "There won't be a party."

The Ruths headed to Claire's apartment for a small impromptu reception and a simple wedding breakfast. Ruth received an unexpected holiday when the rain postponed opening day. A day later, the Yankees became the first team in major league history to appear with uniform numbers of their backs. Ruth wore number 3 to represent his third spot in the batting order. "It is expected that he will make '3' as famous as the '77' Red Grange wore at Illinois."

Opening day was bitterly cold with overcast skies that reduced the expected attendance to 10,000 fewer than projected. Before 40,000, Ruth stepped in for his first at bat of the season. With the count at 2-2, he tagged Red Ruffing's next offering for a 402-foot ride that landed in the leftfield seats. As he headed to third base during his home run trot, he blew a kiss and tipped his cap to Claire, who was seated in box number 173 with her mom beside the third base dugout. "You better stop that kiss-throwing, Babe. The players will be telling you about it next time," his wife warned after the game.

Lou Gehrig, wearing number 4, and playing in his 579th consecutive game since his pinch-hit appearance for "Pee Wee" Wanninger in June of 1925, sent one into the right field bleachers for his first home run of the season. "Gehrig, with no bride to tip his cap to, did it anyway."

"By all means, you must go to Boston," Colonel Ruppert told Mrs. Ruth in reference to the Yankees' first road trip in 1929. "After all, it's your honeymoon, you know."

Baseball wives accompanying their husbands on the road was prohibited, but the Yankees were willing to bend the rule for the Babe. Feeling that the presence of his wife would force him to behave on the road, Ruppert invited Mrs. Ruth to travel with the team throughout the season. "We feel you have done a great deal for him since the two of you met. You would be a good influence while he is traveling."

Could the Yankees win a fourth consecutive pennant? Would they win another World Series? "New York in a breeze," Ruth answered when asked about his pennant prediction. "No, I don't believe the Yankees can get into the World Series for a fourth straight time," said a now retired Ty Cobb. "I'm picking the A's."

Ruth reported to St. Petersburg at 225 pounds, but looked better than the previous spring, according to one writer. His first order of business was to hit the golf links. He won two trophies at the Jungle Club—one for the longest drive of 244 yards, and the other for winning a southpaw tournament. Huggins also played, but struggled so much at one point that a writer asked what he was trying to do. "I can beat Connie Mack in golf right now," he replied. "But can you beat him in baseball?" the writer asked. "We'll come to that later," said Huggins.

"That's seven in a row for us," Durocher said following a Yankees 6–3 win over Boston as Waterfront Park. But while New York was winning, Ruth and Gehrig were not hitting. Through the first five exhibition games, they had not homered. "Don't bother me about that," Huggins told the sportswriters. "What I want to see is pitching."

Pitching would be a question mark for the 1929 Yankees. Injuries and lack of depth had forced their best hurlers to pitch overtime down the stretch of the 1928 season. Pipgras, a twenty-seven-game winner in 1928, was back, and so was Waite Hoyt. Herb Pennock was questionable since he was coming back from a season-ending injury. To be safe, Huggins deactivated his star lefty for the entire exhibition season. "Any time Huggins says the word, I'm ready to work," said Pennock, adding that his arm felt fine.

The manager was counting on his younger pitchers, Hank Johnson, Shealy, and Heimach, to improve. "He is a 'change of pace [pitch]' away from becoming the best pitcher," Huggins said of Heimach. "He is the third fastest lefty in the league [after Grove and Walberg of the A's]." He was also hoping for Moore to regain his 1927 status, and had two rookies: Ed Wells, the 1928 leader in Southern Association wins with twenty-five, and a hard-throwing rookie named Roy Sherid. "He's fast," Huggins said about Sherid, "and he knows how to keep the fastball low, right down there where they can't hit it." Tom Zachery was also back following a good homestretch in 1928 after coming over from Washington.

Another concern for Huggins was his infield, which fell off in 1928, mostly due to Lazzeri's arm injury, Dugan's slowing up with age, and Koenig's sub-par fielding season. Lazzeri was in shape when he reported, but it was said that his arm was still hurting. "Arm perfect," Lazzeri assured after the exhibition season.

The plan to improve the spongy left side of the Yankees infield was to start Durocher at shortstop and Koenig at third base in place of Joe Dugan (who had been sent to the Boston Braves). "I like third," said Koenig, "I feel at home here. It's the easiest position in the game. You don't have to have good hands. All you need is a strong throwing arm and cast iron ribs."

"The only question about Durocher was if we could make Koenig into a third baseman," said Huggins. "That seems to have been accomplished. I'm pleased with what Koenig has shown. Leo is a sensational little shortstop and I have faith that he will do even better than his warmest admirers expect. I knew last year that Durocher could play shortstop for the Yankees."

Huggins assured there was no competition at shortstop with Durocher and a highly-touted rookie infielder named Lyn Lary, a .314 hitter the previous season at Oakland of the Pacific Coast League. His strongest asset was said to be his defense. The manager, however, pointed to some flaws in the rookie's fielding. "He takes grounders with his hands too far back and he's off balance on most of his throws."

Bill Dickey would be the Yankees' starting catcher. He had begun the 1928 season as one of four catchers on the Yankees' roster. Figuring it was better to play him than to sit him on the bench, the Yanks sent Dickey to Hartford. Little Rock of the Southern Association appealed to the commissioner's office, claiming they had placed a bid for his services. Landis agreed, and Dickey played in Little Rock until the Yankees recalled him in August. "I will stand pat or fall with the catchers I started the season with," Huggins said upon Dickey's return. "I only brought Dickey up from Little Rock to give him a chance to watch how things are done in the majors."

It was believed that Dickey's powerful bat would compensate for Durocher's lack of hitting, but that did not stop the mouthy shortstop from popping off. Aware he may face Red Sox pitcher Ed Morris in the first series of the season, and knowing he could get the hurler's goat, Durocher sent Morris a telegram: "Dear Cousin, you better get hot right away or we will make it hot for you."

"Where does that kid get off sending me a cousin card?" asked Ed Morris. "Why, you know I was the reason he was shifted to a switch hitter. He wanted to be near the bench when I was pitching."

"Injuries have held us back, but that does not explain everything," said Connie Mack as he sat on a chair on the porch of the Royal Palm Hotel in Fort Meyers and talked with reporters. The Athletics manager, hoping for 1929 to be his first pennant winner since 1914, was less than happy over the progress of his team. Burning him up the most was his players' electing to hold out over their exorbitant salary demands. "The day is not far off when millionaires will be buying up the ball clubs and running them as a hobby. That will ruin the sport."

The Athletics came to St. Petersburg to play the Braves at Waterfront Park. After a morning workout at Lake Crescent Park, the Yankees attended the game to watch their chief rivals–all except for Ruth, who went fishing. The Yankees were delighted to see the 1928 American League runner-up blow a 6–3 lead and lose 7–6. "It looks like another walkover for the Yankees," Gehrig said without even a smile to Mickey Cochrane when their paths crossed after the game. "Pennants aren't won in March, but in October," replied Cochrane.

Following the end of their season in St. Petersburg, Ruth and the Yankees headed to Waco, Texas, and played before 11,000 in a 4,000-seat ballpark. "The fans in the Southwest are the most enthusiastic," said Ruth. "They won't even leave a guy alone when he's on the field." During the game, around 300 barefooted boys in overalls surrounded Ruth in right field. The game was delayed for ten minutes while Ruth signed scorecards and shook hands. "But

19. Remarried—1929

I'm not kicking," said Ruth. "I understand that the fans are just curious. It's the traveling from town to town and the rough fields that get my goat."

In Oklahoma City, Ruth stirred the crowd during batting practice with his longest drive, the ball clearing the fence and four sets of railroad tracks before landing atop train shed. The fans had behaved throughout the game, but their mood became restless when dark clouds began to approach. In the eighth inning, a rash of fans entered the playing field and grouped around Ruth with scorecards and baseballs, much to the dissatisfaction of the spectators in the box seats hoping to see Ruth homer before it rained. When the fans on the field failed to respond, the box seat customers began to heave their seat cushions. Umpire Bick Campbell ran towards the mob in the outfield until he had second thoughts and retreated. Three policemen ran to Ruth's rescue, but they were trampled by the enthusiastic crowd. Ruth, his jersey torn to shreds, pulled away from the mob and sprinted to the exit. He made it to his car and drove away.

The Yankees headed on their first trip to the west after going 6–4 in April. The road trip did not get off to a promising start. Hoyt, appearing to be the best pitcher on the staff by completing the only two games of the young season, yielded eight runs in six innings to give Chicago an 8–6 lead. In the seventh inning, Ruth hit one into the upper deck in right field. Gehrig, who had belted one over the right field roof in the second inning, followed by hitting one that landed in almost the same spot as Ruth's blast, and Meusel made it three circuit blasts in a row by knocking one off the top of the centerfield wall and legging it out for a home run. One inning later, Gehrig completed a 4-for-4 day by making his third home run of the game; the second time he hit three in one game in his career. Ruth hit another one before 40,000 during the next game, and Pipgras, off to a slow start, won his first game of the season.

Bob Meusel hit a grand slam in the top of the tenth in the third game of the series to break a 3–3 tie. The game appeared to be in hand, but the way the Yankees' pitching was going, no lead was safe. Huggins was forced to call Waite Hoyt in relief when Heimach and Moore failed. Hoyt did the job, although it was too close for comfort for Huggins, who seemed to take every game to heart.

The Yankees' pitching looked like it might get on track when Hoyt, Johnson and Pipgras pitched complete-game victories to extend the Yankees' winning streak to eight and lift them into first place. But just when there was hope, the staff yielded 13 runs on 21 hits in a 13–7 loss in Detroit. Soon the hitting began to slump, and the Yankees lost five straight to fall from first place.

"Two sharp thrusts: one from the left and the other from the right." Pennock, ineffective in three previous starts, hurled a complete-game win, Pipgras followed by pitching a one-hit shutout, and Heimach shut out the Red Sox to persuade writers to ask if "the Yankees pitching was now on track." Just when the pitchers looked like they were in stride, the hitters produced just 10 runs as the Yankees dropped three of their next four. "What's wrong with the Yankees?" a writer asked. When May concluded, the Yankees record was a disappointing 20–16 with a team batting average of just .277. Ruth, Gehrig, Lazzeri, and Dickey were all batting over. 300, and Combs was at .298, but Meusel was at .243. Huggins decided to bench him to give Cedric Durst a chance to play every day. The manager reasoned that Meusel's slump was due to a recent illness. "Everybody knows that Bob can hit."

Koenig was batting just .273. and was not fielding like Huggins had hoped. "My dogs [feet] are terrible," said Koenig. "They need rest." Huggins granted him his wish. The manager talked about switching Koenig back to shortstop. "If Durocher doesn't hit well enough to hold his job, shortstop is an open position again."

Durocher, hitting just .228, had committed 6 errors in his last 21 games to convince Huggins to give Lary a chance at shortstop. "It's just a trial for a few days." After having a long talk with Durocher, Huggins put him back in the lineup.

Before the game on June 2, Lou Gehrig walked through the tunnel leading from the New York clubhouse at Yankee Stadium to the field for batting practice with the other eight players in the starting lineup. He was surprised to see reserves Durst and Byrd among the other starters. "Where you going?" asked the first baseman.

"Didn't you hear?" responded Byrd. "Ruth is out of the game. I'm going to field for him."

"I'm going to bat for him," said Durst.

Byrd, playing in place of Ruth in right field, made three dazzling catches, and Durst, batting in Ruth's third spot in the batting order, hit a two-run homer in a Yankees 6–1 win.

The previous day, Ruth had hit his tenth homer of the season before withdrawing from the game due to an unconfirmed report that he had suffered a "heart attack." At his apartment on Eighty-Eighth Street, he laughed while lying comfortably on a couch as he listened to a radio report about his condition. "You tell them that I'm far from a dead one," Ruth had told his wife, who was busy denying access to visitors. "I'm used to that," he said with a grin. "They have had me dead four times since I joined the Yankees. I don't mind that as long as the undertaker doesn't take it too seriously."

He was diagnosed with a deep chest cold. Doctor King, who was not going to take a chance, sent him to St. Vincent's as a precautionary treatment against pneumonia. An examination revealed there were slight heart murmurs. After being discharged, Ruth would remain at home while under the care of Doctor King.

The traveling and heavy workload wore out Ruth. The Yankees had no off days due to the demand for Ruth. When the New Yorkers received a break in their schedule, they traveled to play an exhibition game against a minor league team. Ruth needed rest, and time away from New York City to recuperate was in order. He mentioned that he intended to be back in action before the Yankees played an important series against Philadelphia, beginning on June 21.

Before leaving on his trip, Ruth and his wife visited Yankee Stadium to watch the Yankees. In the first game, the Yankees pounded out seventeen runs in a lopsided win over the Browns. Ruth stood and cheered when Gehrig hit his first of two homers on the day. He wanted to toss his hat onto the field when Gehrig hit his second until his wife discouraged him from doing so.

During a busy morning of packing, Ruth was asked where he and his wife were heading. "Where you can't find me," replied Ruth. Their big black limousine headed off before disappearing somewhere along Riverside Drive.

Cedarcrest, Maryland, is isolated, "but they found us anyway," said Mrs. Ruth. The Ruths admitted that it was impossible for them to hide from publicity. Ruth felt well enough to go fishing. He said he would head back to New York in a few days for a golf engagement, and would put on a uniform to practice two days later. "They are bound to crack sooner or later," he said about the Athletics. "We will be at our best when we meet the Athletics next week."

The Yankees were winning without Ruth. They scored thirty-four runs in three wins over the Tigers. Gehrig hit two home runs in the series to bring his season total to 17 in 51 games. Meusel, returning to the lineup after a two-week absence, went two-for-two in one game with a homer, and went 4-for-5 in a 13–2 win over Boston in the next series. In that win over Boston, Ruth entered the game in the sixth inning.

"It is almost the single opinion in the baseball world the outcome of these two crucial series will determine the character of the remaining pennant race," someone said about the upcoming meeting between the Yankees and Athletics. "If Mack's players can win 3 of 5 games [in New York], nothing will shake their confidence thereafter," said Browns manager Dan Howley. "I'm rooting for the Yankees," said Bucky Harris, now managing the Tigers. "If the Yankees can knock them down 4 out of 5, it will give the rest of the season a chance."

"I don't think the Yankees will find us a bit worried," said Connie Mack. "I have more confidence in this team than I have had in years."

Philadelphia came to Yankee Stadium with a 40–13 record and a 7½-game lead. Before 70,000, they added another game to their league lead behind the pitching of Grove and a combined nine hits by Simmons and first baseman Jimmie Foxx in an 11–1 win. In the nightcap, Ruth struck out with the bases loaded in the bottom of the first. "A heavy gloom settled over the crowd." Ruth gained his redemption in the bottom of the seventh when he tagged a two-strike pitch for a three-run homer to right field to give New York their first lead of the day, 5–3. One inning later, Ruth "crushed into the ball with terrific force and sent it high into the right field bleachers." With the Yanks now ahead 8–3, Ruth retired for the day.

Before another 70,000 the next day, the Athletics won the first of two games, 8–3. In the second game, Pipgras began by walking two and serving up home run to Simmons. After that, Pipgras held the powerful A's to three hits and a walk to allow the Yankees to rally and tie the game, 3–3. The Yankees' hurler was still in the game in the fourteenth inning, and had faced the minimum since the top of the second. The Yankees won the game in the last of the fourteenth on a bases-loaded single by Lazzeri.

The final game of the series drew 43,000 to total the series attendance at 183,000. Gate receipts were close to $200,000. The Athletics won, 7–4, to take 3 out of 5 in the series, but the Yankees remained confident. "The fight isn't over by any means," said Ruth, who also added that his team "did not hit as well as they should have."

"I don't think we can be counted out yet," said Huggins.

Before traveling to Philadelphia the following week, the Yankees split a pair in Washington while the Athletics swept the Red Sox to increase their lead to 10½ games. At Philadelphia, Huggins selected Hoyt to pitch the first game, and he managed to hold Simmons hitless and Foxx to one hit, but the other A's picked up the slack in a 6–3 win.

Mack went with Grove in the next game, and the A's supported him by giving him a 3–0 lead. In the top of the fifth, Ruth tagged Grove for a two-run homer to right center. Later in the game, he hit another one over the right field fence, his fifteenth of the season, to tie the game, but the A's pulled it out in the bottom of the eighth. As the Yankees dressed after the game, Al Simmons opened the door and peeked inside their clubhouse. "Hey, you birds!" he called out. "We'll win the pennant by ten games," and then slammed the door.

20

The End of the Road—1929

"We're licked this year, but next year we'll have a winner."—Miller Huggins

The Yankees looked like the dynamic team from the previous three seasons by winning 22 of 29 games in July, but were unable to gain on the Athletics, who managed to add another half game to their lead over their second-place rivals by winning 24 of 32. Just two wins in their first seven games in August dropped New York 11½ back prior to the Yankees' next trip to Philadelphia. The three-game series began on a weekday, yet that did not prevent a record crowd from jamming into Shibe Park. Over an hour before game time, all 33,000 seats were filled. Another 10,000 were permitted to pack the aisles or sit on the grass along the outfield wall. Some climbed to a spot within the steel girders beneath the upper deck. Every rooftop that overlooked the field was packed to its fullest. Fans unable to get tickets scaled the right field wall and slipped through the fortified barbed wire. Others climbed to the upper branches of the tall trees that overlooked the outfield fence.

In the series' first game Ruth smacked one over the wall with the bases full. Meusel, Lazzeri, and Koenig also homered in a 13–1 Yankees win. The Athletics bounced back to win by a run in the second game. Hoping to win the final game of the series to gain another game on New York, Mack sent left-hander Rube Walberg to the mound. Huggins countered by starting right-handed hitting Sammy Byrd in place of Combs. The strategy worked as Byrd clubbed a two-run homer to give the Yankees a 6–3 lead. The A's rallied to cut the lead to one and threatened in the fifth when Cochrane singled. Huggins called for Moore, and the relief specialist of two seasons ago finally found his old form by allowing one hit in five innings and preventing Simmons from hitting the ball out of the infield. He began by inducing Simmons to hit one on the ground that the Yankees infield turned into a double play. An inning later, he struck out two batters to end a Philadelphia threat, and he finished the game by getting Simmons to ground out. At Cleveland, the Indians continuously batted Moore's sinker into the ground, resulting in a double play in each of the last four innings in a 4–2 Yankees win. In the top of the eighth, Ruth came within one of reaching a milestone by tagging his 499th home run of his career.

With a capacity crowd of 25,000 at League Park for the second game of the series, Ruth smacked an inside curve by Indians hurler Will Hudlin with a "great lifting swing." The ball sailed down the right field line and cleared the tall fence for a home run. As Ruth trotted around the bases, the cheers became an ovation. Aware of the significance of his home run, he immediately dispatched someone to find the ball.

Jack Geiser, a forty-six-year-old from New Philadelphia, Ohio, was in the right place at the right time. He was on his way to catch a bus after visiting relatives when he saw a baseball ricochet off a doorstep. He immediately "pounced on it and thrust it into his pocket." He headed to the gate at League Park, where an alert attendant noticed something in Geiser's pocket. "What do we have here?" asked the attendant.

"A ball came over the fence," replied Geiser.

"I know the guy who might give you something for that," the attendant said. "Come with me."

Geiser was bewildered as he trailed the attendant to the box seats behind the New York dugout as the Yankees were heading in after the bottom of the inning. Ruth saw Geiser holding a baseball and knew right away. "Gimme that, will you?" he asked. "I'd like to have that as a souvenir." Geiser, lost for words, wanted to have it for himself, but realizing what it meant to Babe Ruth, he handed him the ball.

"Eddie," Ruth called to Eddie Bennett, "give me a new baseball and a fountain pen."

Ruth signed the ball, and then asked team trainer Doc Woods to lend him twenty dollars. "Here, kid, wrap this around the ball and take it home with you," he said as he handed over a signed baseball with a twenty-dollar bill.

It was a great moment in Ruth's career that Huggins had missed. Experiencing migraines throughout the series in Philadelphia, the manager remained in his hotel room during the series in Cleveland.

Miller Huggins was a sick man before the 1929 season had begun. How many knew how ill he really was is unknown, but one person aware was Rogers Hornsby. "Miller Huggins is a very sick man," he said back in September of 1928 when informed of Urban Shocker's passing. "He's been in there day in and out when he should have been in bed. I'm making a prediction that Huggins will not be living a year from now."

20. The End of the Road—1929

The 1929 season had taken its toll on the manager. He constantly worried about his hurlers, often displaying his anxiety by pacing the dugout from corner to corner when the opposition rallied against his struggling pitching staff. "The wear and tear of running a championship team is becoming too much," he confessed to *New York Sun* sportswriter Joe Villa. "I have made enough money in salary and investments to permit me to enjoy the rest of my life at my home in [St. Petersburg,] Florida." According to the *Chicago Tribune*, Miller Huggins was worth more than $250,000.

Ruppert and Barrow, aware that their manager was exhausted due to his tendencies to overwork and worry, pleaded with him to take time off, but he was reluctant. His plan to retire following a fourth consecutive pennant had changed. Hearing the cries change from breaking up the Yankees to "rebuilding the Yankees," Huggins felt an obligation to manage the Yankees back to the top before retiring.

The manager returned to the dugout and stayed on the job through the rest of the road trip. One day during the trip, the exhausted manager reminisced with Ford Frick and a few other sportswriters about the good old days of the Yankees. "I owe a lot to Colonel Huston," he said, a bit whimsically. "If it hadn't been for the Colonel I probably would have been a bust."

"Why, what do you mean?" asked one of the sportswriters. "The Colonel was one man who never did give you a break. He was always panning you."

"That's just it," Huggins said with a smile. "The Colonel thought I was so rotten, and said so in so many columns of spaces so many times, that nobody expected anything from me. Even the little things I happened to do stood out like mountains. It was one of those cases where a bouquet of roses was wrapped in every crate of raspberries the Colonel tossed."

Desperate to generate a stronger hitting attack to pick up the slack for his team's sub-par pitching, Huggins changed his lineup by batting Combs third, Ruth fourth and Gehrig fifth. The new batting order worked for thirteen runs on eighteen hits, with Combs getting four hits, and Ruth making three to lift his season average to .359. However, the pitching staff allowed eighteen runs for New York's fourth consecutive loss. The New York bats produced just two hits the next day in a 3–0 loss. They did manage to salvage the last two games of the series, with Waite Hoyt winning one of those games for his first win in over two months.

The Yankees were blanked three games in a row in St. Louis. Their string of consecutive scoreless innings reached thirty-two before Ruth snapped it with his thirty-fourth home run. Nonetheless, the Yankees lost again to finish a disappointing 7–12 on the road trip.

The team returned to Yankee Stadium trailing the A's by thirteen games with less than forty to play. George Pipgras, nowhere near his twenty-seven-win performance from the previous season, pitched his best game of the season. With the support of the Yankees turning four double plays, and two outstanding fielding plays by Cedric Durst, he took a no-hitter into the eighth inning. In that inning, Simmons beat out a slow roller for the first A's hit. In the ninth, with two outs, and Pipgras clinging to a 2–0 lead, Cochrane drilled one over Sam Byrd into deep leftfield. When Byrd finally retrieved the ball, he made a great throw to Durocher, who wheeled and threw a strike to Dickey in time to tag Cochrane to end the game. A week later, the Athletics got their revenge against Pipgras in Philadelphia with a six-run third inning en route to a 10–3 win. In the second game of the twin bill, New York overcame a 4–0 deficit to take a 5–4 lead. In the bottom of the ninth, with the tying run on first and the Yankees two outs away from a one-run victory, Mule Haas dropped a hit into leftfield. Meusel fielded the ball and threw to rookie third baseman Lynn Lary. His throw hit Max Bishop (the lead runner) and rolled away. Haas advanced on the throw, rounded second base, and running with his head down, he failed to notice that the Bishop was occupying third base until he was halfway to the base. Lary, after retrieving the ball, was unaware that Haas was trapped between the bases, and also failed to hear the shouts of his teammates. When he did notice, his throw to second base was too late. Bishop broke for home on the throw and slid across the plate with the tying run.

Huggins was fuming. He stepped out of the dugout and slowly paced toward Lary as his players gazed in despair. "What the hell are you doing?" he asked. The rookie shook his head and made no reply. Huggins looked him over before walking away. As he headed back to the dugout, he beckoned to the bullpen for a relief pitcher. He turned to take another look at Lary, and then sent in a replacement for his third baseman.

Lary took a seat next to his manager on the dugout bench. "Why was I replaced?" he asked. "I'll let you know in the clubhouse," replied Huggins. The rookie got up and quietly headed to the locker room.

The A's quickly capitalized to score Haas and win the game. Later that evening, there was a rumor that Lary was carried from the clubhouse when an irate teammate slugged him. He was back in the lineup the following day in a 10–2 Athletics win to complete the series sweep. "It's all over," Huggins said. "It's impossible for us to catch them now."

It was now time for the Yankees to focus on building for the future. The first sign of the rebuilding process came when the Yanks sold Gene Robertson to the Braves. Shortly after the season, Bob Meusel, clearly past his prime, was sold to the Reds. Byrd, Durst, and a minor league prospect named Dusty Cooke were candidates to take Meusel's place in 1930. Koenig and Durocher

20. The End of the Road—1929

were expected to play elsewhere in 1930 or in a reserve role with the Yankees. Lary was a starting possibility. So was a minor league infield prospect named Ben Chapman. With the pitching staff being the most critical department, the Yanks purchased a promising hard-throwing left-handed teenager from the San Francisco Seals named Vernon "Lefty" Gomez.

As the 1929 season headed into its final weeks, Huggins entered the clubhouse one day with a red blotch beneath his left eye. The players and coaches were concerned. "Go see a doctor because I have a red spot on my face?" replied Huggins. "Me?—who took the spikes of Frank Chance and Fred Clarke?" Sportswriter Ford Frick, also very worried about the manager's appearance, pleaded with Huggins. "Listen, when I see a doctor this time it will be a tough, tough pull," Huggins replied quietly. "I'm not going to get well in one or two days. This one is going to be serious. So I want to straighten up everything first. Then I will fight this sickness."

In the second game of a double-header at Yankee Stadium, Hoyt was shelled after three innings. He went to the clubhouse and was surprised to see Huggins lying on a training table with a heat lamp shining on his cheek in an attempt to dissolve the red spot.

HUGGINS: "What happened?"
HOYT: "Hauser hit a long one and here I am. I pitched him where I always pitch him—high and outside—but he hit this one."
HUGGINS: "How old are you?"
HOYT: "I was thirty this month."
HUGGINS: "Well, I'll tell you this. You're getting older. After thirty, you can't do what you did when you were twenty-five or twenty-six. You've got to take care of your condition. We've got two weeks to go. Go down and get your paycheck—go home. I'll see you next spring—but stay in shape this winter. That's my advice to you."

A few days later, on a cold, misty afternoon at Yankee Stadium, on "one of those days that seems to seep into your bones," Durocher and Miller Huggins were alone in the clubhouse prior to the game. The young Yankees shortstop watched his manager stand before a mirror and pick at his sore. "He looked sick, and he had a wracking cough," said Durocher. "He looked thinner than ever, like he was shrinking away."

"Mr. Huggins, why don't you go home?" advised Durocher. "We're not going anyplace. We can't win the pennant and we've got second place clinched. You're sick. Please. Why don't you go home?"

"Maybe you're right, son," Huggins said, "maybe I should."

The manager headed to the dugout to inform his right-hand man. "Art, I'm going home. Look after the club."

"I think you're wise," said Fletcher. "See a doctor, get a good night's sleep, and you'll be all right tomorrow."

Huggins turned and slowly made his way down the dugout steps and walked through the runway for the last time. He went back to his apartment, where he lived with his sister, Myrtle, and contacted Yankees doctor Edward King, who advised him to check into St. Vincent's Hospital. After an examination, it was reported that the Yankees manager was a "very sick man." He was suffering from skin disease known as erysipelas. "Huggins has worked himself down to his last ounce of energy, as he usually does during his pennant races," said Ed Barrow. "I am afraid that he has weakened himself so that his physical condition is such that he cannot ward off a trouble that might otherwise be considered lightly. We tried to persuade him to take a rest, but he refused to do so."

The sore was diagnosed as merely a carbuncle, although in the manager's case it had turned lethal and began to poison his body. Pus began to form in his blood and fluid filled his lungs. When his fever skyrocketed to 105 the following morning, the patient's status was changed to "grave" condition. Doctor King responded by performing two blood transfusions in an era before the importance of blood typing was fully understood. When asked for an update following the transfusions, King said Huggins "seemed brighter." Huggins was in pain but never complained. "How much chance do I got, Doc?" he asked. "We are very hopeful," the doctor answered.

With their manager in their thoughts and prayers, the Yankees prepared to hear the worst as they traveled to Boston. Ruth, with forty-six home runs for the season, knocked out two hits to lift his season average to .346 in a 5–3 Yankees win. That evening he ventured to Cambridge, Massachusetts, as a guest speaker at the Catholic Club. He asked his audience to pray for Huggins's recovery, and to ask their friends to do the same. "If prayers can help, the old boy ought to pull through."

Myrtle and Arthur Huggins were at their brother's bedside the entire day and through the night. Fearing the end may be near, Huggins sold his stocks and signed his will. (The timing of his stock sales was perfect, since the stock market would crash a few weeks later.)

On September 25, the Yankees were in action before 7,000 fans at Fenway Park, including Connie Mack and his 1929 American League champion Philadelphia Athletics, who were in town to play a series beginning the following day.

Back in New York, Huggins's two siblings, his close friend Bob Connery, a minister, a house physician, a few friends, and two nurses were at his bedside while Ruppert and Barrow sat in the hallway by the door. Two more blood

20. The End of the Road—1929

transfusions were performed, but his condition failed to improve. "His lowered vitality resulted in rapid spread of the infection, which we were unable to curb," said Doctor King. With his temperature now 107, he had slipped into a coma. He briefly came out of it, was unable to recognize his sister, and fell back into a state of unconsciousness. At 3:16 that afternoon, the door of the manager's hospital room opened and the nurses emerged with the news the two Yankees officials dreaded to hear: Miller Huggins was dead.

Word was received at Fenway Park during the third inning. Boston Red Sox officials debated if they should tell the New York players. They decided to wait, but someone from the front office lowed the outfield flag to half-mast. Unaware of the news, not noticing the position of the outfield flag, the Yankees continued to battle. Following the completion of the fifth inning, the megaphone announcer began to announce the news to the crowd while a Red Sox official entered the New York dugout to break the news to the Yankees and instruct them to line up for a moment of silence. Stunned by the news, the Yankees were too numb to immediately reply. A choked sob was heard in the dugout. Combs wept without shame. A writer began to approach Ruth, but the Babe waved him off as he brushed away his tears.

Both teams lined up along the baseline before their respective dugouts. Connie Mack and his Athletics, and the rest of the crowd of 7,000, stood, removed their hats, and observed one minute of silence. It became so quiet that the only noise heard was the traffic in the street from outside of the ballpark. The announcer broke the silence and both teams headed back to their dugouts. "Well," Yankee's coach Charley O'Leary said with a sob as he walked with the players, "we'll have to finish this game—let's get it over with."

21

Legacy

"Miller Huggins passes into baseball history as one of the great managers of all time. Too bad he can't read the encomiums now being passed on upon him by the many of the same persons who said of him that he would never do as a big league manager."

—Westbrook Pegler

"They call Yankee Stadium 'the house that Ruth built.' If I built it, Hug supplied the material."

—Babe Ruth

"I always felt that Miller Huggins never received full credit for his managerial skills. He was one of the best managers the American League ever had and credit for his pennant triumphs must go to him."

—Connie Mack

The New York Yankees stood before the grave of their former manager as they bowed their heads in a mute tribute to the man who had guided them to six pennants and three World Championships. "Lou Gehrig was the most affected of the players," said Cliff Morton of the *Cincinnati Enquirer*. "No one will ever know how much Miller did for me," said Gehrig.

As the team continued to meditate, Babe Ruth stepped forward and placed a flower on the grave in representation of the New York Yankees. Ford Frick also approached the manager's final resting place with a flower on behalf of the New York Sportswriters. "And for years after that, a delegation of writers made a pilgrimage to the cemetery each year to place a wreath on Hug's grave," according to Ruth.

The Yankees had arrived in Cincinnati on the morning of June 2, 1930. When the players stepped off the train, their spirits were dampened by the memory that their former manager was present the last time they were in this city. They taxied to the Spring Grove Cemetery to pay their respects to Miller

Huggins. Following the brief ceremony, they journeyed to Crosley Field to play the Reds in an exhibition game.

The list of managerial candidates for the Yankees was only a few. The job had been offered to Huggins's right-hand man, Art Fletcher, but acknowledging his unpleasant managing experience with the Phillies, and aware of the toll that managing the Yankees had taken on Huggins, he elected to stick to coaching. When Ruth pondered over the candidates, he spoke a thought that came to mind: "What's the matter with me?"

"You can't manage yourself, so how are you going to manage the Yankees?" asked Ruppert. Ruth backed his credentials, and to his joy the Yankees owner seemed impressed. Ruppert told him he'd think about it for a few days.

Was Ruppert really considering Ruth for the job? He once told Mrs. Ruth that she had done a great deal for him since they had met, and that he believed she would serve as a good influence. Others agreed. "I've noticed an improvement in Ruth since he got married," said American League umpire Brick Owens, backing his opinion with examples of Ruth's hustle and determination in the outfield. But was this enough to convince Ruppert?

A few days passed; no word from Ruppert. Ruth was about to phone the Yankees owner when he noticed the newspaper headlines. His former teammate and Yankees pitcher Bob Shawkey accepted the job.

The denial of the New York managing job disappointed Ruth; nonetheless, he maintained his good spirits. He phoned Shawkey to congratulate him and assured he'd give him his best effort. He also wanted a higher salary, and once again mentioned $100,000 per season. "Ruth has taken more money from the Yankees than I have," Ruppert said in response to Ruth's salary demand.

Ruth's three-year contract of $70,000 per season had expired after the 1929 season. Ruppert stood pat on his offer of $75,000. Ruth was willing to compromise for a three-year contract at $85,000 per season. "I'm good for $25,000 a year for life [through endorsements] even if I quit baseball today," he said. "A lot of people in New York are rioting for bread," a friend told Ruth, in reference to a riot at the Union Station breadline. "They're broke. There's a depression. And you're holding out for $85,000 while they're starving. It makes a bad impression and is hurting baseball."

"Why don't people tell me these things." replied Ruth.

On March 8, Ruth and Ruppert sat at a table before a group of sportswriters outside of the Princess Martha Hotel in St. Petersburg. The contract was for two seasons at $80,000 per season—$5,000 more than the president's salary. "You will never hear of a ballplayer getting that kind of money," Barrow told a reporter. "Even if another Babe Ruth comes along, he would never be a novelty."

The Yankees' 1930 season began on a disappointing note. Expected to do better than finishing eighteen games behind the A's as they had in 1929, New York lost their first five games. It was said the problem was due to lack of hitting, but that didn't bother the new manager. "It's the best problem to have," Shawkey said. "Everyone knows the Yankees will begin to hit." He was right, but the big problem continued to be lack of pitching depth. "We need relief pitching, badly," the manager admitted. Two trades were made during the month of May to bolster the pitching staff. Outfielder Cedric Durst was sent to Boston for pitcher Red Ruffing, and Waite Hoyt, now past his prime, was traded with Mark Koenig to Detroit for pitcher Ownie Carroll (and two position players). Ruffing would develop into one of the best pitchers in the league, while Carroll would be pitching elsewhere before the end of the season.

With the departure of Koenig and Durocher (sold to the Reds after the 1929 season), Lyn Lary became the starting shortstop. Rookie Ben Chapman played second base and Lazerri played third until they traded positions in mid-season. Another rookie, Dusty Cooke, and Sammy Byrd alternated in leftfield. Combs, Dickey, and Gehrig continued to be productive in the everyday lineup, as was Babe Ruth, off to a great start with 14 home runs through the first forty games. Ruth was among the league leaders with a .375 batting average and 40 RBI.

Ruth concluded the 1930 season with forty-nine home runs (three better than 1929) to win his fifth consecutive home run title. He hit .359, drove in 153 runs, and crossed home 150 times. The Yankees won 86, two fewer than 1929, finishing sixteen games behind the pennant-winning Philadelphia Athletics, and eight behind the Washington Senators for a disappointing third place. Shawkey was fired and once again Ruth inquired about the position. Once again, Ruppert told him no, backing his decision with a list of Ruth's mistakes before 1926. "Was there any fault with my conduct in 1930 or efforts to make Shawkey's year a success?" Ruth asked. Ruppert said no. "You really earned the big money I paid you." Nonetheless, the Yankees owner didn't even tell him he'd let him know. Joe McCarthy was Ruppert's man. He had shaped the Cubs into a winner after inheriting a last-place team in 1926 and managed them to the 1929 National League pennant. He became available when the Cubs fired him following a second-place finish in 1930, and Ruppert wasted no time in hiring him. "Did they have to go to the National League for a manager?" asked Ruth.

Babe Ruth wore the Yankees uniform for four more seasons, 1931–1934. He would star in one more Yankees World Series championship, in 1932. By 1934, at age thirty-nine, he was slowing up, especially in the field. The Yankees believed the time had come for the great player to retire. Others agreed, but not Ruth. He wanted to continue to play and eventually make a transition to managing. He wanted the Yankees job, but the Yankees did not want him, nor did the other American League clubs. He was waived by Ruppert, and went unclaimed by the other owners in the circuit. "Somebody should have had more compassion when they maneuvered him out of the American League," said Detroit Tigers slugger Hank Greenberg. But there was an owner who was interested.

Wanting to capitalize on Ruth's fame, Emil Fuchs, the owner of Boston's National League franchise, signed him to a contract to play, serve as the team's vice-president and assistant manager, and apparently with an agreement for Ruth to manage the Boston Braves in 1936 (although Fuchs had no intention of hiring him to manage). He was also assured a share of the team's profits, but there were no profits to be received. The Depression was now in full tilt. The Braves were awful, and not even Ruth's popularity could rescue them. Before the month of May was over, Ruth, having his worst season, announced he was calling it quits to officially end his playing career. In response, the Braves terminated his contract. He later claimed that Fuchs had doubled-crossed him.

Ruth maintained his ambition to manage. In 1934, he managed Connie Mack's all-star team through their tour in Japan. Some believed this was a sign that he would get the A's job, but when asked, Mack laughed. "His wife would be managing the team in a month," he said.

Ruth's second wife took over. Unlike in his first marriage, Ruth agreed to let Claire handle their finances. The days of reckless spending and tipping fifty dollars for a five-cent sandwich were over. When Babe needed money he would ask Claire to write a check. She also curbed his eating habits. Ballpark food was off limits; however, Ruth would sneak out of the dugout during a game and head to a concession stand where he could enjoy hot dogs, peanuts, soda, and his favorite snacks.

Babe, Claire, Dorothy, and Julia moved into a spacious apartment on Riverside Drive. Dorothy, delighted to have her dad back in her life, was happy to be rid of the name Marie Harrington. And she was no longer assumed to be Dorothy Kinder. Everyone now knew her as Dorothy Helen Ruth, the daughter of Babe Ruth. But something that still troubled her was the strange disappearance of her mother. She received her answer when putting together a scrapbook for her father and came across the articles about the fire that took Helen's life.

Unfortunately, Dorothy was not entirely happy in her new surroundings. Her stepmom's favoritism to her own daughter put her in a no-win situation she would have to endure for the next ten years. Her father, busy with his own

The Ruth family: Left to right: Julia, Babe, Dorothy, and Claire (National Baseball Hall of Fame, Cooperstown, New York).

affairs, was unaware. She slept under the same roof and ate at the same table as her stepsister, "but that's all we had in common. Claire had every intention on raising her own daughter in her own image."

Dorothy loved her father and believed he tried his best to be a good dad. "Babe was a good father, considering the circumstances," she would later say. "He never deliberately neglected me, and I know he loved me very much."

Opportunity knocked for another possible managing position. Ruth signed to coach the Brooklyn Dodgers during the 1938 season with the hope of piloting the team in 1939. At the conclusion of the season, the Dodgers fired the manager, but opted to go with a rookie manager named Leo Durocher. Sadly, Ruth would never get the chance to fulfill his desire to lead a major league team. "Despite his faults, baseball didn't do right by him," said Greenberg.

Arthur Daley (*New York Times*): "He [Huggins] won six pennants in spite of virtually insurmountable difficulties."

Did Miller Huggins ever regret his decision to manage the Yankees? "If I were ten years younger, I would never sign as a big league manager," he once

21. Legacy

> MILLER J. HUGGINS
> 1878   1929
> AS A MEMORIAL AND TRIBUTE TO AN OUTSTANDING
> SPORTSMAN AND A SPLENDID CHARACTER, WHO
> AS MANAGER OF THE NEW YORK YANKEES AND
> RESIDENT OF THIS CITY CONTRIBUTED TO ITS FAME
> AND THE BETTERMENT OF BASEBALL, THE CITIZENS OF
> ST. PETERSBURG DEDICATE THIS GROUND, WHICH
> FOREVER SHALL BE KNOWN AS
> MILLER HUGGINS FIELD

Miller Huggins was honored in 1932 when his plaque became the first to be erected at Yankee Stadium. A plaque (pictured) was also placed at Lake Crescent Park in St. Petersburg to show that the field had been named in his honor (St. Petersburg Museum of History).

said. He was the most accomplished manager of his era: an astute businessman who read the daily stock report and had career interests outside the game of baseball. "I would go into business for myself," he once said. "I can take over a ball club and I know it would be a worthwhile investment." Although never the sole owner of the ball club, he did partner with his good friend and minor league ball club owner Bob Connery by investing in his St. Paul Saints.

Twice during his twelve years of managing the Yankees, Huggins considered a career change. He loved roller-skating, believed there was a future in it, and envisioned it as a great business opportunity. During his playing days he served as a manager and director of a rink in Cincinnati. He inspected roller rinks when his teams were on the road, and often mentioned how he would love to someday see the rinks in Europe.

He considered a career transition into real estate during his business partnership with Colonel Ruppert. The two men opened an office in St. Petersburg, where Huggins found his law background to be useful when making deals. But after a few years he decided he favored managing. "Baseball and real estate don't mix," he reasoned, "and I like the game better of the two." He sold his real estate earnings for a reported $150,000, which made him financially secure to the point where he could have retired before the 1929 season, but never regretted his decision to lead the Yankees. "Miller said it always had been worth it," said Myrtle Huggins.

John Kieran of the *New York Times* wrote: "Ruth was never a bigger fellow than the day he admitted he was wrong and Huggins was right."

In the end, Babe Ruth had the utmost respect for his manager. "He ran the club wisely and well, and what he said he always meant. Only the players who worked under him really knew him.

"He was the best friend I ever had in baseball. He was more like a father than a manager to me. And if a fellow could follow the path that Miller Huggins pointed out, he would never go wrong."

On May 30, 1932, Miller Huggins became the first former New York Yankee to have a plaque erected in his honor at Yankees Stadium. During a pregame ceremony, forty-five thousand fans greeted Mayor Jimmy Walker with a mix of cheers and boos as he stood at the microphone by home plate. "New York will always hold Miller Huggins in affectionate memory," he told the crowd, "and the fans will always remember him as an intelligent sportsman and a game one." And then the entire Yankee Stadium crowd roared its approval.

Miller Huggins went down in history as a great manager, who was loved and respected by all who knew him.

Chapter Notes

Introduction

—"'He's an old man. He isn't the Babe that he used to be,' the fans say": *New York Evening Journal*, June 29, 1925.
—"The Yankees are a collection of individuals who are convinced their manager is a sap": *New York Times*, February 4, 1964.
—"sharp quick [batting] strokes proved effective": Edward J. Prindle, *The "Reach" Art of Batting* (Philadelphia: A.J. Reach, 1904), page 28.
—"hitting home runs were frowned upon by the fraternity": ibid.

Chapter 1

—"Gentlemen, we have just bought Babe Ruth from Harry Frazee of the Boston Red Sox": Frederick G. Lieb, *The Boston Red Sox* (New York. G.P. Putnam's Sons, 1947), page 182.
—"You can't do this to me, Harry": Lieb, *Red Sox*, page 183.
—"I'm sorry, Ed: I've got to do it": ibid.
—"The Ruth deal was the only way I could retain the Red Sox": Daniel R. Levitt, *Ed Barrow* (Lincoln: University of Nebraska Press, 2008), page 163.
—"Those are the only friends that so-and-so has": Lieb, *Red Sox*, page 178.
—Huggins-Ruth dialog: Leigh Montville, *The Big Bam* (New York: Broadway Books, 2006), page 99; Robert W. Creamer, *Babe* (New York: Fireside, 1992), page 211.
—"Huggins' word is the law": Jim Reisler, *Babe Ruth* (New York: McGraw-Hill, 2004), page 24.
—"Look at ya! Too fat and old to have fun!": ibid.
—"And that goes for him too": ibid.
—"As for this shrimp": ibid.
—"He is one of the most selfish and inconsiderate ballplayers": *New York Times*, January 7, 1920.
—"He thought of only himself": *Chicago Tribune*, January 7, 1920.
—"I learned to fear and hate the coppers": Creamer, page 29.
—"These we used on Babe Ruth": Montville, page 23.
—"I used to get my discipline the old-fashioned way": William R. Cobb, *Babe Ruth: Playing the Game* (Mineola, NY: Dover, 2011), page 4.
—"He just wouldn't go to school": Creamer, page 32.
—"I guess I am too big and ugly for anyone to come see me": Brother Gilbert, *Young Babe Ruth* (Jefferson, NC: McFarland, 1999), page 4.
—"I was a catcher": *New York Sun*, July 14, 1926.
—"That guy out there—getting his brains knocked out": Bob Considine, *The Babe Ruth Story* (New York: Penguin, 1992), page 7.
—"I pitched to everyone I could get to catch me": *New York Sun*, July 14, 1926.
—"You mean I can eat anything I want, and it won't cost me anything?": John Tullius, *I'd Rather Be a Yankee* (New York: Macmillan, 1986), page 35.
—"I wouldn't have believed it if I hadn't seen it": Tullius, page 34.
—"We've got twenty-seven other fellows on this club, George": Tullius, page 35.
—"Excuse me, I have to piss": Reisler, page 21.
—"I can't live with this man Ruth": Lieb, *Red Sox*, page 120.

—"He can do anything": Leigh Montville, page 34.
—"Jack, you have a great young pitcher in Ruth": Frederick G. Lieb, *The Baltimore Orioles* (New York: G.P. Putnam's Sons, 1955), pages 141–142.
—"Hon, how about you and me getting married?": Marshal Smelser, *The Life that Ruth Built* (Lincoln: University of Nebraska Press, 1975), page 56.
—"I can't take credit for changing the game": Edward Grant Barrow, *My Fifty Years in Baseball* (New York: Coward-McCann, 1951), page 89.
—"In the spring of 1919 I had a sore arm": *New York Sun*, July 14, 1926.
—"He pitched the first game against us and won it with a triple": Stanley "Bucky" Harris, *Playing the Game* (New York: Grosset & Dunlap, 1925), page 126.

Chapter 2

—"When Ruppert and Huston agreed to buy the Yankees": Barrow, page 123.
—"At last, I've written my John Hancock on those papers": *New York Times*, January 12, 1925.
—"Money talks": ibid.
—"The way to make money is to put others to work for you": Frank Graham, *The New York Yankees* (Carbondale: Southern Illinois University Press, 2002), page 22.
—"Never do anything you can hire someone else to do for you": Phil Weintraub, *The House that Ruth Built* (New York: Little, Brown and Company, 2011), page 132.
—"No chance": Graham, page 22.
—"It was an orphan ball club without a home of its own": Harvey Frommer, *Remembering Yankee Stadium* (New York: Stewart, Tabori, and Chang, 2008), page 28.
—"I like you, Donovan": Graham, page 31.
—"No, you won't do. For one thing, you're too old": Graham, page 33.
—"Get Miller Huggins": ibid.
—"All right, to please you, I'll go": Graham, page 34.
—"There is something about that fellow that I like": "Miller Huggins as I Knew Him," by Bill Slocum (Miller Huggins file at the A. Bartlett Giamatti Library, Cooperstown, NY).
—"in which juries never sleep": J.G. Taylor Spink, *Judge Landis and Twenty-Five Years of Baseball* (New York: Thomas Y. Crowell, 1947), page 18.
—"I don't room with him. I room with his suitcase": Montville, page 109.
—"Oh God, oh my God, please bring Charlie back": Mike Sowell, *The Pitch that Killed* (New York: Macmillan, 1989), pages 143–144.
—"Most fans got the wrong idea of the play": *New York Sun*, August 18, 1926.
—"The accident crushed the two teams' spirit": ibid.

Chapter 3

—"Probably nowhere in all the imaginative field of fiction": *New York Times*, August 17, 1948.
—"She was just a kid when they got married": Creamer, page 281.
—"We made more dates for Babe than he could have ever dreamed of": Waite Hoyt, *Babe Ruth as I Knew Him* (New York: Dell, 1948), page 9.
—"I paid a guy to move them the hell out": Hoyt, page 13.
—"Landis was a personality, a man of great mental strength": Spink, page 74.
—"Baseball men were pretty scared": Spink, page 64.
—"Who is he?" *New York Sun*, October 3, 1928.
—"The Giants gave me $5 for signing": William A. Cook, *Waite Hoyt* (Jefferson, NC: McFarland, 2004), page 9.
—"Not me": Barrow, page 129.
—"They are moving to Goatsville": Frommer, *Remembering Yankee Stadium*, page 28.
—1920 home attendance and gate receipts: Lyle Spatz and Steve Steinberg, *1921: The Yankees, the Giants, and the Battle for Baseball Supremacy in New York* (Lincoln: University of Nebraska Press, 2010), page 36.
—"We aim to make our new park the finest baseball plant in the world": Spatz and Steinberg, page 62.
—"The players had many friends": page 83.
—"Regardless of the verdict of juries": Spink, page 84.
—"I'll bet he'll be one of the most talked about hitters in the country this season": Reisler, page 55.
—"Oh, you are, are you?": Spink, page 104.

Notes—Chapter 4

—"Who does that big monkey think he is?": ibid.
—"Aw, go tell that old guy to jump in the lake": Spink, page 106.
—"Well, what do you want?": Levitt, page 294.
—"Play ball, you big bum": Smelser, page 244.
—"Hit the big stiff": *New York Times,* May 26, 1922.
—"Anyone who wants to fight": Creamer, page 258.
—"But I did mean to hit that bastard in the stands": Creamer, page 259.
—"If you ever put me out of the game again": *New York Times,* June 21, 1922.
—"If you don't like it, come under the stands": Creamer, page 261.
—"If that monkey says anything": Hoyt, page 11.
—"For God's sakes, Pipp": ibid.
—"Now stop that": Creamer, page 264.
—"You birds ought to fight every day": Graham, page 82.
—"Oh, you found out about that": Dorothy Ruth Pirone, *My Dad, the Babe* (Boston: Queen Press, 1988), page 24.
—"But when we put her in an incubator": ibid.
—February 2, 1921, at the Presbyterian Hospital: Pirone, page 25.
—"I should say not ... that baby is mine, mine, mine!": ibid.
—June 7, 1921, at St. Vincent: ibid.
—"Obviously he confused it with his own birthday": ibid.
—"Don't you think that Dorothy is a dead image of her father?": Pirone, page 23.
—"Nice going, Two Head!": Weintraub, page 57.
—"Lay it over for him!": Weintraub, page 142.
—"Throw it in the dust!": John Devaney and Burt Goldblatt, *The World Series* (Chicago: Rand McNally, 1981), page 95.
—"How did McGraw make you look so foolish?": Weintraub, page 65
—"Mr. Ruth for a case of bootlegger beer": Montville, page 128.
—"Do you know who I am?": ibid.
—"About five dollars each": Weintraub, page 66.
—"Babe Ruth is not only a great athlete, but a great fool": Weintraub, page 67.
—"So help me, Jim, I will!": Montville, page 158.

—*Chapter 4*

—"Let me tell you something": *New York Sun,* September 29, 1929.
—"Pipe the new mascot": *New York Evening Journal,* September 28, 1929.
—"I'm Miller Huggins": ibid.
—"Nice going, Mr. Little Everywhere": ibid.
—Huggins penciled in March 27, 1878, on his 1918 draft registration card: Miller Huggins file at the A. Bartlett Giamatti Library, Cooperstown, New York.
—"Don't do it, Miller": *New York Evening Journal,* September 27, 1929.
—"Either I'm a lawyer or a ballplayer": ibid.
—"Cincinnati fans are so touchy over the deal": Frederick G. Lieb, *The St. Louis Cardinals* (New York: G.P. Putnam, 1944), page 43.
—"It's just like a woman to replace Bresnahan with the Little Shrimp": Lieb, *Cardinals,* page 49.
—"The Little Miracle Worker of the West": Leo Thatchenberg, "The Travails of Miller Huggins" (Miller Huggins file at the A. Bartlett Giamatti Library, Cooperstown, NY).
—"Mr. Britton, I've got a chance to get a good infielder": *New York Evening Journal,* September 29, 1929.
—"Huggins's Folly": ibid.
—"That rookie ought to be back on the farm": ibid.
—"Gentlemen, I want the two of you to be the first to know": Lieb, *Cardinals,* page 59.
—"But I need a man to run all the affairs as club president": Lieb, *Cardinals,* page 61.
—"There was never a sounder leader": *St. Louis Dispatch,* September 26, 1929.
—"He thought a certain club official had doubled crossed him": ibid.
—"He told me he wanted to get away": ibid.
—"I told him if he could find such a club, I give him his release": *St. Louis Dispatch,* September 26, 1929.
—"His record, considering he had very little money": Miller Huggins files at the A. Bartlett Giamatti Library, Cooperstown, NY.
—"They had reason to believe that any shackles placed on them by Huggins would be struck off by Huston": Spatz and Steinberg, page 198.
—"At that particular moment my whole world was falling down": Levitt, page 154.

—"I'll never pitch another ball for this ball club again!": Sowell, page 40.
—"If necessary, we'll go to the courts": Graham, page 39.
—"Picked to lead Yankees": Thatchenburg.
—"I was never on a club where a fellow was as disliked as much as Mays": Sowell, page 22.
—"Ruth could never accept managerial discipline": Thatchenburg.
—"You're too little to be around a ball club": *New York Evening Journal*, September 30, 1929.
—"You really wouldn't have tossed me off the train, would you?": ibid.
—"Stick it out": Weintraub, page 183.
—"Mite Manager": Spatz and Steinberg, page 86.
—"Babe Ruth cost him about five years of his life": /Levitt, page 403.
—"You're the manager, and you're going to get no interference or second guessing from me": Barrow, page 126.
—"You can pat Moran but you can't kid Gleason": Eliot Asinof, *Eight Men Out* (New York: Henry Holt, 1987), page 88.
—"You can't hug Miller": Spatz and Steinberg, page 213.
—"The club began to play as though it took some interest in the game": Spatz and Steinberg, page 195.
—"scowled and said a lot of caustic things to nobody in particular": Spatz and Steinberg, page 297.
—"The fact that he made an error that possibly cost us a World Championship": Barrow, page 133.
—"Yankees training on Scotch": Graham, page 74.
—"If a guy wanted it, he found it": William B. Mead, *Two Spectacular Seasons* (New York: Macmillan, 1990), page 71.
—"Oh sure, I remember you now": Graham, page 76
—"Like to play the horses?": Graham, page 77.
—"Why not come to Chicago with us?": ibid.
—"each player sign his name beneath his picture": ibid.
—"I'll bet you one hundred bucks that he's a detective": Frank Graham, *All-Time All Stars* (New York: Signet, 1977), page 181.
—"You're nuts": ibid.
—"Is there any one of you who wishes to deny that this is his signature under his picture?": Graham, *Yankees*, page 78.
—"All right, sucker. I'll take cash or a check": Graham, *All Stars*, page 181.
—"I'm running a ball club, not a fight club": Graham, *Yankees*, page 82.
—"What for, you stupid [expletive]!": Sowell, page 303.
—"Miller Huggins has managed his last game with the Yankees": Miller Huggins file at the A. Bartlett Giamatti Library, Cooperstown, New York.
—"I won't fire the man who brought us two pennants": Weintraub, page 174.
—"I'm through": Graham, *Yankees*, page 88.
—"Look, Ed, I'm sick of it too": ibid.

Chapter 5

—"The Yankees are the champions": *New York Times*, October 16, 1923.
—"automobiling": Weintraub, page 98.
—"blackmail": ibid.
—"I would give a year of my life": Frommer, *Remembering Yankee Stadium*, page 35.
—"Be smart here, George, two men on": Weintraub, page 29.
—"to allow Huston to receive his full share of the glory of Yankee Stadium": *New York Times*, May 22, 1923.
—"It was too good to refuse": ibid.
—"I am the sole owner of the Yankees": Weintraub, page 179.
—"hello": Mrs. Babe Ruth, *The Babe and I* (New York: Avon, 1959), page 20.
—"I don't know what hotel you are at": Mrs. Babe Ruth, page 21.
—"I wonder who wrote the note for him": ibid.
—"Tell him I'll have dinner with him tonight": ibid.
—"I'll be delighted to have you both": Mrs. Babe Ruth, page 22.
—"Aren't there any restaurants in Washington?": ibid.
—"Lord, Miss Hodgson, I can't go into any restaurants": ibid.
—"Don't worry": ibid.
—"was the very model of a Southern citizen lawyer": Mrs. Babe Ruth, page 16.
—"very, very, strict": ibid.
—"He just couldn't get home fast enough": ibid.
—"There isn't a decent woman in New York": Mrs. Babe Ruth, page 17.
—"Be here by nine this morning,": Mrs. Babe Ruth, page 18.

—"Thanks, keed": Mrs. Babe Ruth, page 23.
—"You know, you drink too much": ibid.
—"So long, keed": ibid.
—"You know, he's a very nice man, but he's really a child at heart": Mrs. Babe Ruth, page 25.
—"I'm a working girl and need my sleep": ibid.
—"a rather substantial sum if he had lost": Dan Gutman, *Baseball Babylon* (New York: Penguin Books, 1992), page 220.
—"What's wrong with me?": Sowell, page 304.
—"Hey Hug, why won't you let me pitch?": Mike Sewell, page 305.
—"He told me he needed lots of work, so I gave it to him": ibid.
—"Carl, I want to tell you that in all my years in baseball": ibid.
—"I think I've seen another Babe Ruth": Weintraub, page 193.
—"broad-shouldered, good-looking kid walking behind him": Hoyt, page 12.
—"Don't use that one, son": ibid.
—"Who was this powerful kid?": ibid.
—"Do you think you can win this time?": *New York Sun*, September 29, 1929.
—"And then, like a bolt of blue, it happened": Hoyt, page 12.
—"By this time, McGraw was in a frenzy": Frederick G. Lieb, *Baseball Registry* (St. Louis: The Sporting News, 1949), page 37.
—"Never did the big Bambino try harder to break up a game": ibid.

Chapter 6

—"It is not remarkable that the stomach ache of Babe Ruth was felt around the world": *New York Herald-Tribune*, April 11, 1925.
—"If I win the pennant this year": *St. Petersburg Times*, March 4, 1925.
—"The World Champions of 1923 lost the pennant last year for one reason—overconfidence": *Washington Star*, April 8, 1925.
—"They didn't perform the fundamentals": *New York Times,* April 12, 1925.
—"or come dangerously close to it": *New York Times*, March 2, 1925.
—"lucked": Howard K. Hilton, *Reach Baseball Guide, 1926*, page 121.
—"Cobb sent me": *New York Sun*, September 14, 1924.
—"I'll get you, Horan, next season!": *New York Sun*, September 23, 1924.
—"I wish them all the luck in the world against the Giants": *Chicago Tribune*, September 30, 1924.
—"I thought I was going to feed the fishes": *New York Times*, March 21, 1925.
—"I used to chop the wood for him": Curtis F. Garfield, *Sudbury 1890–1989: 100 Years in the Life of a Town* (Porcupine Enterprise, 1999), page 43.
—"Okay, if that's the kind of guy you are, go ahead": *Evening Independent*, March 11, 1925.
—"hog fat": *New York Times*, March 13, 1925.
—"Say it isn't true, Babe": *Evening Independent*, March 12, 1925.
—"Yes, I owe that money": *Evening Independent*, March 11, 1925.
—"If Babe Ruth is broke, then Midas was a pauper": *Evening Independent*, March 12, 1925.
—"Hail to the Chief": *New York Times*, March 2, 1925.
—"This is yours": *Evening Independent*, March 2, 1925.
—"but I'll be down to 215 by opening day": *New York Times*, March 2, 1925.
—"Just what our Babe weighs is somewhat of a mystery": *Evening Independent*, March 2, 1925.
—"ceremonial pitch": *St. Petersburg Times*, February 24, 1925.
—"Ruth is old and fat and his best days are behind him": *New York Times*, March 12, 1925.
—"Dog racing is a great sport": *St. Petersburg Times*, March 3, 1925.
—"Go out to the lot this morning and bag a few flies": *New York Daily News*, March 12, 1925.
—"Hug, I can't": ibid.
—"to set a broad jumping record": *New York Times*, March 12, 1925.
—"Guess some fly balls over there would do the Babe some good": *Evening Independent*, March 12, 1925.
—"Why didn't you come up with that ball?": *St. Petersburg Times*, March 6, 1925.
—"Yeh? If I came up with the ball": *St. Petersburg Times*, March 6, 1925.
—"Why don't you blow out of here?": Weintraub, page 96.
—"So I heard": *The Sporting News*, April 9, 1925.
—"Don't walk him!": *Atlanta Journal*, April 4, 1925.
—"Sure I am going. Don't we play today?": *New York Times*, April 6, 1925.

—"All I can say about Ruth is unless he learns to use good judgment when he eats": *New York Herald-Tribune*, April 9, 1925.
—"I will do your act today, Babe": *Ashville Times*, April 8, 1925.
—"It was my longest ever": ibid.
—"I tipped one for you today, Babe": *New York Times*, April 8, 1925.
—"Every bone hurts in my body": *New York Times*, April 9, 1925.
—"I went everywhere in town, trying to find a size 48": *New York Daily News*, April 9, 1925.
—"Meet me. The report that I am dead is a lie": *New York Evening Journal*, April 10, 1925.
—"How do you feel?": *New York Evening Journal*, April 10, 1925.
—"Cheer up ... I'm all right": *New York Herald-Tribune*, April 10, 1925.
—"I'm sick, I'm in agony, but I am not dead": *New York Evening Journal*, April 10, 1925.
—"The big fellow doesn't take care of himself": *New York Times*, April 10, 1925.
—"He's careless": ibid.
—"That comes as a shock": *New York Daily News*, April 13, 1925.

Chapter 7

—"It isn't what you used to be; it's what you are today": *New York Evening Journal*, March 15, 1926.
—"I guess I'll have to take the doctor's advice": *New York Times*, April 12, 1925.
—"We are ready for the bell to sound": *New York Evening Journal*, April 11, 1925.
—"I knew Shocker had the earmarks of a great pitcher": *Philadelphia Record*, October 1, 1929.
—"Not only will he win games for us": *Atlanta Journal*, April 4, 1925.
—"I'm no prophet, but I say Shocker will win twenty games for this team this year": *New York Times*, April 5, 1925.
—"The greatest outfield prospect in a decade": *New York Times*, April 12, 1925.
—"He's fast, hits to all fields, and gets on base often": *New York Times*, March 18, 1925.
—"When I passed the one-thousand mark, I lost interest in the matter": *New York Times*, May 7, 1925.
—"A great weakness": *New York Times*, April 12, 1925.
—"the best fielding shortstop since [Rabbit] Maranville": *New York Times*, April 12, 1925.
—"They don't seem to miss me much": *New York Times*, April 15, 1925.
—"I guess we won't get bigger crowds until Ruth is back in the lineup": *New York Daily News*, April 20, 1925.
—"It's easier to be in bed when you know you're not missing anything": *New York Times*, April 21, 1925.
—"The Yankees have rarely looked worse than they did today": *New York Times*, April 23, 1925.
—"Robbed by the umpires": *New York Times*, April 24, 1925.
—"I suspect Huggins' opinion of [umpire] Ormsby is not high": ibid.
—"Johnson is dressing": *New York Evening Journal*, April 25, 1925.
—"Why in the hell don't you make them send up a pinch hitter?!": *New York Daily News*, April 24, 1925.
—"The hit should be null and void": *New York Sun*, April 24, 1925.
—"Our left on base totals reads like the national census": *New York Times*, April 29, 1925.
—"The Yankees have now plummeted to the depths of humiliation": *New York Times*, May 2, 1925.
—"I'm sticking with Scott": *New York Sun*, April 25, 1925.
—"I don't know how long they will keep me here": *New York Times*, May 3, 1925.
—"What's the trouble with you?": ibid.
—"Collectively or individually?": *Washington Times*, May 2, 1925.
—"I mean man against man": ibid.
—"I never knew what pain was until this time": *New York Times*, May 3, 1925.
—"Without Everette in the lineup": *New York Times*, May 7, 1925.
—"He is young and has a natural appetite for ground balls": *New York Sun*, May 8, 1925.
—"excellently ... anxious to get out": *New York Times*, May 23, 1925.
—"All I need is a little more exercise to strengthen my legs": *New York Times*, May 23, 1925.
—"I go down south to lose weight and I get sick": *New York Times*, May 25, 1925.
—"The Yankees cannot possibly be this bad": *New York Times*, May 25, 1925.
—"If he's a slugger, then I'm the reigning prince of Hindustan": *New York Times*, May 28, 1925.

—"What an outburst of hoots and sepulchral moans": ibid.
—"Take him out!": *New York Times*, June 14, 1925.
—"in no condition to play": *New York Times*, June 2, 1925.
—"The Big Bam looked pale and thinner through the shoulders": *New York Morning Telegraph*, June 4, 1925.
—"He received a burst of applause when he came to bat for the first time": *New York Morning Telegraph*, June 4, 1925.
—"In the good days he would have scored standing up": *New York Times*, June 2, 1925.
—"The spirit was willing, but the flesh was weak": *Washington Times*, June 3, 1925.
—"The old dogs won't work fast": *New York Evening Journal*, June 2, 1925.
—"just for luck": *New York Sun*, June 4, 1925.
—"Miller Huggins took his favorite lineup and shook it to pieces": *New York Times*, June 3, 1925; *New York Telegraph*, June 4, 1925.
—"The fans were sorry to see Wally go": *New York Times*, June 3, 1925.
—"Well, where have these guys been all season?": *New York Daily News*, June 4, 1925.
—"From now on they'll be a hard outfit to beat": *New York Evening Journal*, June 3, 1925.
—"It was one of those games that you could fall asleep at any time": *New York Times*, June 18, 1925.
—"I guess some of you guys would like to be fired back to a championship outfit": *New York Evening Journal*, June 24, 1925.
—"He has improved wonderfully since replacing Scott": *New York Sun*, July 21, 1925.
—"You guys haven't a chance in the world": *New York Evening Journal*, June 27, 1925.
—"No club but the current Yankees could permit a play like that": *New York Times*, July 17, 1925.
—"How two base runners with their eyes open in plain daylight": *New York Times*, July 30, 1925.
—"My boys are original": *New York Journal*, June 26, 1925.
—"Tough": *New York Evening Journal*, June 30, 1925.
—"There is absolutely nothing to it": *New York Times*, June 27, 1925.
—"That's news to me": ibid.
—"I'm through": Creamer, page 291.
—"The farm has become a nuisance": *New York Times*, June 29, 1925.

—$100,000: Pirone, page 38.
—"It feels like somebody sticking me with a pin": *New York Evening Journal*, June 29, 1925.
—Dialog with Ford Frick and Miller Huggins: *New York Evening Journal*, June 29, 1925.
—"I have practically made up my mind to retire": *New York Evening Journal*, August 28, 1925.
—"In the first game there was no fire to the Yankees game": *New York Times*, July 16, 1925.
—"I was visiting the homes of some personal friends": *Chicago Herald Examiner*, August 31, 1925.
—Dialog of Huggins and Ruth: *New York Sun*, July 23, 1925.
—"New York is not patient with ball teams": *New York Sun*, July 21, 1925.
—"$100,000 beauty": *New York Sun*, July 31, 1925.
—"Oh, goody, goody. Let's give three cheers": *New York Sun*, August 18, 1925.
—"Will you get Colonel Ruppert's backing on this?": Barrow, page 141.

Chapter 8

—"Ruth has been a bad boy this season": *St. Louis Post-Dispatch*, August 29, 1925.
—"Sorry Hug, I had some business to attend to": *New York Times*, September 4, 1955.
—Huggins-Ruth dialog: Dave Anderson, "Sport of the Times," Miller Huggins file at the A. Bartlett Giamatti Library, Cooperstown, NY; Graham, *All Stars*, page 184.
—"I just want him to understand things": *New York Sun*, August 31, 1925.
—"Then I will see [Jake] Ruppert": *Chicago Daily News*, August 31, 1925.
—Landis-Report dialog: *New York Sun*, August 31, 1925.
—"I will back Huggins to the finish": *Chicago Daily News*, August 31, 1925.
—"Holy Smokes": *New York Sun*, August 31, 1925.
—"If Huggins is the manager [in 1926], I'm through with the Yankees": ibid.
—"Huggins is making me the 'goat'": *New York Times*, August 31, 1925.
—"The fine is a joke": *New York Times*, August 31, 1925.
—"Can you imagine a fellow who hit about .240 when he was playing": Tom Stanton,

Ty and the Babe: Baseball's Fiercest Rivals (New York, St. Martin's Press, 2007), page 122.
— "The truth to the matter is that Huggins is incompetent": *New York World*, August 31, 1925.
— "If Huggins is a baseball manager, I can swim the English channel": *Chicago Herald Examiner*, August 31, 1925.
— "because I thought it was the proper play": *New York World*, August 31, 1925.
— "Anyway, it's too hot to sleep in St. Louis": *Chicago Tribune*, August 31, 1925.
— "He was afraid that Peckinpaugh would get his job": *Chicago Herald Examiner*, August 31, 1925.
— "Well, what do you think of it?": *Chicago Daily News*, August 31, 1925.
— "I appreciate the contrary of being given the opportunity to defend myself": *Chicago Daily News*, August 31, 1925.
— "Of course it means drinking": *Chicago Tribune*, August 30, 1925.
— "I have tried to overlook Ruth's behavior for a while": *New York Times*, August 30, 1925.
— "Will the five-thousand-dollar fine be in cash?": *Chicago Tribune*, August 30, 1925.
— "He charges me with excessive drinking": *New York Sun*, August 31, 1925.
— "Anything Miller Huggins says goes with me": *Chicago Tribune*, August 31, 1925.
— "Huggins, despite of what Babe Ruth says": *New York World*, September 1, 1925.
— "Find us a customer, someone who will take Ruth's contract and his upkeep": ibid.
— "If Ruth comes back here and says he's sorry": ibid.
— "That will be up to Huggins": ibid.
— "When I think that Ruth has learned his lesson": *New York World*, September 2, 1925.
— "Leave him alone": Creamer, page 296.
— "Come to the [Concourse] hotel, boys, later on": *New York World*, September 2, 1925.
— "Are you going to quit the Yankees?": Creamer, page 296.
— "What about you and Mrs. Hodgson?": ibid.
— "The Bambino is going to have to explain about the rumors": *New York Evening Journal*, September 1, 1925.
— "I know absolutely nothing about those affairs": *New York Sun*, August 31, 1925.
— "She couldn't cope": Creamer, page 297.

— "I have heard both sides, and Huggins is handling the matter": *New York Sun*, September 1, 1925.
— "Ruth is not running the Yankees": *New York World*, September 1, 1925.
— "Hello, Miller": *New York Times*, September 2, 1925.
— "May I put on a uniform?": *New York World*, September 3, 1925.
— "and soon Ruth was all alone, thinking over his mistakes": ibid.
— "What's the matter, Babe?": Cobb, page 3.
— "Hello, is this you, Hug?": *New York Times*, September 5, 1925.
— "Gosh, I'll go stale": *New York World*, September 4, 1925.
— "The main thing is Ruth must convince me": *New York Times*, September 4, 1925.
— "Well, Hug, I'm here": *New York Times*, September 7, 1925.
— "They come in bunches like bananas": *New York Times*, September 8, 1925.
— "Koenig hits well, looks good, and was tidy in the field": *New York Times*, September 9, 1925.
— "It has been a shame the way balls have traveled through our infield": *New York Evening Journal*, August 31, 1925.
— "since the unhappy days of Frank Chance": *New York Times*, October 4, 1925.
— "It seems like poetic justice": *Washington Evening Star*, October 1, 1925.
— "His progress has been amazing this year": *New York Times*, October 4, 1925.

Chapter 9

— "Babe Ruth not only will stage a comeback next season": *New York Times*, December 26, 1925.
— "Losing your pep?": *New York Times*, January 3, 1926.
— "Ruth weighed 254": Leigh Montville, "How the Babe Got Fit," *Parade Magazine* (April 30, 2006): page 12.
— 682,000 permits and thirty-five million dollars: *St. Petersburg Times*, February 28, 1926.
— "Let's go get breakfast, fellows": *St. Petersburg Times*, March 1, 1926.
— "Well, vacation has ended": *New York Evening Journal*, March 1, 1926.
— "It's the first time since he joined the Yankees that he was first in anything except the dining room": *New York Evening Journal*, March 2, 1926.

Notes—Chapter 9

—"Hey, Hug, this guy is hooking 'em": *New York Evening Journal*, March 2, 1926.
—"He's a sure bet": *New York Sun*, March 2, 1926.
—"At 190 pounds, he's built more like a fullback than an infielder": *New York Sun*, September 16, 1925.
—"Poosh 'em up Tony": *New York Sun*, July 16, 1926.
—"Ever since I was a kid I wanted to be a big league player": *New York Sun*, April 4, 1926.
—"My folks often told me about it": *New York Sun*, April 1, 1926.
—"Like it better than the Czar": *St. Petersburg Times*, March 6, 1926.
—"Is there anything I can do for you to make your stay more pleasant?": ibid.
—"The Hugman looked as bad this afternoon": *New York Times*, March 10, 1926.
—"It was like one of those games where the fat men play the thin men": *New York Times*, March 12, 1926.
—"I am not much of a baseball historian but I do remember that in 1919": *New York Times*, March 15, 1926.
—"a rather sour strike on Lazzeri": *New York Times*, March 16, 1926.
—"I'm not a man for a few words": *New York Evening Journal*, March 17, 1926.
—"A few more words and I would have socked that guy,": ibid.
—"If Miller Huggins knew how to manage a ball team": Levitt, page 226.
—"One of the Yankees was complaining": *Washington Post*, March 14, 1926.
—"They aren't a ball team; they're just a lot of players": Levitt, page 226.
—"That made us fighting mad": Babe Ruth, *The Babe Ruth Story* (New York: Signet, 1992), page 143.
—"I feel sometimes I would like the take the newspapermen, one by one": *New York Evening Journal*, March 19, 1926.
—"In all the years I've directed the New York team": *New York Sun*, March 19, 1926.
—"dangerous operation": *New York Times*, October 3, 1925.
—"The big fellow has come to his senses": *New York Sun*, March 30, 1926.
—"There's no doubt about it, the Yankees are going to win the pennant": *St. Petersburg Times*, March 4, 1926.
—"They had a few old fellows who happened to come through for them last season": *New York Times*, March 2, 1926.
—Yankees club bulletin: *New York Sun*, March 23, 1926.
—"Meanwhile, what does he think my batters will do?": *New York Times*, March 27, 1926.
—"Well, there is one way I am sure to stop the Yankees": *New York Times*, March 31, 1926.
—"Old Hickory": *New York Times*, April 1, 1926.
—"He must have been a considerable citizen to have a bat named after him": ibid.
—"The Brooklyn Dodgers outfielders are getting dizzy": *New York Times*, April 2, 1926.
—"The Yankees have the greatest hitting club ever assembled": *New York Times*, April 6, 1926.
—"There seems to be nothing that the Yankees cannot do": *New York Times*, April 9, 1926.
—"a screamer": *New York Times*, April 10, 1926.
—"No, I don't want to predict that": *New York Sun*, April 13, 1926.
—"You have to excuse me; I do not speak the English very well": *New York Sun*, April 16, 1926.
—"This is the hardest hitting club I ever had": *New York Times*, April 16, 1926.
—"I'm not so worried about the pitchers": ibid.
—"People who were taking the afternoon constitutional saw the stranger in the sky": *New York Times*, April 21, 1926.
—"It was warm enough to take off your overcoat": *New York Times*, April 22, 1926.
—"to break the World's standing high jump record": *New York Times*, April 28, 1926.
—"It was one of the gamest throws of the decade": *New York Times*, May 19, 1926.
—"It looks like now that the only thing that can stop the Yankees is another amendment to the Constitution": *New York Times*, May 2, 1926.
—"How did those birds ever win eight straight?": *New York Times*, May 4, 1926.
—"Let's see that hand": *New York Times*, May 9, 1926.
—"We've always been good friends and the first thing he did when he saw me": *New York Times*, May 11, 1926.
—"a huge modern looking four engine plane": Von Hardesty, *Lindbergh* (New York: Harcourt, 2002), page 22.

—"All the Yankees need now is good pitching": *New York Times*, May 12, 1926.
—"better than Ward": *New York Times*, May 10, 1926.
—"Ruth went hitless for the first time in a week": *New York Times*, May 19, 1926.
—"Getting hold of a straight one": *New York Times*, May 20, 1926.
—"It would have gone over the stand at Yankee Stadium": *New York Times*, May 26, 1926.
—"The Yankees must be stopped or the pennant will be a joke": *New York Times*, May 30, 1926.
—"You can't hit what you can't see": *New York Times*, June 29, 1926.
—"Out a week": *New York Times*, May 15, 1926.
—"The Yankees at some point or another are due for a slump": *New York Times*, June 14, 1926.
—"Look at the Babe": *New York Sun*, June 25, 1926.
—"Don't worry, Mr. Ruth": ibid.
—"I did nothing of the kind": *Philadelphia Evening Bulletin*, September 28, 1926.
—"What the hell ... Let's eat": *New York Sun*, June 25, 1926.
—"We'll have you fixed up with a room, the first one, Mr. Ruth": ibid.
—"He fanned": ibid.
—"This damn charley horse": ibid.
—"The Babe liked my mother": Mrs. Babe Ruth, page 26.
—"How did you like what Grove did to your boys?": *New York Sun*, June 29, 1926.
—"Jack Dunn seemed unreasonable to meet": ibid.
—"but not as much as Johnson had a number of years ago": *New York Sun*, July 7, 1926.
—"I'm losing too many ball games": *New York Times*, July 6, 1926.
—"He may not last the season": *New York Sun*, July 7, 1926.
—"The Yankees will crack": *New York Times*, July 12, 1926.
—"Like all clubs, good or bad, they will have their unlucky spells": *New York Sun*, June 30, 1926.

Chapter 10

—"You may say a lot of uncomplimentary things about the Yankees": *New York Times*, July 22, 1926.
—"What's the matter with the Yankees?": *New York Sun*, July 9, 1926.
—"What about Koenig?": ibid.
—"The crowd could hardly believe its eyes": *New York Times*, August 1, 1926.
—"If the Indians can't gain on the Hugman at home": *New York Times*, August 11, 1926.
—"I engineered the whole party": *New York Sun*, August 10, 1926.
—"I'm not what I would call a good hitter": *New York Sun*, September 1, 1926.
—Koenig refused to speak to Ruth until they shook hands on the last day of the season: Dave Newhouse, "A Golden Team's Sole Survivor" (SI Vault).
—"I don't think we got good enough pitching": *New York Sun*, September 24, 1926.
—"with terrific speed": *New York Times*, September 12, 1926.
—"Babe, I admire a man who can win over a lot of tough opponents": Ruth, page 144.
—"Beat those fellows today, that's all I ask": *New York Times*, April 4, 1928.
—"to let those fellows know what one sportswriter thinks of them": Barrow, page 143.
—"If I had known, I would have knocked Mike out of the way": *New York Sun*, September 16, 1926.
—"The result was an absurd condition to play": *New York Times*, September 19, 1926.
—"We're playing rotten ball": *New York Times*, April 4, 1928.
—"I believe it's good luck. I've worn it all year": *New York Sun*, September 27, 1926.
—"It took more than luck": ibid.
—"It's nothing": *New York Sun*, September

Chapter 11

—"He [Pete Alexander] had a curveball that did a lot of queer things": *New York Evening Journal*, October 5, 1926.
—"Horace, we will not only get the ball": Charlie Poekel, *Babe & the Kid* (Charleston, SC: The History Press, 2007), page 50.
—"They seem a bit out of their class": *New York Sun*, October 2, 1926.
—"Hello, kid!": ibid.
—"I feel plenty good, but I got to have the trainer to tape me up a bit": ibid.
—Dialog with the Cardinals and a policemen: *Chicago Tribune*, October 3, 1926.
—"Will it rain?": *New York Sun*, October 3, 1926.

—"Babe is the color of a nice red brick house": *New York Times*, October 3, 1926.
—"The credit goes to Pennock": *New York Time*, October 3, 1926
—"Alex will never last": *New York Times*, October 4, 1926.
—"Get in there!": ibid.
—"We couldn't hit Alexander. That's all there's to it": *New York Times*, October 4, 1926.
—"We'll win the series, I'm sure of it": *New York Sun*, October 4, 1926.
—Dialog of Graham, Huggins, Ruth, and Koenig: *New York Sun*, October 4, 1926.
—"It Ain't Gonna Rain No More": *New York Times*, October 6, 1926.
—"It's for a sick kid": Poekel, page 51.
—"To Johnny Sylvester": *New York Evening Journal*, October 7, 1926.
—"I'll knock a home run for you in Wednesday's game": ibid.
—"It's the same old story, but I have to say it": *Chicago Tribune*, October 6, 1926.
—"I can't see the Cardinals as a ball club": ibid.
—"The Babe is waving that wand over the plate": *New York Times*, October 7, 1926.
—"Oh, what a shot!": ibid.
—"That's a World Series record—three home-runs in one World Series game": ibid.
—"I said we would start hitting, didn't I?": *New York Times*, October 7, 1926.
—"I look to have the boys keep the hitting up in the next three games": *Chicago Tribune*, October 7, 1926.
—"I don't think there is anything that can stop us": *New York Times*, October 7, 1926.
—"Boy, was that a darling": *Chicago Tribune*, October 7, 1926.
—"no. 1, 2, and 3": ibid.
—"Ball": *New York Times*, October 8, 1926.
—"It was low": ibid.
—"Now watch the play": *New York Times*, October 8, 1926.
—"You can't beat a fighting spirit like that": *New York Times*, October 8, 1926.
—"I have to say it, but ordinary pop ups": *Chicago Tribune*, October 8, 1926.
—"I had a bunch of fine fellows out there this afternoon": *New York Times*, October 8, 1926.
—"We kicked the game away from Sherdel": *New York Sun*, October 8, 1926.
—"We're just one game behind, that's all": *New York Times*, October 9, 1926.

—"Alexander has a world of speed today": *New York Times*, October 10, 1926.
—"They can't beat us now": *Chicago Tribune*, October 10, 1926.
—"Alexander stopped them and won": ibid.
—"We didn't hit": *Chicago Tribune*, October 10, 1926.
—"but some 'friends' got hold of him and thought they were doing him a favor": Lawrence S. Ritter, *The Glory of Their Times* (New York: Macmillan, 1966), page 236.
—"This is the way Alex holds them": *New York Sun*, October 12, 1926.
—"one of the best catches of the series": *New York Times*, October 11, 1926.
—"Oh, Meusel": ibid.
—"Poosh-em up Tony!": ibid.
—"Then from around the corner of the bleachers": *Chicago Tribune*, October 11, 1926.
—"he walked like a man in no hurry to go anywhere": *New York Times*, October 11, 1926.
—"Like a fighter who fidgets in the corner": *New York Sun*, July 8, 1927.
—"Can you do this, Alex?": Ritter, page 236.
—"Alexander now pitching for St. Louis": *Chicago Tribune*, October 11, 1926.
—"Alexander's arm goes up": *New York Times*, October 11, 1926.
—"I thought we were going to pitch him low and outside?": Ritter, page 237.
—"The Yanks must score or the Championship will go to St. Louis": *New York Times*, October 11, 1926.
—Dialog of Alexander and Hildebrand: Lieb, *Cardinals*, page 125.

Chapter 12

—"Nobody worked harder to win a championship last season than Babe": *New York Sun*, March 4, 1927.
—"Two gentlemen to see Mr. Johnny": *New York Sun*, October 12, 1926.
—"Gosh": ibid.
—"the last ball used in the first game of the World Series": Poekel, page 83.
—"Goodbye, Johnny": *New York Sun*, October 12, 1926.
—"Johnny's a fine looking boy": Poekel, page 85.
—"I am already counting the days until I can get up": ibid.

—"You and I have a lot to remember about the 1926 World Series": Poekel, page 97.
—"I want to settle down for a while": *Detroit News*, November 4, 1926.
—"I want to be traded if Cobb is the manager next year": *Boston Globe*, May 8, 1927.
—"swung his last bat in a baseball game": *Detroit News*, November 4, 1926.
—"I am going to be forty on December 18": ibid.
—"The Indians finished second last season": *New York Times*, November 29, 1926.
—"a baseball scandal which may surpass all previous exposes": *Chicago Tribune*, December 21, 1926.
—"There are two fellows going out of the game absolutely clean": *Chicago Tribune*, December 22, 1926.
—"a dirty deal": *Chicago Tribune*, December 24, 1926.
—"Ty Cobb and Tris Speaker never again will play ball or manage in the American League": *Chicago Tribune*, January 13, 1927.
—"I am mighty glad that Commissioner Landis has cleared Cobb and myself": *Chicago Tribune*, January 28, 1927.
—"It wouldn't be good for baseball": ibid.
—"Yes, I want Ty Cobb": *Chicago Tribune*, February 5, 1927.
—"This will be my last year in baseball": *Philadelphia Evening Bulletin*, February 8, 1927.
—"I was determined to get Speaker": *Washington Post*, February 1, 1927.
—"There's nothing else to say": *New York Sun*, March 1, 1927.
—"The bitching between Ruppert and Ruth should not be taken seriously": *New York Times*, February 12, 1927.
—"You're crazy": *New York Times*, February 16, 1926.
—"Ruth is in perfect condition": *New York Times*, February 27, 1927.
—"He and I had met in 1921": Jack Dempsey, *Dempsey* (New York: Harper and Row, 1977), page 207.
—"It's a bad match, as I see it": *New York Sun*, September 23, 1926.
—"I still think he's a great fighter and I doubt that Tunney could beat him": ibid.
—Dialog between Ruth and Dempsey: Dempsey, page 208.
—"Babe Ruth Comes Home": *Chicago Tribune*, March 2, 1927.
—"Get your one hundred thousand, Babe!": *New York Sun*, March 2, 1927.

—Dialog of Ruth and hotel operator: *New York Sun*, March 2, 1927.
—"Nicely": *New York Sun*, March 2, 1927.
—"May we say you are delighted beyond words, Mr. Huggins?": *New York Sun*, March 3, 1927.
—"It's a big gamble": *Chicago Tribune*, March 3, 1927.
—"I'll get what I asked for from Colonel Ruppert": *New York Sun*, March 19, 1927.
—"To hold or not to hold": *St. Petersburg Times*, March 8, 1927.
—"There are lots of trains heading back to St. Louis": *St. Petersburg Times*, March 12, 1927.
—"Overall, he looks fit": *St. Petersburg Times*, March 8, 1927.
—"Up with the sun and to bed with the chickens": ibid.
—"Well, I kissed that one": ibid.
—"He can't pitch": Wilcy "Cy" Moore files at the A. Bartlet Giamatti Library, Cooperstown, New York.
—"I don't care": ibid.
—"I am glad to be here now, with the Yankees": *New York Sun*, March 8, 1927.
—"He's a good batter": *New York Sun*, March 15, 1927.
—"Fort Myers was once a dead city": *St. Petersburg Times*, February 27, 1927.
—"I can hardly be charged with an error on that": *St. Petersburg Times*, March 8, 1927.
—"I want to take this opportunity to express my appreciation": *New York Sun*, March 28, 1927.
—"Who's going to win the American League, Ty?": *New York Sun*, March 18, 1927.
—"While I was in the National League": *New York Sun*, March 19, 1927.
—"This game is a forfeit to the Braves, nine to nothing!": *Philadelphia Inquirer*, March 18, 1927.
—"We want Cobb!": *Philadelphia Inquirer*, March 19, 1927.
—"They will need more strength at short and second": *New York Sun*, March 18, 1927.
—"If our club develops a few more pitchers": *New York Sun*, April 9, 1927.
—"Cobb will have those A's 'nuts' by the time the season is half over": *Philadelphia Inquirer*, April 22, 1927.
—"With good pitching and breaks this team would run away with the pennant": *New York Times*, April 10, 1927.
—"Cobb mishandled the pitchers, and they never recovered": ibid.

—"No use in kidding ourselves": *New York Sun*, March 18, 1927.
—"The White Sox haven't enough besides pitching to take them to the top": *New York Sun*, April 9, 1927.
—"The Browns are not going to win every day": *New York Times*, March 3, 1926.
—"You tell the public what you think of the team": *New York Sun*, April 8, 1927.
—"It looks like a capacity crowd": *New York Sun*, April 13, 1927.
—"glorious hand": *New York Sun*, April 13, 1927.
—"No lefthander this writer has seen in the last forty years": *New York Sun*, April 13, 1927.
—"It took four innings for New York to size up": ibid.
—"Although Cobb is in his fortieth year": ibid.
—"Black spots before the eyes from looking at Grove's speedsters?": *Philadelphia Inquiry*, April 14, 1927.
—"Unless I am dead wrong, Moore is another Cy Young": *New York Sun*, April 14, 1927.
—"I thought you would like to know, Mr. Ruth": Tom Meany, *Babe Ruth* (New York: Grosset & Dunlap, 1951), page 139.
—"Now who in the hell is Johnny Sylvester?": Tom Meany, page 139.

Chapter 13

—"He's coming to see me pitch?": *New York Sun*, June, 17, 1927.
—"I'll be in Paris tomorrow": *Cleveland Press*, May 20, 1927.
—"It's like getting into a death chamber": ibid.
—"He can't make it!": ibid.
—"He's off!": ibid.
—"I didn't think he'd make it": *New York Sun*, May 20, 1927.
—"He must have been moving better than one hundred miles per hour": *Cleveland Press*, May 20, 1927.
—"Yes, that's a good park to hit in": *New York Sun*, May 14, 1927.
—"I have a better club than I had in 1926": *New York Sun*, May 19, 1927.
—Moore and Graham dialog: *New York Sun*, May 20, 1927.
—"The Yankees celebrated by knocking Emil Levsen out of the box": *New York Times*, May 22, 1927.
—"Sock one on the nose!": ibid.
—"We underestimated the Yankees": *New York Sun*, May 27, 1927.

—"Our boys are trying hard to win": ibid.
—"I dunno. But I'll be in there swinging": *New York Times*, June 15, 1927.
—"Push em-up, Tony!": G.H. Fleming, *Murderers' Row* (New York: William Morrow, 1985), page 185.
—"even sniffed it as if it was pretend of filled with iron": *New York Times*, June 12, 1927.
—"Lindy's coming!" *New York Evening Journal*, June 17, 1927.
—"New York City is yours": *New York Times*, June 17, 1927.
—"I never expected anything like this": *New York Times*, June 17, 1927.
—"I feel a homer coming": *New York Times*, June 17, 1927.
—"I had been saving that home run for Lindbergh": ibid.
—"Gee, Dad. That's a peach": *New York Evening Journal*, June 17, 1927.
—"It's very sad that the great exhibition of the Bust-em twins": *New York Times*, June 17, 1927.
—"Lindy! Lindy! Lindy!": *New York Evening Journal*, June 17, 1927.
—"It's too bad that you couldn't have been here earlier": ibid.
—"where six men and two boys fell on it": *New York Times*, June 24, 1927.
—"I never had to force Lou Gehrig's development as a first basemen": *New York Sun*, June 25, 1927.
—"I never had his likes before": *New York Sun*, June 23, 1927.
—"It tickled me to pitch that victory over the Red Sox": *New York Sun*, June 24, 1927.
—"I just mix 'em up—fast ones and slow ones": ibid.
—"He relies on a fellow's experience of being able to pitch without being told": ibid.
—"hee-haw": John Mosedale, *The Greatest of All* (New York: Warner, 1975), page 152.
—"Well, all I hope is you drop twenty straight": *Washington Post*, July 5, 1927.
—"There are few flingers who can win without thinking": *Washington Post*, July 7, 1927.
—Dialog with Bump Hadley and the Washington veteran pitchers: *New York Sun*, July 7, 1927.

Chapter 14

—"Miller Huggins has the strongest team seen in the majors": *New York Sun*, July 21, 1927.

—"It isn't broke": *New York Sun*, July 7, 1927.
—"It sounds funny": ibid.
—"I was hoping to have a good year at second base": *New York Sun*, June 29, 1927.
—"With any speed he would have made four bases on the drive": *Detroit News*, July 9, 1927.
—"I was a bum hitter in the Sally League": *New York Sun*, August 29, 1927.
—"I was fouled": *Washington Post*, July 22, 1927.
—"How are we going to catch a team that rarely loses?": *Washington Post*, July 18, 1927.
—"We are out so far": *New York Sun*, July 22, 1927.
—"Most of the other teams, barring the Indians": ibid.
—"I see John McGraw said the Orioles were the best team the game ever saw": ibid.
—"I don't think the Yankees could touch the old Red Sox": *New York Sun*, September 28, 1927.
—"Not once this season have I come up to the plate with the determination": *New York Sun*, August 3, 1927.
—"This is the most disappointing season of my career": *Cleveland Press*, July 11, 1927.
—"Cobb, Collins, and Wheat have done everything I've expected of them": ibid.
—"A club with great batting that is getting the best pitching in the American League": ibid.
—"When Connie Mack tells me he does not need me": *New York Sun*, August 23, 1927.
—"The Cubs pitching will smother the New York hitters": *New York Sun*, August 17, 1927.
—"A slump?... Back in 1908": *New York Sun*, August 24, 1927.
—"You know what's the most distressing feeling in the world?": *New York Sun*, September 7, 1927.
—"While it is not likely he will go as high as fifty-nine": *New York Sun*, September 7, 1927.
—"Taking pity, we let them win the twenty-second game": Considine, page 152.
—"What are my plans for the World Series?": *New York Sun*, September 16, 1927.
—"like the tail of a comet": Mosedale, page 24.
—"Ladies and gentlemen of the radio audience: we are in Chicago": *Pittsburgh Press*, September 23, 1927.
—"The most impressive spectacle that any of us have ever seen": ibid.
—"Now I want to get one point clear": Dempsey, page 218
—"Dempsey has Tunney down!": *Washington Post*, September 23, 1927.
—"Go to a neutral corner!": Jack Dempsey, page 219
—"Come on and fight": ibid.
—"I realized the time had come to hang up my gloves and leave the ring": ibid.
—"a fastball right through the middle with a three and two count": *New York Sun*, September 30, 1927.
—"Hopkins should be grateful": ibid.
—"What did you say his name was?": ibid.
—"a tall, good-looking chap, his black hair shower-pasted": Mosedale, page 213.
—"You'll not hit any home runs off of our pitchers": Fleming, page 367.
—"Come out to the ballpark": ibid.
—"Gee! They're big guys!": *New York Sun*, October 10, 1927.
—"Holy Smoke!": ibid.
—"If you made mistakes they beat you": Devaney and Goldblatt, page 117.
—"When will Hug learn that Pipgras will never make it as a pitcher?": *New York Times*, October 7, 1927.
—"I don't think we'll come back here": *New York Times*, October 7, 1927.
—"Torn scorecards floated down from the upper deck": Mosedale, page 230.
—"Paul Waner in right field and Lloyd Waner in center each took a few steps": Mosedale, page 232.
—"Let's try a squeeze play, Hug": Ford Frick, "Huggins a constant planner saw Yanks 1930 winner" (Miller Huggins file at the A. Bartlett Giamatti Library, Cooperstown, NY).
—"Listen, we don't have to take a chance at all": ibid.
—"You called it, Hug!": ibid.
—"Nice work, gang": ibid.

Chapter 15

—"Throw the Yankees out of the league and give the other teams a chance!": *New York Sun*, May 29, 1928.
—"I ain't going to demean myself by chasing after golf balls": *New York Sun*, February 29, 1928.
—"Sixty-one or bust": *St. Petersburg Times*, March 7, 1928.
—"Why don't you change up and hit into leftfield?": ibid.

Notes—Chapter 15

—"Would you rather hit .400 than hit sixty-one homers?": ibid.
—"He says he's quit and I'm going to take his word": *New York Times*, March 9, 1928.
—"I hurt my arm during the training trip last season": *New York Times*, March 12, 1928.
—"I come to say goodbye, Hug": *New York Sun*, April 10, 1928.
—"Sure Robertson is a good ballplayer": *New York Times*, March 3, 1928.
—"He's as fine a young shortstop as I ever saw in a southern training camp": *St. Petersburg Times*, March 6, 1928.
—"Never lose that self-assurance that you are the best": Leo Durocher file, A. Bartlett Giamatti Library, Cooperstown, New York.
—"Oh God!": Leo Durocher, *Nice Guys Finish Last* (New York: Simon and Shuster, 1975), page 33.
—Dialog with Huggins and Durocher: Durocher, page 33–34.
—"Overconfidence, lack of pitching, and the unseen uprising of a strong rival": *New York Times*, April 8, 1928.
—"It's not easy to win three pennants in succession": *New York Sun*, April 10, 1928.
—"Even if they don't": *New York Times*, April 7, 1927.
—"Cobb was a great help last season": *St. Petersburg Times*, March 22, 1928.
—"I really wanted to retire": *New York Times*, March 2, 1928.
—"I am unable to run back and pull down those long line drives like I used to": *New York Sun*, March 19, 1928.
—"Everything is fine and we have enjoyed a great training season": *St. Petersburg Times*, March 29, 1928.
—"When you try to bat you have to squint your eyes like this": *New York Times*, March 31, 1928.
—"one of the most disastrous spring training campaigns": *New York Times*, April 11, 1928.
—"They're playing possum": *New York Sun*, March 27, 1928.
—"You are starting another season": *New York Sun*, April 13, 1928.
—"I wonder if Al Simmons is listening down at the hospital": *Philadelphia Record*, April 14, 1928.
—"We're going to knock the A's off again": ibid.
—"Whiff him!": ibid.
—"Max gathered it up and threw to Joe Hauser": ibid.
—"Here we go, and on to first place": ibid.
—"They're all right": *New York Times*, April 13, 1928.
—"This game shows me that there isn't anything wrong with this ball club": *New York Sun*, April 13, 1928.
—"If some old Philadelphia furniture hadn't interrupted its flight": *New York Times*, April 14, 1928.
—"Boston extends you hearty greetings on your season": *Boston Globe*, April 11, 1928.
—"hitless wonder": *New York Times*, April 13, 1928.
—"two-hundred right-handed and two-hundred left": Ruth, page 165.
—"pulling for": *New York Times*, April 12, 1927.
—"He did fine": ibid.
—"You get in my way again, you fresh busher": Durocher, page 35.
—"Well, kid, the next time he comes to bat": ibid.
—"Now what are you going to do?": Leo Durocher, page 36.
—"I am not conceding the pennant to the Yankees this year": *New York Sun*, April 23, 1928.
—"It was a Ruthian shot of the first order": *New York Sun*, May 2, 1928.
—"Hey, cousin, are you going to pitch today?": *New York Sun*, May 8, 1928.
—"A game young man": *New York Sun*, May 21, 1928.
—"I don't know what to do with all of this spare time": *New York Sun*, May 16, 1928.
—"How do you beat a team that scores seven runs a day": *New York Times*, May 15, 1928.
—"So thick were the fans in leftfield": *New York Times*, May 25, 1928.
—"I'm tired": *New York Sun*, May 26, 1928.
—"What pleased me today was Gehrig's home run": ibid.
—"about eighty years of spit balling": *New York Times*, May 27, 1928.
—"It looks like they have knocked the armchair out from under me again": *New York Times*, May 29, 1928.
—"Break up the Yankees": Barrow, page 152.
—"Get other American League clubs to go out and buy high-class players like we have done": *New York Sun*, May 31, 1928.
—"The Athletics are so far behind that it will cost them ten cents": *New York Times*, June 4, 1928.
—"I'd rather wait until we make a swing around the west before I commit myself": *New York Times*, May 29, 1928.

—"I'll be right when the warm weather comes around": *New York Times*, June 8, 1928.
—"The rape of the Red Sox was now complete!": Lieb, *Red Sox*, page 187.
—"I found the way to acquire control is to pitch in games": *New York Sun*, July 28, 1927.
—"Pipgras needs a lot of work": *New York Sun*, May 11, 1927.
—"traveled at unbelievable speed": *New York Times*, June 11, 1928.
—"One of the hardest hit balls of his career": *New York Times*, June 11, 1928.
—"Your correspondent was certain that the ball had gone into the stand": *New York Times*, June 14, 1928.
—"But I played some outfield in Milwaukee last year and hit .333": *New York Sun*, August 2, 1928.
—Dialog of Yankees during batting practice: *New York Sun*, June 29, 1928.
—"It was an authentic wallop": *New York Times*, June 29, 1928.
—"It's all over but the shouting": *New York Times*, July 2, 1928.

Chapter 16

—"Flowers bloom and their fragrance fills the air": *New York Times*, September 8, 1928.
—"I thought for sure he was hurt badly on that play": *New York Sun*, July 4, 1928.
—"Babe Ruth's wife lives over there": *Boston Herald*, January 13, 1929.
—"We always thought that 'Mrs. Kinder' had been divorced from Babe Ruth": ibid.
—"a young matron with no social aspirations": *Boston Post*, January 15, 1929.
—"They frequently went out at night by themselves": ibid.
—"That would be a terrible way to die": ibid.
—"I remember that dog": *Boston Post*, January 17, 1928.
—"I was the only person in the neighborhood who knew": *Boston Post*, January 17, 1929.
—"Dorothy Kinder": *Boston Post*, January 15, 1929.
—"No woman likes to hide her love": Mrs. Babe Ruth, page 26.
—"I'm a Catholic, I'm married, and I have a kid": Mrs. Babe Ruth, page 27.
—"He didn't have much besides his spitter in the last few years": *New York Sun*, July 7, 1928.
—"I've had a bum heart for some time": Marty Appel, *Pinstripe Empire* (New York: Bloomsbury, 2012), page 159.
—"Oh, sure": ibid.
—"I'm going to Denver to fight this thing": ibid.
—"Nothing mattered if you put a baseball into his hands": *Rocky Mountain News*, September 10, 1928.
—Dialog of the Yankees during batting practice: *New York Sun*, July 10, 1928.
—"whack!": *New York Times*, July 19, 1928.
—"a charming little lady": *New York Times*, July 20, 1928.
—"Give her a wristwatch": ibid.
—"It started three weeks ago and spread through the arm and into the hand": *New York Sun*, July 24, 1928.
—"If you ask me": *New York Sun*, July 11, 1928.
—"Once upon a time there was a Yankee pitcher who lasted the full nine innings": *New York Times*, August 1, 1928.
—"I gave them the best I had in the way of pitching": *New York Sun*, August 2, 1928.
—"Boy, is he fast": *New York Times*, August 10, 1928.
—"a walloping blow": *New York Times*, August 11, 1928.
—"The burden is on the A's": *New York Sun*, August 13, 1928.
—"They have showed that they are a great club": ibid.
—"The clients applauded furiously": *New York Times*, August 16, 1928.
—"He may be out a few days or several weeks": *New York Times*, August 23, 1928.
—"Isn't this a swell break?": *New York Sun*, August 22, 1928.
—"When did your arm go lame?": ibid.
—"I don't expect Lazzeri to play regularly for the rest of the season": *New York Times*, August 27, 1928.
—"He's a smart, clever southpaw who has plenty of experience": *New York Times*, July 24, 1928.
—"You'll be working today, Zach": *New York Times*, September 27, 1929.
—"left the Detroit batters swinging in empty air": *New York Times*, August 28, 1928.
—"Going to jump?": *New York Times*, September 1, 1928.
—"pull Lazzeri's arm out of its socket to make sure he would be out until October": *New York Sun*, October 31, 1928.
—"There are two things Grove is doing this year": *New York Sun*, September 1, 1927.

—"Nobody told me a thing": ibid.
—"Where do you think you're going?": *New York Times,* September 7, 1927.
—"I am hoping that the A's play Hauser and Hale": *New York Sun,* September 6, 1928.
—"They're liable to be groggy": ibid.
—"Not since 1886, when the double-header habit was introduced into baseball": *New York Sun,* September 6, 1928.
—"Bring on the A's!": *Washington Post,* September 9, 1928.

Chapter 17

—"I want to take this occasion to thank every member of the team": *New York Sun,* September 29, 1928.
—"I got a reserve ticket": *New York Times,* September 10, 1928.
—Receipts totaled $115,000: *New York Times,* September 10, 1928.
—"Get me a morning paper": *Rocky Mountain News*: September 10, 1928.
—"I'll be better today": ibid.
—"conscious to the last and unaware of the pending tragedy.": ibid.
—"He played the game to the last": ibid.
—"They broke out with the thunder": *New York Times,* September 10, 1928.
—"We broke their hearts today": *New York Times,* September 10, 1928.
—"I hit a curve ball, about the fastest he could throw": ibid.
—"We ought to play them every day": ibid.
—"The same old A's": ibid.
—"I'm just lucky against the Macks": *New York Sun,* September 12, 1928.
—"What a jinx these Yankees are to me": ibid.
—"That kid has nerve": *New York Sun,* September 17, 1928.
—"It was the worst blow I ever got when I was forced to quit against the champions": *New York Sun,* September 16, 1928.
—"There were only four men between me and the victory": ibid.
—"Guess it's time to get out of the game and play with my kids": *New York Times,* September 18, 1928.
—"the squarest man in baseball": ibid.
—"I feel safer here": *New York Sun,* September 19, 1928.
—"I will miss Koenig if he can't play": *New York Sun,* September 20, 1928.
—"Even a blind pig will find an acorn if he keeps rooting long enough": *Chicago Tribune,* September 23, 1928.
—"There's a man hitting out of turn": Durocher, page 37.
—"That's the way I want you to play, son": ibid.
—"Whee, what a relief that it's over at last": New York Sun, September 29, 1928.
—"It's all over!": *New York Sun,* October 3, 1928.
—"It's going to take more than a slap on the kisser to keep me out": *New York Sun,* October 1, 1928.
—"Pipgras and Hoyt have pitched 11 of 13 games": *New York Sun,* October 2, 1928.
—"I hate to be kept waiting in getting my base hits": *New York Sun,* October 3, 1928.
—"Can you beat that kid?": ibid.
—"I pitched him a screwball": *New York Sun,* October 6, 1928.
—"He's pitching better than he was in that other inning": Bill Slocum, "Miller Huggins as I knew him," Miller Huggins file at the A. Bartlett Giamatti Library, Cooperstown, New York.
—"My fortunes lay in the fact that I couldn't hit the corners": ibid.
—"We couldn't beat anybody with the kind of pitching we got": ibid.
—"How can I write my piece when I am sitting on a bridge game?": ibid.
—"But the train moves so fast that I can't hit the keys": ibid.
—"He should've caught it": *New York Sun,* October 8, 1928.
—"A guy would be safer in the World War": ibid.
—"We played terrible, terrible": ibid.
—"Where did Ruth hurt you?": ibid.
—"He's all right. The Babe didn't hurt him": ibid.
—"You can't do this": Lowell Reidenbaugh, *Sporting News Selects Baseball's 50 Greatest Games* (St. Louis: Sporting News Publishing Company, 1986), page 213.
—"Ruth isn't out. Sherdel will have to pitch all over to him": ibid.
—"But it's legal!": ibid.
—"The National League is a hell of a league": Smelser, page 383.
—"We were as crazy as a bunch of wild Indians": Ruth, page 162.
—"Go away": Ruth, page 163.
—"Don't do it, Mr. Ruth": Montville, *Big Bam,* page 279.
—"Did anyone see my false teeth?": Ruth, page 163.

Chapter 18

—"This thing has licked me": *Framingham News*, January 16, 1929.
—"The dentist and his wife aren't usually home at this hour": *Boston Post*, January 15, 1929.
—"Mrs. Kinder has been confined to her home": ibid.
—"That's not a electric light": ibid.
—"Are you going to turn on an alarm?": *Boston Post*, January 16, 1929.
—"Mrs. Kinder is in the house": *Boston Post*, January 15, 1929.
—"choking smoke": *Boston Herald*, January 14, 1929.
—"severely burned about the body": *Boston Post*, January 13, 1929.
—"artificial respiration": *Watertown Sun*, January 17, 1929.
—"your house is on fire": *New York Morning Telegram*, January 14, 1929.
—Dialog with O'Hearn and caller: *Boston Herald*, January 14, 1929.
—"sister-in-law": *Boston Post*, January 15, 1929.
—"Arthur, isn't this a tough break to get?": *Boston Post*, January 15, 1929.
—"half-sob": ibid.
—"Oh, Babe Ruth, he's a buddy of the doctors": ibid.
—"Mrs. Kinder had married when very young": ibid.
—"His story is a damnable lie": *Boston Post*, January 15, 1929.
—"It isn't true": *Boston Post*, January 16, 1929.
—"and the police do not have all the facts behind the death of my sister": *Boston Post*, January 14, 1929.
—"I am sure Mrs. Ruth did not take drugs or sleeping pills": *Boston Post*, January 17, 1929.
—"There is nothing about the body that is inconsistent with death in a burning building": *Boston Herald*, January 14, 1929.
—"The wiring of the house gave indications that amateurs tinkered with them": *Boston Herald*, January 14, 1929.
—"She never told anyone that she was his wife": *Boston Post*, January 16, 1929.
—"What I'm going to say I can say in very few words": *Boston Globe*, January 15, 1929.
—"Her death comes as a great shock to me": *New York Sun*, January 14, 1929.
—"Never!": *Boston Post*, January 17, 1929.
—"We're going to make every effort to have Dorothy with us": ibid.
—"There has been no evidence that a crime was committed": *Boston Herald*, January 14, 1929.
—"There's the Babe": *Boston Post*, January 18, 1929.
—"Over here, Babe": ibid.
—Lou Gehrig's letter: *Boston Herald*, January 16, 1929.
—"Forever rest in peace": *Boston Herald*, January 17, 1929.
—"I'm proud of you, Babe": *Boston Post*, January 15, 1929.
—"These were happy times": ibid.
—"Oh-oh-oh-Helen-oh-oh": *Boston Post*, January 17, 1929.
—"Oh-oh, wait": ibid.
—"I've made all the arrangements": *Boston Herald*, January 17, 1929.

Chapter 19

—"We're not going on a honeymoon": *New York Sun*, April 18, 1929.
—"drab, gray waiting room": Pirone, page 51.
—"When that didn't work, they simply told me to shut up": Pirone, page 41.
—"Trust in God: everything will be all right": Pirone, page 47.
—According to another source, that had been arranged by Ruth's lawyer: *Boston Post*, January 19, 1929.
—"I give and bequeath unto my husband, George Herman Ruth": *Boston Herald*, January 30, 1929.
—"slighted": Pirone, page 48.
—"Shocked": *Boston Herald*, January 30, 1929.
—"Mrs. Ruth's family is delighted that Dorothy is fully provided for": *Boston Herald*, January 31, 1929.
—"beloved ward": *Boston Herald*, January 31, 1929.
—"Claire is going to be your new mother": Dorothy Ruth Pirone, page 51.
—"She's not my mother, and she will never be my mother!": ibid.
—"You've done very nicely toward us": *Boston Herald*, January 18, 1929.
—"I want to do right by you": ibid.
—"If I'm getting married, it's news to me": *Chicago Tribune*, April 16, 1929.
—"I want a license": *Chicago Tribune*, April 17, 1929.
—"When?": *New York Sun*, April 16, 1929.
—"Hello, Babe": *New York Times*, April 18, 1929.

—"looking pretty and charming, and a trifle sleepy": *New York Sun*, April 17, 1929.
—"I do": ibid.
—Dialog with reporter and Ruth: *New York Times*, April 18, 1929.
—"It is expected that he will make '3' as famous as the '77'": *New York Times*, April 18, 1929.
—"You better stop that kiss-throwing, Babe": *Mrs. Babe Ruth*, page 28.
—"Gehrig, with no bride to tip his cap to": *New York Times*, April 18, 1929.
—"By all means, you must go to Boston": *Mrs. Babe Ruth*, page 61.
—"We feel you have done a great deal for him since the two of you met": ibid.
—"New York in a breeze": *New York Times*, March 3, 1929.
—"No, I don't believe the Yankees can get into the World Series": *New York Sun*, May 10, 1929.
—"I can beat Connie Mack in golf right now": *New York Times*, March 3, 1929.
—"Don't bother me about that": *New York Times*, March 18, 1929.
—"Any time Huggins says the word": *New York Times*, March 28, 1929.
—"He is a 'change of pace [pitch]' away from becoming the best pitcher": *New York Times*, March 7, 1929.
—"He's fast": *New York Times*, March 22, 1929.
—"Arm perfect": New York Times, March 9, 1929.
—"I like third": *New York Sun*, March 6, 1929.
—"The only question about Durocher was if we could make Koenig into a third baseman": *New York Sun*, March 31, 1929.
—"He takes grounders with his hands too far back": *New York Times*, March 30, 1929.
—"I will stand pat or fall with the catchers I started the season with": *New York Sun*, August 13, 1928.
—"Dear cousin": *New York Sun*, March 30, 1929.
—"Injuries have held us back": *Washington Post*, March 15, 1929.
—"The day is not far off when millionaires will be buying up the ball clubs": ibid.
—"It looks like another walkover for the Yankees": *New York Sun*, March 30, 1929.
—"The fans in the Southwest are the most enthusiastic": *New York Sun*, April 9, 1929.
—"But I'm not kicking": ibid.
—"Two sharp thrusts: one from the left the other from the right": *New York Times*, May 19, 1929.

—"the Yankees pitching was now on track": ibid.
—"Everybody knows that Bob can hit": *New York Times*, June 4, 1929.
—"My dogs [feet] are terrible": *New York Sun*, May 31, 1929.
—"If Durocher doesn't hit well enough to hold his job": *New York Times*, June 4, 1929.
—"It's just a trial for a few days": *New York Sun*, May 20, 1929.
—"Where you going?": *Washington Post*, June 3, 1929.
—"heart attack": *New York Times*, June 8, 1929.
—"You tell them that I'm far from a dead one": ibid.
—"Where you can't find me": *New York Times*, June 12, 1929.
—"but they found us anyway": *New York Times*, June 16, 1929.
—"They are bound to crack sooner or later": *New York Times*, June 16, 1929.
—"It's almost the single opinion in the baseball world": *New York Times*, June 21, 1929.
—"If Mack's players can win 3 of 5 games": *New York Sun*, May 31, 1929.
—"I'm rooting for the Yankees": *New York Times*, June 21, 1929.
—"I don't think the Yankees will find us a bit worried": *New York Sun*, June 18, 1929.
—"A heavy gloom settled over the crowd": *New York Times,* June 22, 1929.
—"crushed into the ball with terrific force": ibid.
—"The fight isn't over by any means": *New York Times*, June 25, 1929.
—"I don't think we can be counted out yet": ibid.
—"Hey, you birds!": *New York Times*, July 15, 1929.

Chapter 20

—"We're licked this year, but next year we'll have a winner": Frick, "Huggins a Constant Planner."
—"a great lifting swing": *New York Sun*, August 12, 1929.
—"pounced on it and thrust it into his pocket": ibid.
—"What do we have here?": ibid.
—"Gimme that, will you?": ibid.
—"Eddie ... give me a new baseball and a fountain pen": ibid.
—"Miller Huggins is a very sick man": *Philadelphia Record*, September 26, 1929.

—"The wear and tear of running a championship team is becoming too much": *New York Sun*, September 26, 1929.
—"I owe a lot to Colonel Huston": Ford Frick, "Huggins took criticism of Huston as boost," Miller Huggins file at the A. Bartlett Giamatti Library, Cooperstown, New York.
—"What the hell are you doing?": *New York Sun*, September 3, 1929.
—"Why was I replaced?": ibid.
—"It's all over": *New York Times*, September 4, 1929.
—"Go see a doctor because I have a red spot on my face?": Ruth, page 175.
—"Listen, when I see a doctor this time it will be a tough, tough pull": Slocum.
—"What happened?": Cook, pages 111–112.
—"Well, I'll tell you this": ibid.
—"Mr. Huggins, why don't you go home?": Durocher, page 45.
—"Art, I'm going home": Graham, page 157.
—"very sick man": *New York Sun*, September 23, 1929.
—"Huggins has worked himself down to his last ounce of energy": ibid.
—"grave": *New York Sun*, September 23, 1929.
—"seemed brighter": ibid.
—"How much chance do I got, Doc?": *Boston Globe*, September 26, 1929.
—"If prayers can help, the old boy ought to pull through": *Boston Post*, September 27, 1929.
—"His lowered vitality resulted in rapid spread of the infection": *Pittsburgh Press*, September 26, 1929.
—"Well ... we'll have to finish this game—let's get it over with": *Cleveland Plain Dealer*, September 26, 1929.

Chapter 21

—"Miller Huggins passes into baseball history as one of the greatest managers of all time": *Washington Post*, September 25, 1929.
—"I always felt that Miller Huggins never received full credit for his managerial skills": *Philadelphia Inquirer*, September 26, 1929.
—"Lou Gehrig was the most affected of the players": *Cincinnati Enquirer*, June 4, 1930.
—"No one will ever know how much Miller did for me": ibid.
—"And for years after that": Ruth, pages 175–76.
—"What's the matter with me?": Ruth, page 176.
—"You can't manage yourself, so how are you going to manage the Yankees?": Ira Berkow, *Hank Greenberg* (New York: Times Books, 1989), page 88.
—"I've noticed an improvement in Ruth since he got married": *New York Sun*, August 9, 1929.
—"Ruth has taken more money from the Yankees than I have": Mead, page 13.
—"I'm good for $25,000 a year for life": Mead, page 14.
—"A lot of people in New York are rioting for bread": ibid.
—"Why don't people tell me these things?": ibid.
—"You will never hear of another ballplayer getting that kind of money": Mead, page 15.
—"It's the best problem to have": *Washington Post*, April 24, 1930.
—"We need relief pitching, badly": ibid.
—"Was there any fault with my conduct in 1930 or efforts to make Shawkey's year a success?": Ruth, page 183.
—"You really earned the big money I paid you": ibid.
—"Did they have to go to the National League for a manager?": *New York Times*, July 30, 1974.
—"Somebody should have had more compassion when they maneuvered him out of the American League": Berkow, page 88.
—"His wife would be managing the team in a month": *New York Times*, July 30, 1974.
—"but that's all we had in common": Pirone, page 59.
—"Babe was a good father, considering the circumstances": Pirone, page 67.
—"Despite his faults, baseball didn't do right by him": Berkow, page 88.
—"He won six pennants in spite of virtually insurmountable difficulties": *New York Times*, February 4, 1964.
—"If I were ten years younger": Slocum.
—"Baseball and real estate don't mix": *Philadelphia Inquirer*, September 26, 1929.
—"Miller said it had always been worth it": Harvey Frommer, *Baseball's Greatest Managers* (New York: Franklin Watts, 1985), page 112.
—"Ruth was never a bigger fellow than the day he admitted he was wrong": *New York Times*, September 26, 1929.
—"He ran the club wisely and well": *Boston Post*, September 26, 1929.
—"New York will always hold Miller Huggins in affectionate memory": *New York Times*, May 9, 1932.

Bibliography

Appel, Marty. *Pinstripe Empire*. New York: Bloomsbury, 2012.
Asinof, Eliot. *Eight Men Out*. New York: Henry Holt, 1987.
Barrow, Edward Grant. *My Fifty Years in Baseball*. New York: Coward-McCann, 1951.
Berkow, Ira. *Hank Greenberg*. New York: Times Books, 1989.
Cobb, William R. *Babe Ruth: Playing the Game*. Mineola, NY: Dover, 2011.
Considine, Bob. *The Babe Ruth Story*. New York: Penguin, 1992.
Cook, William A. *Waite Hoyt*. Jefferson, NC: McFarland, 2004.
Creamer, Robert W. *Babe*. New York: Fireside, 1992.
Dempsey, Jack. *Dempsey*. New York: Harper and Row, 1977.
Devaney, John, and Burt Goldblatt. *The World Series*. Chicago: Rand McNally, 1981.
Durocher, Leo. *Nice Guys Finish Last*. New York: Simon and Shuster, 1975.
Fleming, G.H. *Murderers' Row: The 1927 New York Yankees*. New York: William Morrow, 1985.
Frommer, Harvey. *Baseball's Greatest Managers*. New York: Franklin Watts, 1985.
_____. *Remembering Yankee Stadium*. New York: Harry N. Abrams, 2008.
Garfield, Curtis F. *Sudbury 1890–1989: 100 Years in the Life of a Town*. Sudbury, MA: Porcupine Enterprises, 1999.
Gilbert, Brother. *Young Babe Ruth*. Harry Rothgerber, ed. Jefferson, NC: McFarland, 1999.
Graham, Frank. *All-Time All Stars*. New York: Signet, 1977.
_____. *The New York Yankees*. Carbondale: Southern Illinois University Press, 2002.
Gutman, Dan. *Baseball Babylon*. New York: Penguin, 1992.
Hardesty, Von. *Lindbergh*. New York: Harcourt, 2002.
Harris, Stanley "Bucky." *Playing the Game*. Grosset & Dunlap, 1925.
Hilton, Howard K. *Reach Baseball Guide, 1926*.
Hoyt, Waite. *Babe Ruth as I Knew Him*. New York: Dell, 1948.
Levitt, Daniel R. *Ed Barrow*. Lincoln: University of Nebraska Press, 2008.
Lieb, Frederick G. *The Baltimore Orioles*. New York: G.P. Putnam's Sons, 1955.
_____. *The Baseball Registry*. St. Louis: The Sporting News, 1949.
_____. *The Boston Red Sox*. New York: G.P. Putnam, 1947.
_____. *The St. Louis Cardinals*. New York: G.P. Putnam, 1944.
Mead, William B. *Two Spectacular Seasons*. New York: Macmillan, 1990.
Meany, Tom. *Babe Ruth*. New York: Grosset & Dunlap, 1951.
Montville, Leigh. *The Big Bam*. New York: Broadway, 2006.
Mosedale, John. *The Greatest of All*. New York: Warner Paperback Library, 1975.
Pirone, Dorothy Ruth. *My Dad, the Babe*. Boston: Queen Press, 1988.
Poekel, Charlie. *Babe & the Kid*. Charleston, SC: History Press, 2007.
Prindle, Edward J. *The "Reach" Art of Batting*. Philadelphia: A.J. Reach, 1904.
Reidenbaugh, Lowell. *Sporting News Selects Baseball's 50 Greatest Games*. St. Louis: Sporting News, 1986.
Reisler, Jim. *Babe Ruth*. New York: McGraw-Hill, 2004.
Ritter, Lawrence S. *The Glory of Their Times*. New York: Macmillan, 1966.

Ruth, Babe. *The Babe Ruth Story*. New York: Signet, 1992.
Ruth, Mrs. Babe. *The Babe and I*. New York: Avon, 1959.
Smelser, Marshall. *The Life that Ruth Built*. Lincoln: University of Nebraska Press, 1975.
Sowell, Mike. *The Pitch that Killed*. New York: Macmillan, 1989.
Spatz, Lyle, and Steve Steinberg. *1921: The Yankees, the Giants, and the Battle for Baseball Supremacy in New York*. Lincoln: University of Nebraska Press, 2010.
Spink, J.G. Taylor. *Judge Landis and Twenty-Five Years of Baseball*. New York: Thomas Y. Crowell, 1947.
Stanton, Tom. *Ty and the Babe*. New York: St. Martin's Press, 2007.
Tullius, John. *I'd Rather Be a Yankee*. New York: Macmillan, 1986.
Weintraub, Robert. *The House that Ruth Built*. New York: Little, Brown, and Company, 2011.

Internet

www.baseballalmanac.com
www.baseballlibrary.com
www.baseball-reference.com
www.SI.com

Articles

Durocher, Leo. "Candid memories of Leo Durocher."
Frick, Ford. "Huggins a constant planner, saw Yanks 1930 winners."
_____. "Huggins took criticism of Huston as boost," Miller Huggins file at the A. Bartlett Giamatti Library, Cooperstown, New York.
Hoyt, Waite. "Babe Ruth as I Knew Him." New York: Dell, 1948.
Montville, Leigh. "How the Babe Got Fit." *Parade Magazine*, April 30, 2006.
Newhouse, Dave. "A Golden Team's Sole Survivor." September 3, 1990.
Slocum, Bill. "Miller Huggins as I Knew Him." September 1929.
Thatchenburg, Leo. "The Travails of Miller Huggins."

Newspapers

Ashville Times
Atlanta Journal
Boston Globe
Boston Herald
Boston Post
Chicago Daily News
Chicago Herald Examiner
Chicago Tribune
Cincinnati Enquirer
Cleveland Plain Dealer
Cleveland Press
Detroit News
Evening Independent
Framingham News
New York Daily News
New York Evening Journal
New York Herald-Tribune
New York Morning Telegraph
New York Sun
New York Times
New York World
Philadelphia Evening Bulletin
Philadelphia Inquirer
Philadelphia Record
Pittsburg Press
Rocky Mountain News
St. Louis Post-Dispatch
St. Petersburg Times
Sporting News
Washington Herald
Washington Post
Washington Star
Washington Times
Watertown Sun

Index

Numbers in ***bold italics*** indicates pages with photographs.

Academy of the Assumption 170
Adelphia Hotel 164
Aiken, Albert 107
Alexander, Pete 99, 107–110, 115–120, 189, 190, 192
Astor Hotel 21

Bailey, Fanny 180, 181, 197, 198
Baker, Frank 30
Ball, Phil 36, 37, 166
Baltimore Orioles (American League) 9
Baltimore Orioles (International League) 8, 9, 10, 98, 102
Baltimore Orioles (National League) 17, 145
Barrow, Ed 5, 13, 28, 42, 44, 65, 72, 76, 79, 87, 105, 128, 165, 215, 218; accepts job as Yankees business manager 40; manager of Red Sox 11, 23; switched Babe Ruth from pitcher to everyday player 11
Barry, Dave 149, 150
Barton, Jimmy 46
Bengough, Benny 49, 77, 89, 167, 172, 183
Bennett, Eddie 49, 90, 151, 214
Bishop, Max 160, 161, 178, 181, 185, 216
Bluege, Ossie 66
Bodie, Ping 18
Boston Braves 73, 89, 206, 223
Boston Red Sox: Babe Ruth years 2, 10, 17, 18; in 1925 67, 69, 72, 73, 82; in 1926 92, 93, 102; in 1927 130, 132, 137, 140; in 1928 161, 164, 166, 167, 174; in 1929 206, 210, 211, 218, 219; in transactions with Yankees 5, 23, 165
Bottomley, Jim 117, 189, 190
Bresnahan, Roger 36
Britton, Helene Robison 35, 36
Brooklyn Dodgers 11, 15, 20, 53, 91, 92, 156, 203
Brother Matthias 7, 81
Burke, Bobby 141
Bush, Joe "Bullet Joe" 28, 32, 44, 51, 52, 64

Byrd, Richard 94, 104, 133, 134, 156
Byrd, Sammy 210, 213, 216, 222

Campbell, Brick 209
Cardwell, Charlie 73
Carlin, Phil 108, 149
Carrigan, Bill 130, 145, 146, 160
Carroll, Ownie 222
Chance, Frank 15, 84, 143, 217
Chapman, Ben 217, 222
Chapman, Ray 19, 20
Chicago Cubs 11, 147
Chicago White Sox: in 1920 19; in 1925 66, 75, 76; in 1926 96, 100, 101, 106; in 1927 130, 136, 141, 144; in 1928 162, 163, 172–175, 186; in 1929 209; World Series scandal of (1919) 18, 20, 22, 25
Cincinnati Reds 97, 221, 222
Clarke, Fred 217
Cleveland Indians: in 1920 19, 20; in 1921 24, 26, 41; in 1925 70–72; in 1926 101, 103–105; in 1927 130, 135, 136; in 1928 161, 163, 173; in 1929 214
Cobb, Ty 24, 41, 48, 128–131, 146, 150, 157, ***159***, 160–162, 166, 173, 178, 185–187, 206; announces retirement from baseball 185; confrontation with Bob Meusel 54, 55; confrontation with Leo Durocher 162; confrontation with Lou Gehrig 55, 71, 94, 102; last career at bat of 184; resigns as Tigers manager 122; rivalry with Babe Ruth 54, 71, 94; signs with Athletics 124; suspected of fixing ball games 123, 124
Cochrane, Mickey 98, 131, 164, 168, 181–183, 208, 213, 216
Cole, Burt 54
Collins, Eddie 128–131, 146, 184, 186, 187
Collins, Pat 68, 69, 92, 93, 97, 111, 153, 160, 166, 167, 184, 186, 187
Combs, Earle: in 1925 65, ***68***, 70, 74, 76, 84; in 1926 91–93, 109, 113, 116, 119; in 1927

249

127, 128, 132, 136, 145, 152–153; in 1928 160, 164, 167, 168, 174, 179, 192; in 1929 210, 213, 215, 219; in 1930 222
Comiskey Park 43, 96, 100, 134, 144, 166, 186, 187
Connery, Bob 36, 68, 218, 225
Cooke, Dusty 216, 222
Coolidge, Calvin 66, 108
Coveleski, Stan 156, 163, 165, 174
Crowder, General 141
Crowley, Art 197, 200
Cullop, Nick 58, 59
Cvengos, Mike 153

Davis, Ike 76
Dempsey, Jack 85, 107, 108, 125, 144, 149, 150; in the long count 149
Detroit Tigers: in 1921 41; in 1924 54, 55; in 1925 71; in 1926 94, 101, 102; in 1927 128, 130, 144, 146; in 1928 163, 173, 175, 176, 186, 187; in 1929 209, 211
Devery, Bill 13, 15, 24
Dickey, Bill 156, 208, 210, 216, 217, 222
Dineen, Bill 30, 108, 114, 185, 187
Dixon, Delores 45, 201
Donovan, Bill 15, 99
Douthit, Taylor 190
Dugan, Joe: knee injury 74, 143; knee surgery 90; in 1923 World Series 52; in 1925 66, 72; in 1926 *88*, 92, 93, 109, 114; in 1928 156, 160, 163, 165, 174, 182, 186, 192; in 1929 197; obtained from Red Sox 5; quote by 64; sold to Braves 207
Dunn, Jack 8, 9, 10, 98
Durocher, Leo: antagonizing Ed Morris 208; antagonizing Fatty Fothergill 187; antagonizing Ty Cobb 162; manager of Dodgers 224; in 1928 156–158, 160–161, 164–165, 175, 177–*178*, 188; in 1929 206, 207, 210, 216, 217; purchased by Yankees 75; sold to Reds 222
Durst, Cedric 69, 128, 136, 189, 190, 192, 210, 216, 222
Dykes, Jimmie 96, 176, 184

Ebbets, Charles H. 23
Ebbets Field 23, 203
Edison, Thomas 128
Ehmke, Howard 46, 146, 185
Evers, Johnny 34

Farrell, Frank 15, 24
Fenway Park 5, 18, 139, 148
Ferguson, Alex 75
Field, Marshall 85
Fletcher, Art 128, 157, 183, 184, 218, 221
Forbes Field 151

Fothergill, "Fatty" 187
Foxx, Jimmie 212
Frazee, Harry 5, 27, 39, 46, 165
French, Walt 184
Frick, Ford 70, 73, 74, 80215, 217, 220
Frisch, Frank 189, 192
Fronck, Rene 95, 105
Fuchs, Emil 223

Gazella, Mike 88, 105, 167, 185
Gehrig, Lou: condolence letter to Babe Ruth 200; confrontation with Ty Cobb 55, 71, 94, 102; consecutive games streak 70–71, 206; discovery of 50; first batting practice with Yankees 50, *51*; in home run race, 1927 132, *138*, 140, 141, 146, 150; Johnny Sylvester 121–122; memory of Miller Huggins 220; in 1925 73, 76, 82, 84; in 1926 *88*, 89, 91, 92, 96, 99, 106, 108, 109, 111, 114, 117, 120; in 1927 132, 138, 140–144, 146, 147, 150, 151–153; in 1928 156, 159, 176, 177, 179, 181, 182, 184–186, 188, 189–192; in 1929 209–211, 215; in 1930 222
Gibson, Sam 129
Gilks, Bob 127
Gleason, Kid 40, 98
Gomez, Vernon "Lefty" 217
Goslin, Goose 140
Grabowski, Johnny 128, 134, 163, 166, 172
Grange, Red 113, 206
Grantham, Larry 152
Gray, Sam 146, 173
Greenburg, Hank 223, 224
Griffith, Clark 99, 158
Griffith Stadium 140
Grimes, Burleigh 53
Grove, Lefty: in 1926 94–96, 98–99, 102; in 1927 130, 131, 146, 150, 162, 176; in 1928 160–162, 165, 167, 176–178, 183, 184; in 1929 207, 212

Hadley, Bump 141, 142
Hafey, Chick 114–117
Haines, Jesse 111, 116, 190
Hale, Sam 177
Harris, Bucky 12, 59, 71, 140–142, 145, 157, 162, 211
Hass, Mule 173, 216
Hauser, Joe 160, 177
Heilmann, Harry 188
Heimach, Fred 174, 177, 182, 183, 187, 207, 209, 210
Herr, Eddie 87
Herrara, Mike 92
Hildebrand, George 119
Home Plate Farm (Sudbury, MA) 52, 69, 73, 82, 98, 126, 197

Index

Hopkins, Paul 150
Horan, Shags 55
Hornsby, Rogers 36, 97, 108, 114–117, 120, 188, 214
Howley, Dan 124, 130, 171, 173, 211
Hoyt, Waite 5, 21, 22, 23, 24, 32, 41–44, 46, 49, 53, 55, 58–61, 63–68, 77–82, 85, 86, 88–90, 93, 95, 97–100, 102, 105, 106, 131, 133, 134, 143, 147, 148, 151, 157–161, 163–169, 171, 174, 175, 178, 180, 182–187, 200, 206, 207, 209, 210, 212–221, 224–226; background of 23; in 1921 World Series 26, 27, 42; in 1926 World Series 109, 110, 112, 114–116; in 1927 World Series 152; in 1928 World Series 189, 190, 193
Hudlin, Willis 163, 214
Huggins, Arthur 218
Huggins, James 35
Huggins, Miller: attempt to buy Cardinals 36–37; background 34, 35; business aspirations 53, 225; death 219; fines and suspends Babe Ruth 77; health issues 40, 214, 215, 217, 218; hired by Yankees 17; in hospital 218, 219; pep talks 105, 159; playing career 2, 34, 35; praised as manager *16*, 36, 37, 106, 220, **225**, 226; in real estate business 85, 225–226; resignation from Yankees 41; St. Louis Cardinals manager 35–37, 68; taking disciplinary action 18, 42, 43, 73–75, 79, 81, 82, **83**, 101, 157, 164, 216; talking about 1925 Yankees 64, 72; talking about 1926 Yankees 95, 99, 100, 110, 112, 113, 115, 116; talking about 1927 Yankees 129, 132, 139, 145, 165; talking about 1928 Yankees 156, 158, 160, 163, 164, 166, 173, 174–176, 185–187; talking about 1929 Yankees 207, 210, 212, 213, 216; under fire as manager of Yankees 1, 3, **38**–40, 44, 72, 90
Huggins, Myrtle 40, 218
Huston, Col. Tillinghast 2, 6, 13, 15, 17, 27, 28, 37, 38, 42, 89, 215; background 14; bid to buy Dodgers 46; selling share of Yankees 44, 46, 47

Jackson, Joe "Shoeless Joe" 25, 96
Jennings, Juanita 170, 201
Johnson, Ban 15, 17, 29, 30, 36, 39, 156, 166–168, 173, 176, 179, 183, 184, 207, 209
Johnson, Ernie 66
Johnson, Hank 183, 184, 207, 209
Johnson, Walter 66, 70, 93, 99, 141, 142
Jones, Sam "Sad Sam" 28, 51, 92, 101, 128, 176
Judge, Joe 140

Keeler, Wee Willie 17
Kelly, Detective 42, 43
Kelly, George 44

Killefer, Bill 116
Kinder, Dr. Edward 126, 195, 198, 199
Kinder, William, Jr. 195, 196, 197, 198
Kinder, William, Sr. 197
King, Dr. Edward 66, 66, 211, 218, 219
Koenig, Mark: debut with Yankees (1925) 82, 84; in 1926 75, **88**, 91, 92, 95, 99–102, 105, 110, 111, 114–117, 119; in 1927 131, 132, 134, 139, 143, 145, 148, 152, 153; in 1928 163–169, 171, 173, 174, 179, 181, 182, 184, 186, 189; in 1929 207, 210, 213; in San Francisco earthquake (1906) 87–88; scouted by Huggins (1925) 68; traded to Tigers (1930) 222
Krichell, Paul 50, 61, 62, 75, 87, 88, 126, 177

Lake Crescent Park 58, 86, 87, 127, 255
Landis, Judge **23**, 25, 27, 28, 43, 50, 78, 123, 124, 129, 163
Lang, Al 57, 58
Lannin, Joe 10
Lary, Lyn 207, 210, 216, 217, 222
Lazzeri, Tony: background 87, 143; movie actor in *Slide, Kelly, Slide* 127; in 1926 **88**, 89, 90–93, 95, 99, 101, 102, 107, 111, 114; in 1927 131, 132, 134, 136, 139, 141–143, 145, 152; in 1928 158, 160, 162–165, 167, 168, 173–177, 182, 183, 185, 188, 191; in 1929 207, 210, 212; in 1930 222; at Salt Lake City 87; vs. Pete Alexander in 1926 World Series 109, 117, *118*; vs. Pete Alexander in 1928 World Series 189, 192
League Park 105, 134, 214
Leonard, Dutch 123, 146
Levsen, Emil 135
Lieb, Frederick 27, 50
Lindbergh, Charles 104, 105, 133, 134, 135, 137, 138, 139
Lisenbee, Hod 140, 150, 151, 162

Mack, Connie: in 1926 95, 102; in 1927 128, 129, 131, 136, 146, 150; in 1928 173, 178, 179, 182–184, 187; in 1929 206, 208, 212, 213, 218, 219; offered Babe Ruth 10; praised by Ty Cobb 185; praises Miller Huggins 220; on Ruth a manager 223; signs Tris Speaker 158; signs Ty Cobb 124
Maranville, Rabbit 65, 128
Marberry, Fred 141
Mays, Carl 26, 27, 38, 39, 41, 42, 47, 49, 51; investigation for fixing games 50; in tragedy of Ray Chapman 19, 20
McCarthy, Joe 222
McGovern, Artie 85, *86*, 102, 124, 125
McGowen, Bill 94
McGraw, John 14, 17, 23, 24, 26, 32, 51–53, 145

McKechnie, Bill 189–192
McLean, Larry 34
McNamee, Graham 108, 109, 112, 115, 116, 149
Merkle, Fred 94, 128
Meusel, Bob: actor *Slide Kelly, Slide* 127; attempt to throw Huggins off train 39–40; background 25–26; confrontation for Detroit Tigers 54–55; confrontation with Ty Cobb 55; contract clause (1921) 26; in 1920 25–26; in 1921 World Series 27; in 1922 28, 32; in 1923 World Series 52; in 1925 61, 69–70, 82, 84; in 1926 91–94, 105–106, 109, 111, 114, 115–117, 120; in 1927 128, 131, 132, 136, 145, 152, 153; in 1928 160, 163–165, 167, 172, 176, 181, 186, 189–192; in 1929 209–211, 213; sold to Cincinnati Reds (1930) 216; suspension of (1922) 28
Miljus, Johnny 153
Miller, Bing 173, 184
Moore, Wilcy "Cy": in 1927 127, 128, 132, 134–136, 139, 140, 145, 148, 151–153; in 1928 155, 157, 173–175; in 1929 207, 209, 213, 214
Moran, Pat 40
Morehart, Ray 128, 136, 143, 155
Moriarity, George 130, 163
Morris, Ed 208
Murderers' Row, origin 37, 38

Navin, Frank 15
Navin Field 134, 143, 144
Nehf, Art 51, 52
Nevers, Ernie 134
New York Giants 14, 15, 23, 24, 26, 27, 32, 43, 45, 51, 52
New York Yankees: add uniform numbers in 1929 206; failure to win 1924 pennant 53–54; history 15; 1927 Yankees, as greatest team 143, *145*, 146; transactions with Red Sox 5, 23, 165; unwelcome tenants by Giants at the Polo Grounds 24; visit Miller Huggins grave site 220

O'Donnell, Cardinal Joseph 96
O'Farrell, Bob 109, 114, 115, 117, 118
O'Leary, Charlie 41, 75, 89, 126, 157, 183, 219
O'Neill, Steve 60, 75
Ormsby, Red 66
Oroll, Ossie 173, 178, 185
Orteig, Raymond 95, 139
Owens, Brick 24

Pascal, Ben 65, 76, 105, 114, 128, 131, 166, 167, 172

Pate, Joe 146
Peckinpaugh, Roger 28, 84, 99, 163; as manager of Yankees 15, 40–42; traded by Yankees 42, 79, 84; winning 1925 MVP 84
Pegler, Westbrook 1, 89, 90, 105, 220
Pennock, Herb: in 1923 51; in 1925 74; in 1926 96, 108, 109, 111, 114, 115, 121; in 1927 143, 144, 152, 153; in 1928 157, 160, 162, 164, 165, 174–175, 188; in 1929 200, 212, 216; obtained by Yankees from Red Sox 5, 51, 165
Pfirman, Cy 191
Philadelphia Athletics: in 1914 10; in 1920 18, 24; in 1921 42; in 1925 67, 82; in 1926 93, 94, 98, 99, 102; in 1927 128–132, 136, 140, 147, 150; in 1928 164–8, 174, 144, 178–185; in 1929 208, 211–213, 216, 217; in 1930 222
Philadelphia Phillies 221
Pipgras, George 5, 75, 128, 156, 161, 163, 164, 167, 172–176, 181, 182, 186, 207, 209, 210, 212, 216; background 165; in Minors (1926) 75; in 1927 128, 152, 156, 166; in 1928 161, 163–166, 167, 172–176, 181–182, 188, 189, 190; in 1929 210, 212, 216; obtained by Yankees from Red Sox 5, 75, 165
Pipp, Wally 15, 27, 30, 43, 46, 50, 70–73, 84, 88
Pittsburgh Pirates 147, 148, 151–153, 189
Polo Grounds 2, 14, 18, 23, 24, 26, 28–30, 41, 43, 44, 106, 134, 167
Pratt, Del 64
Princess Martha Hotel (St. Petersburg, FL) 57, 86, 91, 126, 155, 221

Quinn, Jack 28, 165, 181; on Chapman tragedy 20

Reinhart, Art 112
Rhem, Flint 112
Rice, Sam 151
Rickey, Branch 17, 36, 37
Robertson, Gene 156, 174, 181, 185, 186, 216
Robinson, Wilbert 15, 39, 53, 91, 92; interview for Yankees managing job 16
Rommel, Eddie 146
Root, Charlie 147
Roth, Mark 75, 147
Ruether, Dutch 101, 111, 139–141, 143, 155, 158
Ruffing, Red 206, 222
Ruppert, Col. Jacob 6, 14, 15, 38, 42, 49, 58, 76, 78, 110, 139, 192, 200, 206, 215, 219, 222–223, 225; announces Babe Ruth deal 2, 5; background 13, 14; buyout of Huston 44, 46; contract negotiations with Babe Ruth 28, 126, 127, 221; hires Miller Hug-

gins 17; interviews Wilbert Robinson 17; loyalty to Miller Huggins *16*, 39, 44, 77, 79; purchase of Yankees 2, 13; vision of Yankee Stadium 24, 47, 180

Ruth, Claire Hodgson: background 48; career as actress and model 48–49; dating Babe Ruth 98, 171; engaged to Babe Ruth 203, 204; first date with Babe Ruth 49; introduced to Babe Ruth 47; invited to travel with New York Yankees 206; marriage with Frank Hodgson 48–49; marries Babe Ruth 204–205; as Mrs. Babe Ruth 204, *205*, 206, 211, 212, 223–*224*

Ruth, Dorothy 3, 45, 57, 65, 73, 98, *196*, 197, 198, 200; at Academy of the Assumptions (Wellesley Hills, Mass) 170–171, 197, 202, 203; on Babe Ruth as a father 224; beneficiary of Helen's will 203; birth *31*–32; child custody battle 199–200; circumstances of birth 170; first meeting with Claire Hodgson 203; growing up in Ruth's second marriage 223–*224*; living in Brooklyn as Marie Harrington 202–203; reunited with Babe Ruth 203

Ruth, George Herman "Babe": attempt to throw Huggins off train 39–40; bid to manage team 222–224; changing the game of baseball 2, 11, 17; child custody battle for Dorothy 199–200; childhood 6, 7; criticizes Miller Huggins 78–79; first home run at Yankee Stadium 46; fitness sessions with Artie McGovern 85, *86*, 125; 500th career home run 214; illness 60–63, 65, 67; informed of Helen's death 197; marital problems 2, 56, 59, 66, 73, 80; married to Claire 204, *205*, 206, 211, 212, 223–*224*; marries Helen, in 1914 10; meets Claire 67; meets Johnny Sylvester 121, 161; 1920 season 17, 19, 24; 1920–21 salary 18; 1921 season 22; 1921 World Series 26–28; 1922 season 28, 29, 30, 32, 33; 1922 World Series 32; 1923 season 51, 54; 1923 World Series 52; 1924 season 54; 1925 season 59, 69, 70, 75, 77, 82, *83*, 84; 1926 season 92, 93, 95, 96, 102, *103*, 106; 1926 World Series 108–118, *119*, 120, *122*; 1927 season 131, 132, 134–137, *138*, 139, 140, 144, 146–150; 1927 World Series 151–153; 1928 season *159*, 160, 161, 165–168, 172, 175, 179, 181–186, 188; 1928 World Series 188–192; 1929 season 206, 210–213; 1930 season 222; origin of nickname "Babe" 81; pays last respects to Helen 200–201; praised Miller Huggins 220, 226; reported dead 19, 61, 210; rivalry with Cobb 54, 71, 94; at St. Mary's Industrial Home for Boys 7, 8, *9*, 48, 81; separation from Helen 73–80; sex exploits 20, 24; signs baseball for Johnny Sylvester 111; signs 1922 contract 28; signs 1927 contract 125–127; signs 1930 contract 221; sixtieth homer, in 1927 151; stomach ache 53, 61, 62; surgery 63, 65; suspensions 28–31, 42, 77; traded to Yankees 2, 5, 6; visits Jack Dempsey 125; "washed up" 1, 58; wedding (second marriage) 204–205; with Baltimore Orioles 9; with Boston Braves 223; with Boston Red Sox 2, 10, 11, 17, 18; with Providence Grays 10

Ruth, George Herman, Sr. 6, 7; death 12

Ruth, Helen Woodford: *196*; autopsy 197, 200; background 10; at ballpark *11*; courtship with Babe Ruth 10; dating Dr. Edward Kinder 126, 169; death 95; funeral 203; lifestyle after separation from Babe Ruth 98, 170; marital problems with Babe Ruth 2, 56, 59, 66, 73, 80; married Babe Ruth 1914 10; nervous breakdowns 7, 66, 69, 126; separation from Babe Ruth 73, 80; as single mom 98; will 203

Ruth, Julia (Hodgson) 46, 98, 223, *224*

Ruth, Katherine 6, 7, 12; death 7

Ruth, Mamie (Mrs. Mary Moberly) 7, 172

Ryan, Rosey 52

St. Louis Browns: in 1922 30, 32; in 1926 95, 109; in 1927 130, 134, 137, 139, 144, 146–148; in 1928 166, 171–173, 185, 186; in 1929 211, 215

St. Louis Cardinals 34–37, 97, 107–120, 188–192

St. Mary's Industrial Home for Boys 7, 8, *9*, 48, 81

St. Petersburg, Florida 56, 57, 59, 85, 87, 89, 91, 126, 127, 155, 206, 208, 215, 221

St. Vincent's Hospital 63, 65, 66, 69, 73, 126, 211, 218

Schacht, Al 141

Schalk, Ray 130

Schang, Wally 5, 23, 42, 52, 71, 72

Scott, Everett 5, 28, 29, 52, 65, 67, 68, 72, 96

Sewell, Luke 135, 136

Shanks, Howie 71

Sharkey, Jack 80, 144

Shawkey, Bob 32, 41, 74, 99, 102, 144, 221, 222

Shealy, Al 156, 163, 174, 187, 207

Sheely, Earl 76, 172

Sherdel, Fred 113–115, 121, 189, 191, 192, 221, 222

Sherid, Roy 207

Shibe Park 134

Shocker, Urban 30, 64, 74, 89, 96, 105, 127, 134, 143, 144, 157, 158, 185; death 181; ill-

ness 155, 156, 171, 180; in 1926 World Series 109
Shore, Ernie 142
Simmons, Al 102, 130, 159, 160, 182, 184, 212–214, 216
Sisler, George 166
Southworth, Billy 109, 114
Sparrow, Ed 40
Speaker, Tris 70, 105, 122–124, 130, 132, 140, 158, *159*, 160, 162, 164, 173, 184; suspected of fixing ball games 123, 124
Spink, Taylor 17, 22, 25
Spirit of St. Louis 104, 133
Sportsman's Park 111, 134
Stallings, Larry 72
Stengel, Casey 75
Stoneham, Charles A. 24
Sylvester, Horace 107, 113
Sylvester, Johnny 111, 113, 116, 121, 122, 132, 161; accident 107; illness 107

Taft, Howard 18
Thevenow, Tommy 109, 110, 117
Thomas, Tommy 147, 162–163, 186
Thurston, Sloppy 141
Tilden, Bill 121
Tunney, Gene 125, 144, 149, 150

Uhle, George 135, 144, 163

Veach, Bobby 41, 45

Waddell, Rube 131, 164, 165
Walberg, Rube 146, 147, 162, 182, 207, 213
Walker, Jimmy (New York mayor and senator) 33, 137, 226
Walsh, Christy 32, 33, 57, 85, 198

Waner, Lloyd 151, 152, 154
Waner, Paul 151, 154
Wanninger, Paul "Pee Wee" 65, 67, 68, 72, 74, 76, 84, 88, 132, 206
Ward, Aaron 43, 52, 71, 72, 74, 95
Washington Senators: in 1920 19, 25, 26; in 1924 53, 55; in 1925 55, 65, 70–72; in 1926 93, 99, 101; in 1927 124, 130, 140–142, 147, 150, 151; in 1928 159, 162, 169, 176, 178, 179; in 1930 222
Wells, Ed 207
Wheat, Zach 128–130, 146
Whitehill, Earl 94, 122
Willard, Jess 149
Williams, Ken 166
Wilson, Frank 89, 90, 129
Wilson, Hack 147
Wilson, Jimmie 191
Wiltse, Hal 172
Witt, Whitey 28, 52, 56, 65, 75
Woods, Doc 60, 73, 89, 101, 108, 109, 143, 214
World Series scandal (1919) 18, 20, 22, 25

Yankee Stadium: capacity increased 161, 180; Dempsey-Sharkey fight 145; first ballpark called stadium 45–46; first game 45, 46, *47*; intended to be best baseball park constructed 24; Lindbergh Day 137, 138, 139; prayers for Lindbergh 135; record crowd 130, 141, 180, *181*, 182, 183
Young, Cy 132
Youngs, Ross 44

Zachary, Tom 137, 141, 147, 151, 175, 176, 186, 188, 207

www.ingramcontent.com/pod-product-compliance
Ingram Content Group UK Ltd.
Pitfield, Milton Keynes, MK11 3LW, UK
UKHW041934140426
5217IPUK00014B/473